# PAUSE FOR TRANSITION

# PAUSE FOR TRANSITION

## AN ANALYSIS OF THE RELATION OF MAN
## MIND AND SOCIETY

*by*

BART LANDHEER
Peace Palace Library

THE HAGUE
MARTINUS NIJHOFF
1957

**PRINTED IN THE NETHERLANDS**

# INTRODUCTION

The idea of the present study is basically a simple one. It attempts to reconcile the concept of social evolution with that of the structural unity of Man, an idea that is becoming increasingly dominant in the exact as well as in the social sciences.

The idea of structure as it emerges from the social field is applied to the human mind as the ultimate cause of society. While pragmatism interpreted the mind as reacting as a whole, the concept of structure places the relation of Man versus his Environment in a different light, and attempts to determine the possible limits of social development.

These problems are analyzed in a number of introductory chapters while the basic approach is illustrated by an analysis of some aspects of the growth of Western civilization. Some fictitious "case-studies" have been added in order to leave room for an imaginative interpretation which sometimes can bring out points which are more difficult to explain in "objective" language.

The starting point of the study was in the social field, and, if references to neural processes are occasionally included, they are, of course, meant as tentative suggestions. This holds also true for the idea which is occasionally submitted that social processes might be ultimately related to energy-processes and energy-transformations. The desire to find a link between the social and the exact sciences is nowadays a common one, and the author felt that there was no reason to omit certain connections which at times appeared to be interesting as well as puzzling.

It has not been the aim to present a scientific study but rather to formulate various aspects of an idea as these accumulated over a number of years. There is no claim to having covered the thinking in any given field but this book is more a presentation of how a number of experiences, studies and observations were translated in the mind of the author.

Such a process might be useful or interesting to others; it also might misfire as being overly individualistic. It is hoped that the first will be the case. If, at times, a lighter tone has been adopted, this was done only because the more exhaustive treatment which was needed did not seem to be possible, and, from an observation which has come to the author that a change in tone or style makes reading less of an effort than when everything is placed upon one level of thought and expression.

The original bibliographical references of Chapters VII-XII (with the exclusion of Chapter IX) were lost during wartime migrations. If they are incomplete, apologies are offered. The author wants to stress, however, that the historical chapters are meant as an illustration of the structural theory which is presented in the first part. The historical materials contained in them have been derived from the works mentioned in the bibliography and do not lay any claim to originality or historical research.

The author is greatly indebted to Professor J. Tinbergen, of the Economic University of Rotterdam, for reading the manuscript and offering many helpful suggestions. He is also much indebted to Mr. Earle Balch, Cultural Relations Officer, at the U.S. Embassy at The Hague, for having cast an expert eye at style and presentation.

Finally, much gratitude is due to Miss A. M. P. Mollema, of The Hague, for having proofread the manuscript and for having prepared the Index.

To publish a manuscript which does not fall into any clear cut category is an hazardous venture, and the author is deeply grateful to the publishing house of Martinus Nijhoff, N.V. at The Hague, for having shown an interest strong enough to make the publication of this work possible.

The Hague, April 1957.                                   B. Landheer

# CONTENTS

# PART I

# DEVELOPMENT OF THE BASIC APPROACH

## CHAPTER I

## ABOUT BASIC CONCEPTS

The idea of the present study dates back a long time. It originated perhaps with the realization — about 20 or 25 years ago — that there seemed to be a severe cleavage between Man as he appeared in the social sciences and the reality of life, although it is undeniable that much of this cleavage has been bridged. But it has been disappointing to the social sciences that much of this process was carried out outside their realm or by thinkers who were motivated more by strong emotional impulses than by ideas which had been derived from the social sciences as such [1]. The interplay between social reality and social thought is a phenomenon which appears to become more visible afterwards when it seems clearer that the success of a philosophy or a theory was not caused so much by its theoretical clarity as by its expression of a social need which had been felt but which had not found any adequate formulation.

One of the most important underlying factors of this relationship between idea and reality seems to be that it is itself subject to change and the degree of change which is natural to one society may be detrimental to another.

If we desire change — as an individual or as a group —, we tend to project our wishes into the image of a more desirable world which then begins to function as a motive for action. The lower the stage of development of individual or group, the stronger the tension between ideal and reality while, as we progress towards realization of a fair percentage of Man's life goals, the more we grow impatient if image and reality do not blend into the unity for which we believe we are striving.

This means that all our ideas and philosophies are placed under a certain perspective [2], and it is not unusual to find implied in the thinking of the 20th century that if reality can be shaped satisfactorily, the ideological superstructure will take care of itself. This idea is appealing through its simplicity but it can be questioned whether its full implications have been understood.

The point of departure of an investigation of this problem must necessarily lie in the concept that the distance between idea and reality is a changing one [3], while the tacit assumption that the decrease of distance means its gradual abolishment could be either a reality or an optical illusion.

Much confusion has been caused by the fact that our social thinking has been largely in terms of national or civilizational groups but much less in terms of mankind as a whole, and insofar as this type of thinking has occurred, it has postulated the growth of *the individual,* abstractly conceived, to a stage of greater maturity as, for instance, in rationalism. The latter type of thinking has caused the popular belief that we are constantly approaching an equalitarian society although social reality offers little to support this contention. It is then assumed that it is only due to insufficient technology or backward social institutions if this society fails to materialize.

Yet, it is not only social reality but social theory which give us cause to examine this whole complex relationship much more carefully.

If we take mankind as a whole, the most salient observation that can be made is its quantitative increase as well as its growing complexity. As human society shows an impressive rate of growth, it would be far more probable that this rate of growth, if not increasing at the same or a higher rate, might at best level off; but it would not be reasonable to expect it to become static. As a result, if the rate of social change changes in intensity, also the projection of our wishes into the future would change in intensity; but they could not be expected to disappear.

If it is also observed that the structure of human society is becoming more complex, due to an increasing refinement of the division of labor, it becomes clear that there are two opposing forces in social reality as well as in social thought, viz. the need for a structured society and a desire for greater equality. Between those two forces some compromise must be achieved, and it falls to the social sciences to be helpful in the struggle for this compromise which might be of decisive importance for the survival of Man.

The idea of the basic equality of Man is appealing to us all, and it has been preached for centuries by religion, philosophy, political ideals, Marxism, economic reform movements, etc. It has been of such overwhelming importance as a motive force in modern society that it has frequently obscured the equally vital requirement of human society, viz. that of structure. Human society shows divisions according to age and sex, labor, professions, political power, ideological power, etc. while even those institutions which aim at greater equality like political parties, religious groups, etc. show themselves a definitely hierarchical structure.

Thus, it would seem that what we need to investigate is not so much any absolute choice between an equalitarian or a structured society but the degree of structure and the degree of individual freedom [4].

It is also essential that social science does not occupy itself with what seems desirable, except as one factor which deserves investigation but rather with the possible forms this relationship can assume in human society. We do not occupy ourselves with a problem that gives room to a considerable degree of free choice because it is determined largely by the quantity of people who make up human society. If X people live in a given territory, and, after Y years, this number has increased 2 ×, it is hardly realistic to assume that it is up to the people themselves to "choose" whether their society will be more or less complex. The need for survival will automatically force the social group into those forms which seem the most effective answer — in terms of its capacity and development — to the challenge [5].

The struggle between existing structure and emerging structural forms is a concomitant of social life, and it might well be that the idea of equality is a psychological mechanism by which these changes are brought about. However, it is not implied that social distance should be regarded as a constant.

In the first place, the structure of a given society is obviously determined by its need-structure, but its need-structure does not reflect only present but also future needs. The relationship between those two need-categories obviously depends a great deal upon the degree of cultural development of the group in question. It is undoubtedly possible to divide human needs in a general way into material ones, like food, shelter, sex, protection, affection, etc., mental ones, like the need for education, technology, legal and governmental organization, etc. and spiritual needs like religious, artistic needs, etc. but, while those needs repeat themselves in a general way in most societies, their complexity seems to be a function of the quantitative quality of the group as well as of the degree of cultural development.

In other words while structure is an absolute attribute of a social group, the complexity of this structure is determined by a number of factors about which we have to seek some clarity.

Although the attribute of structure is increasingly stressed in contemporary social science, the explanation of this fact has not found the same amount of attention because it is seen as a postulate, like the rationalistic idea of equality, more than as a reality.

We have operated so long with the concept of an abstractly conceived individual that our thought-patterns are reluctant to admit the more complex idea of the structured group which also holds less emotional appeal as a motive force for possible action. As a result of our rationalistic thought-habits, we still think of Man in a conceptualization which we attempt to give permanence so that it gives no room to the factor of change which should be our starting-point.

However, if we attempt to think of Mankind as a structured group, we can arrive at some conclusions that — although they must needs remain primitive for the moment — cast a different light on the process we are dealing with. The "universe" of our study, namely "Man", existed first in scattered small groups over a period of almost half a million years, according to the findings of contemporary anthropology; then he suddenly begins to increase at a rapid rate, living in more complex groups, and, in a general way, we are still in this stage of greater increase and of greater complexity. It is logical that Man of the first stage cannot be equal to Man of the later stage. Thus, the idea of structure does not only involve the differentiation of age, sex and division of labor over one generation but we must assume a further differentation in terms of cultural stages. We are also faced with the difficult problem, stressed by Toynbee [6], that mankind went through a very long static period which has been followed hitherto by a very short one of more dynamic development.

How do we explain this fact? Rationalism has not offered much of a solution except the suggestion that Man only gradually becomes rational, while evolutionary thinking has also submitted a theory of stages, stressing, however, more the relation of Man $\rightleftarrows$ Natural Environment than the problems which arise from the expansion of mankind.

One observation seems justified at this point: if Man shows a tendency to live in increasingly larger and more complex groups, the relation of Man to his fellow-creatures gains in importance over that between Man and his natural environment. Thus, Man must needs go through stages which make possible this increasing adaptation to the social group. As these stages came late, there must have been a preceding adaptation in the long period of pre-literate society in which either the adaptation to the natural environment or some inner psychological development took place which formed a condition for the later stage of expansion.

In the primitive stage, Man finds himself in a world which seems hostile and irregular. Nature appears as a whimsical and malevolent force with which Man has to develop some working relationship. He can either placate it by appeal to deities or attempt to discover its regular processes or seek a shortcut via unusual means of causation, as in magic. The factor of knowledge, in terms of actual control over natural processes, is small in this stage, and it is largely through reactions of the imagination that Man seeks to cope with his environment. The imagination magnifies both the positive and the negative aspects of life, and its function could be regarded as a first groping toward a reality which is as yet distant so that the present appears as depending upon forces which are far beyond the control of Man [7].

Nevertheless, it has been stressed that the difference between pre-literate and more fully developed societies is one of degree, rather than an absolute one. The basic needs of Man have to be met in both societies; in both there is a certain amount of knowledge — but that of preliterate societies is generally small — while, in both, those forces which seem to control human life are presented via the process of symbolic thinking. The crucial distinction does not lie in the realm of basic needs but in the relation between intellect and imagination or — to put it differenly — between knowledge and symbolic thinking or belief.

Thus, if Man changes, it would seem that the reaction of the intellect gains in importance after some inner balance has been reached in a period in which image-thinking has been of overwhelming importance. The more experience Man gathers, the more he is struck by the regularities in Nature, and by concentrating on these regularities he develops himself gradually a more rational pattern of thinking.

The long static period of Man would appear as the stage in which the possibilities of life are projected into weird and often incom-prehensible forms by the imagination while only very gradually a concept of reality emerges which enables Man to turn his energy outward. In other words, a sort of introvert stage precedes in which Man's energy is used for the building up of basic mental patterns, and only after those have been formed, is energy set free which can be channelled into different reactions.

The dynamic stage of social life presupposes a certain development of Man himself, viz. that of rational reactions, and if this would mean that we are dealing with stages of growth, we would gain a picture of society different from that which presupposes organic equality. In addition to the visible differentiation of age and sex groups which occurs within one generation, we would have to take into account far more complex factors of organic growth which are *reflected in but not caused by society.*

It has been one of the puzzling aspects of the social sciences that they explain social processes in terms of other social processes, and only very recently has social anthropology attempted to relate social processes to Man's need-structure but the interpretation of this need-structure has been static so that social change does not find any proper explanation. If social change is to be explained from Man's basic need-structure, it is quite obvious that this structure itself must undergo change, or, ulti-mately, *Man's organic structure itself.*

It should be mentioned, however, that these efforts are not new: Plato based his social philosophy upon his theory of Man's mental structure, although he did not attempt to relate mental to organic processes [8]. If this were possible, such a theory could only emerge in any satisfactory manner from combined efforts of the social and the exact sciences, and this possibility is at best in its very initial stages.

Thus, the present study has only the goal to develop a structural theory, insofar as observations of society seem to justify this, and to present suggestions about a possible explanation of the need-structure — and the mental reactions, which appear to be its outcome — in terms of energy-exchange processes [9]. Whether these suggestions are of any value could only be determined by exact scientists and not by a sociologist, but, on the other hand, there is no reason not to indicate the direction toward which social observation seems to point.

The basic theory is ultimately a simple one: the observation of society leads to the conclusion that society has a structure which is formed around economic, socio-political and symbolic institutions. These institutions, although their interrelationship and their specific weight in given societies differ, occur in almost all societies. If this social structure is to be explained from Man's needs, these needs themselves must show a corresponding structure, and, as society has changed, there must be a corresponding change in Man himself.

Man has shown himself capable of adjusting to increasingly complex social structures, but, as the more complex societies form a better guarantee of individual need-fulfillment, adjustment to them can be considered as a derived need of the individual. In other words, the social forms of need-fulfillment may be more complex and involve restraint, but they ultimately lead to more adequate satisfaction of more needs or of more people.

A theory of this type requires in the first place an analysis of Man's possible attitudes or behavior-patterns in terms of his need-structure; secondly, the factors influencing the emergence of one or the other behavior-pattern have to be investigated while, thirdly, it will become evident that the sequence of these behavior-patterns in Man's social history gives cause for the assumption of certain specific changes in his need-structure. As was stated above, the possible relation of this need-structure and its change to bio-organic energy processes is no more than a very tentative suggestion.

It must also be stressed that the starting point is the processes of growth of mankind as an interrelated whole but not those of the artificially isolated individual.

Only if we reason from mankind as a whole does it become at least conceivable that the energy-total of the individual — if this expression is permitted for the time being — might be not a constant but a variable.[9]

If the growth of mankind is seen as a biological process, it becomes much more acceptable that the individual units of a given stage (viz. the individual of a given culture-period, taken over a long time) would differ from the individual unit of another stage (viz. the individual of another period), since they both present different stages in the life-process of mankind as a whole. Thus, it would be logical to assume differences in energy-distribution or composition [10].

If we regard the biological life-process as one in which energy is changed into different forms under the cohesion that is involved in the attributes of the species, it is logical that a higher energy type is gradually transmitted into lower forms — as it is not the additional energy received during the life-process which explains life. The unfolding of energy is a spending of energy, as ancient philosophies have frequently stressed. Consequently, if we attempt to analyze the life-process of mankind as a whole, we obtain a totally different perspective from that of the orientation toward political goals, as, for instance, greater prosperity and more political rights.

This perspective might help to explain the much greater emotional and mental tensions which prevail in earlier cultural periods and which have become almost incomprehensible to most of us. In fact, much confusion is caused by the idea that greater cultural maturity is a "higher" type of life. It has this quality from the point of view of the individual who looks back to more primitive stages, but whether it is a "higher stage" in terms of organic energy-processes is a totally different question.

Perhaps this becomes clearer if we take the life-stages of the individual: childhood, adolescence, maturity, and decline. In terms of success in coping with the natural and social environment, it is quite obvious that maturity probably constitutes the highest stage. But philosophically speaking, the preceding stages are the condition of the later ones so that they must contain the energy-forms which evolve in these later stages. We cannot change the life-stages by the supply of outside-energy — at least, this has not succeeded so far — so that the only permissible assumption is that these changes come from within. In other words, the inner energy-transformation process must be the exact opposite of what is outwardly visible, and the terms higher and lower — or, from the social viewpoint, civilized-rational and primitive-irrational — must be reversed if they reflect organic energy-stages.

As little is known about the energy-structure of Man, or perhaps it is more correct to say that little of it which seems conclusive is known to the author of this study, the only way to approach the topic is to see what conclusions can be drawn from the phenomenon of social structure in relation to that of organic structure. It might be added, however, that a real study of Man would involve biochemistry, biophysics, biology, and neurology as well as psychology and sociology. Yet we see at present more attempts for coordination of the social sciences which all deal with outward phenomena than a coordination of the exact and social sciences which might find out about the underlying structure of the "social cell" or "social atom" [11]. A unified approach to society, viz. seeing it as a totality, may be stimulating for a comparable attitude toward the human individual.

The struggle which has and is being waged in the world between individualistic and collectivistic theories has no bearing on this approach as collectivism has generally seen the state as the dominant social group. The debate, therefore, was largely one about the extent of control to be exercised by the state but this is a political topic rather than one that belongs to social science as a strictly scientific discipline.

If the study of Man starts with the human species rather than with the individual, it takes this study out of the realm of political and emotional controversy, and it places it upon the same footing which has been followed in the exact sciences for a long time. Botany does not study daffodil A or daffodil B but analyzes the phenomena related to the species "daffodil", viz. the structure, life-conditions, processes of growth, etc. Of course, there is no need to stress that this is the approach of contemporary social anthropology, which, however, has not created as yet a wholly satisfactory link with physical anthropology and the other exact sciences which deal with Man as a part of Nature.

However, if the structure of Man and the structure of society are made the focal points of a study, it is essential to recognize that a group of individuals can only be regarded as constituting a social group if they possess at least awareness of one another [12]. If this awareness is lacking, there is no social group or society; so we must take into account the widening of social awareness which has taken place throughout history and which now embraces all of mankind, with a few minor exceptions.

If we isolate a smaller group for the sake of study, be it a kinship, a professional, an economic, a national or a civilizational group, we are definitely operating with a presupposition which limits the validity of our findings because, in reality, these groups are within the orbit of society as a whole. The structural aspects of mankind as one society influence the situational conditions of any subgroup, or, to put it in a different way, a certain amount of awareness of the existence of all other people is present in the consciousness of the vast majority of people, however weak it might be as a motive for action. Ideas and attitudes are the outcome of the life-goals of the individual as a group-member, and the more essential the role of a given group is to his life-goals, although this may not appear clearly or directly in his own mind, the larger this group looms in his consciousness.

Throughout history, the individual belonged to a number of groups, but each period shows a specific group which plays a dominant role in terms of the influence which it exercises over the life of the individual. In early social stages this is mostly the family or wider kinship group, later on the territorial societies like kingships, empires, provinces, nation-states, etc. although we get many variations in regard to the degree of centralization and cohesion.

The group which exercises the largest influence is most instrumental in shaping the patterns of our thinking so that we think either in familial, tribal, economic, national, religious patterns, etc. [13] All these patterns still occur in western society, but it will probably not raise a controversy if it is stated that our thought-patterns are predominantly those shaped by the nation-states, although there is some emergence of regional patterns as, for instance, in Western Europe. Global thinking is still very limited; yet it is undoubtedly a "conditio sine qua non" for the emergence of a global society in the real sense of the word.

Consequently, if we make the concept of structure our starting point, we are on more familiar ground if we apply it to the national state with its now familiar structure of caste and class and functional groupings than when we apply it to either the individual or to global society. Our thought-patterns have been influenced by the nation-states and their cultural forms for so long that our thinking can only with difficulty separate itself from its presuppositions which are regarded as absolute. If we speak about freedom, we mean our individual rights in relation to the state; if we think of prosperity, it is in terms of a government which allots us so much or so little; if we think of freedom of thought, we mean freedom from state-control, etc.

If seen in terms of the individual or mankind as a whole, these familiar concepts acquire a different perspective.

But it is the very goal of social science to probe beyond the obvious and the familiar, and it is certainly not accidental that the great thinkers of our period like Freud, Gandhi, Marx, Toynbee and Spengler all operated in terms of processes which occur in that part of human consciousness that is beyond social control or with those social groups which go beyond the limitations of the nation-state.

If Man is to build a different world, he will need different thought-patterns, while the choice seems to lie between the individual as he "really" is, or mankind under that same perspective, or a combination of those two forms. Much of the submerged part of the individual's life may be at the root of our social frictions, and we have made great strides toward the discovery of the influence of early pressures on later behavior [14].

On the other hand, it is equally obvious that a complex society cannot exist without a great deal of rational restraint although we cannot formulate clearly as yet what amount of rational restraint is feasible over long periods in relation to the organic and psychological structure of Man. There are ample warnings that a completely rational society is not possible but a formula which aims at a workable division between the rational and the irrational remains to be found. Many contemporary social studies point to the weight of emotional satisfaction as well as to the importance of a set of beliefs which have to be wide enough and human enough to allow a compromise with the rational part of life [15].

Man needs the small group which gives him the sense of "belonging" as an individual as well as ideals which define his role in relation to mankind. The rational thought-patterns of the nation-state have not met those needs, although the social welfare state of the present is operating strongly in that direction, albeit often in a paternalistic fashion.Whether it really gives an answer of lasting value is open to discussion. As long as the nation-state cannot create an international mechanism which gives room for the changes in function of the individual state in world society, we are still faced with the accumulation of hidden tensions which will emerge at one moment or the other. Our thinking about international problems is rational-legalistic and equalitarian while, in reality, differences in terms of population and technological power grow instead of diminishing, in spite of well-meant isolated efforts to the contrary [16].

We tend to close our eyes to those problems for which only hard, sincere and unselfish thinking might offer tentative solutions.

If one thinks of the magnitude of the problems with which mankind is faced, it is evident that the social sciences are no more than a small voice which, from the quietude of the study, can merely offer a few ideas or try to elucidate a point here or there. It should and cannot pretend to offer any ready-made theories or — and this is worse — hint at theories which would help to give control over social life. If we can create a more permanent social structure, social science will undoubtedly be in a position to operate with factors of greater regularity, but there is a vast difference between regularity and prediction. Prediction lacks the element of awe which is essential in science as it is in life. And it is in this realm that we need a renewal of ideals because a life that would succumb entirely to regularity would be just as unbearable as one which is an unbroken sequence of crises.

Apart from the concept of structure, it is the idea of the rhythm of life which, in Western science and in Western thinking, is not receiving its proper share.

Another point which deserves some consideration is the degree of complexity of social science and social theory. The fact of the greater success and prestige of the exact sciences has often tended to create a terminology in the social sciences which seems more complex than the field of study requires. We deal with Man, and although this search takes place upon the theoretical level, basically human problems are at stake from which we cannot detach ourselves and should not detach ourselves as we do when we study Nature. Social science has a social goal, viz. to make a contribution to the knowledge and improvement of human society, and this goal should remain constantly in our minds.

The assumption that a theory which would be "correct" would therefore also have an ethical justification is wholly untenable. If some theory claims that such and such a development *has* to occur, we are in the realm of speculation, and there is no reason why speculative theories, however interesting they might be, should disguise themselves as scientific theories if the latter term implies absolute knowledge. If it is granted that science — exact or social — is a manifestation of the society whence it emerges, it becomes immaterial whether our theories are presented as speculative or as "exact". The "exactness" in this case is purely relative to the assumption of "all other factors remaining equal", and all abstraction which is faithful to its own basic assumptions has this merit, although its value in relation to "reality" is determined by the segment of reality that is covered by the assumptions. It is probably undeniable that modern scientific methods enable the scholar to analyze a larger part of reality than was hitherto possible, but it may not be useless to point out that the difference between this part of reality and the unknown factor "reality" may still be considerable and that it is at least likely that the chasm can never be bridged by human knowledge [17].

An additional point is that a number of observations in the exact sciences can eliminate the factor "time" while, if this same procedure is applied in the social sciences, we tacitly operate upon the basis of a static society, even though history discloses convincingly that, in social life, more factors change than remain permanent or, it might be justifiable to say, *all* factors change. Thus, "change" in time and space is a basic category of the social sciences so that valid scientific laws would be possible only insofar as the factor "change" itself can be computed in a scientifically acceptable formula.

The social sciences are, in a way, four-dimensional while parts of the exact sciences but not, for instance, biology or geology are three-dimensional. The distinction may be frequently more relative than absolute but it is a crucial one.

If science is seen as four-dimensional, the conclusion would follow that each social stage has its specific "science". Again this is more evident in the social than in the exact sciences although for the latter as well much proof can be submitted to support this thesis [18].

It is the goal of this study to consider this problem in the light of the possible structural attributes of the human mind, rather than in terms of an absolute distinction between rational and irrational attitudes. This distinction has too much the flavor of the prejudice of attitudes in certain civilizational stages which are more a hindrance than a stimulus for the development of a functioning world society. Each social group, in time as well as in terms of its position in the social structure, has its own mental pattern, and an equalization of these patterns might make social cooperation impossible instead of easier, although this is obviously again a matter of degree rather than an absolute difference.

Or perhaps even the term "mental" is misleading in this respect unless it is considered to include emotional and spiritual factors; the mind contains far more than the relatively small percentage of ordered rational thought-processes, which are reflected in normal social behavior.

Ultimately, it is the individual with all its attributes but as a manifestation of the species "Man" which will be placed at the basis of this study. This individual is the only reality which is before us but it is a reality that should not be isolated, even in theory, from the setting in which the life-drama unfolds itself and from the general natural laws which seem to govern and control the actions of the player, who appears in the most startling variety of roles.

## CHAPTER II

# THE CIRCUMFERENCE

If Man is an animal, he is at least a complex one. In fact, the distance between him and the other primates seems so tremendous that Man's position deserves to be reconsidered, not in terms of his likeness but his unlikeness to other animals. It has been said that Man is a "culture-bearing" animal, and in this term is implied everything that is specifically human: technology, government, science, art, religion, philosophy, language, etc. All these activities are mental, and it is the mind which furnishes the great question mark in regard to the distinction between Man and the other animals. Is Man simply more intelligent or does he possess a sort of "mind-stuff" that does not occur in the rest of Nature?

The opinions of scholars and scientists are divided. Religion is uncompromising in its attitude but at least it is definite. It claims a specific attribute for Man called "spirit" that only he possesses. Philosophy was inclined to regard "reason" as a quality that only Man has, although many contemporary and earlier schools of philosophy do not share this view. Psychology is more definitely than these latter schools of philosophy committed to the opinion that the difference between Man and animal is one of degree and not an absolute one.

A few attempts have been made to reconcile the various theories, and of those the most notable one is that of the German philosopher Max Scheler [19]. He attempted to prove that the psychic reactions of the higher animals re-occur in Man but that Man possesses a level of reaction which is absent in the animal world. His idea of various reaction levels is not new: it occurs in other modern schools of psychology and it is a point that is made, more or less explicitly, in a number of philosophic systems. There are also philosophers of history who explain the development of culture in terms of the dominance of one psychic reaction-form over others [20].

In its simplest form, the idea can be explained in the following manner. The human organism receives certain stimuli, either coming from the organism itself or transmitted via the senses from the outside world, which are registered or appear in the conscious mind. Let us assume that the mind translates the message it receives into the sensation "I-am-hungry." To this message, a more or less immediate reaction is possible or seems at least possible. If the individual in question is walking along a street and just passing a grocery store, he can

walk over and take an apple from the basket that is standing next to
the door. In reality, this reaction will be rare, although it might occur
in cases of extreme hunger, abnormal psychological reactions or conscious anti-social behavior. In most cases, the impulse has in the meantime been transferred to a different level upon which it is coordinated
into normal social behavior. The person may decide to buy an apple,
or, if he has no money, to go home and borrow some from his sister, etc.
In other words, before arriving at any action, a number of additional
factors are considered and weighed as to their proper significance, so
that the whole reaction becomes one which presupposes the capacity of
the use of the intellect. It could be called a "rational reaction" or "a
social reaction" because it involves adjustment to the patterns of group
behavior and its various taboos.

In contrast to it, the term "natural reaction" could be applied to
the first reaction. This is a short term one while the second one can
be called a „long term reaction", since it involves the consideration of
factors which affect the individual over a long period, as, for instance,
the implications of his actions in terms of the social group to which
he belongs. This second type of action involves training and selective
choice, and consequently, presupposes associative memory as well as intellect [21]. Most animal psychologists nowadays maintain that the higher
animals also possess this reaction although undoubtedly not to the
same degree of complexity. The greater complexity of this reaction in
Man is based upon a higher degree of intellect but not upon a psychic
reaction that is qualitatively different. It makes Man purely a more
intelligent animal.

The human being, however, possesses the possibility of a third
reaction, and this one — and this is the point made by Scheler and other
philosophers — does not occur in the animal world. It is the capacity
to suppress the action of eating altogether, for instance out of religious
fervor, for patriotic reasons, in order to save the life of a child, etc. It
means that Man is capable of blocking or unblocking his desires, of
seeing himself and his environment objectively and of placing himself
in a wider context in which his own animal life becomes relatively unimportant.

This reaction presupposes the capacity of abstract thought, either in
terms of image-thinking or idea-thinking, because it is this quality which
enables Man to see himself objectively and to act in such a fashion.
Sociologically, this reaction can be interpreted as a mechanism for
group-survival because it enables Man to sacrifice himself when necessary for the survival of the group. This does not mean, of course,
that the individual himself sees it in this fashion but is seems to be

one of the functions of this reaction. Another of its functions is the transmission of culture, because culture is transmitted in its abstract forms, as art, science and religion, but not in its concrete aspects, which would have no significance for a subsequent generation. As such it has frequently been referred to as the symbolic faculty of the mind, but why this function should exist, has not always been convincingly explained.

Psychology has stressed that frustration appears to stimulate this faculty through the process of sublimation but an attempt to explain why it is present deserves priority over an explanation of the way in which it functions. Sublimation as a subconscious process and asceticism as a conscious one are both techniques by which this faculty receives additional energy so that it becomes more active.

The first problem is, however, the question why it should exist, and secondly, whether there is proof that it does not occur in the animal world. The capacity for self-sacrifice does not furnish this proof because there are numerous instances of it in animal life, also in terms of the precedence of group survival over individual survival. The aspect of abstract thought seems more rewarding: there is definitely no evidence of this capacity among animals, and there is no transmission of any form of "culture". As a result, there is no history in animal life because it does not possess continued culture patterns that run through a number of generations. Animal life repeats itself with each generation; human life does not. Animal life is static; human life is dynamic. It is absolutely illogical to explain the changes in human life from the environment; the environment of animal life changes the same way without showing any comparable results.

There seems to be no other possibility than to admit the specific faculty of abstract and symbolic thinking in Man, and to regard this as the specific attitude that does not occur in any other form of life.

Plato drew attention to the vexing question of how it is possible that different ideas co-exist in the mind at the same time [22]. His suggestion was that there might be different kinds of "mind-stuff", because if the mind were of one substance there would be no possibility of conflicting ideas. A stimulus would create an idea A, but it could not result in co-existing ideas A, B and C unless there were at least different levels of reaction. He assumed that the mind had three parts: the appetitive mind, the realm of knowledge in the sense of control-knowledge, and reason as the capacity of thinking in abstract, metaphysical ideas which belong to the spiritual realm and through which Man participates in the supernatural and eternal.

His thinking in this respect was influenced by Pythagorean philo-

sophy, and, indirectly, perhaps even by ideas which occur in Buddhism.
In Buddhism we find the same notion of Man as a "mixtum com-
positum," a combination of various forms of energy which interact with
one another [23]. This interaction occurs partly within the conscious
mind, and it is the relation between the various types of energy which
establishes harmony. In addition, the Greeks saw human life as but one
instance of the total life-process, which consists of the changes of lower
forms of energy into higher ones. At a given point, the process reverses
itself so that life itself becomes eternal as a transition from lower to
higher forms, an ultimate reversal, and a subsequent re-occurrence of
the same process. According to Aristotle, the number of possible forms
was so infinitely great that, although according to mathematical
probability the same form could re-occur, practical probability would
be of a relatively low order.

In Man, this process of life occurs in very complex forms. In the
human organism, less complex forms of energy are changed into more
complex ones but the entire process occurs within the limits which the
structure of the species imposes. In fact, species is the specific relation
between the energy forms. This means that in Man the total life process
repeats itself: it shows a development from less to more complex energy
forms, ultimately a breakdown, and, possibly, a renewal of the process.
It seems that in Man this transition occurs in the gradual formation of
more complex patterns but in an extremely intricate manner.

The most difficult aspect is the role of the conscious mind. No psychologist claims that the conscious mind reflects all processes in the
organism. A great part of organic activity is automatically regulated
without reaching the conscious mind. Philosophically speaking, a possible assumption would be that only these processes reach the conscious
mind which can be influenced or adjusted by conscious behavior. For
instance, the activity of breathing is not normally reflected in the conscious mind, but if it becomes difficult, it does penetrate, warning the
organism back to a normal condition.

However, a stimulus which reaches the conscious mind can be reacted
to in various ways, as was outlined before. Does this mean that within
the conscious mind various forms of energy occur so that a stimulus
can be transmitted into energy A, B or C, or does it mean that purely
the strength of the stimulus determines what region of the brain a
stimulus reaches? In other words, does the possibility of the co-existence
of ideas mean that there are quantitative or qualitative differences
between psychic reaction levels?

Contemporary science gives no conclusive answer to this question.

The processes can be viewed in analogy to those of mechanics: a stimulus of intensity 0-20 penetrates to one level of the brain, one of intensity 20-40 to the next level, one of intensity 40-60 to the highest one. [24]

Tremendous complexity is added, however, because the mind is not a mechanism but part of a living organism, so that every stimulus is weakened or re-enforced by the conscious mind itself. Our conscious processes determine to a certain measure what level of reaction a stimulus reaches, but there seems to be no possibility of determining this measure exactly.

Let us return to our original example of the sensation of hunger. There are three basic factors involved: the intensity of the sensation as it emerges from the organism into the conscious mind; the manner it is dealt with by the conscious mind, namely as a motive for immediate action, postponed and controlled action or suppression of action; and, third, the influence of the environment, which may awaken or re-enforce any of the possible reaction patterns. The environment then can still be separated into a natural and a social one but this additional difficulty will be omitted for the time being.

It is obvious that only one type of action results from the various possible reaction patterns. Our mind selects one out of a possible number of actions; our freedom consists in the choice, not in the action itself. The action is an occurence that is bound to time-space and cannot be repeated. In other words, "free will" ultimately means that our conscious mind can increase or decrease the intensity of a stimulus, and thereby contribute to the ultimate formation of the action-pattern. It would be erroneous, however, to consider this factor as more than a contributory one, as the others, namely original stimulus and influence of the environment, are at least of equal importance.

Returning, however, to the general problem of the relation between stimulus and conscious mind, we have to face first the baffling difficulty that this relation varies in stages of physiological growth as well as of cultural development. This makes it essential to attempt at least to relate mental development to physiological as well as to cultural growth. To do this in detail is a task which our present state of knowledge does not permit, but it is feasible to ask in what stage of life the various basic psychic reaction patterns seem to evolve and in what manner their interrelationship changes. The stress will be placed upon the way they become evident in social life rather than in the life of the individual as the general approach is more conducive to the formulation of some sort of theory.

It is logical to assume that the life of the individual as well as of the social group starts out with a relatively unformed mind. Man has not gathered experience; he has had no opportunity to observe regularities in Nature or human responses; the world appears as mysterious, threatening and whimsical. His emotional insecurity and lack of experience make him react with his entire mind to every event, so that practically every stimulus penetrates those sections of the mind which respond in the way of imaginative thinking. His mind has as yet no definite neural reaction patterns which diminish stimuli to such an extent that they can be absorbed by standardized patterns.

The sun rises, but it has not risen so often that the event hardly penetrates the conscious mind. It is an event of the utmost importance which ends the ominous darkness and promises new life, so that it is awaited with anxiety. If the sun does not appear, the mind creates the image of a power preventing it from doing so, or the sun itself becomes this power, as uncertain and unpredictable as the mind of the person who creates the image.

But the sun continues to rise, day after day in the same place, or so it seems, and the mind gradually gets attuned to the process. The regularity of the process creates a regular response, leading to the impression that the process *must* be regular. An explanation is sought for the regularity, and Man begins to weave his theories around that part of life which seems to be in terms of regular and re-occurring processes. Whatever remains uncertain, unpredictable and haphazard is still the realm of personalized anthropomorphic deities which reserve a part of life for direct intervention while they are satisfied to operate the rest of the universe in a mechanical way. [25]

It is Man himself, however, who has gained some control over life but is still powerless in regard to its most basic aspects. This philosophy, this interpretation of life, reflects the stage in which he finds himself.

The rising of the sun no longer causes the same psychic reaction. As a physical stimulus from the outside world it has not changed in its chemical and physical proportions. It is still a stimulus of energy-type XI/50, and of intensity AB 533. But the way in which the mind receives it has been changed; the response of the conscious mind is different; it "processes" the stimulus in a different fashion.

What has taken place in the meantime? The constant receiving and processing of stimuli has given a certain structure to the mind. The re-occurrence of events with a certain regularity has led to more standardized reaction-patterns; the neural response has been developed to a higher extent in patterns which themselves possess a certain regularity.

The increasing awareness of the partial regularity of life leads to the effort to interlink these regular events, in terms of "cause and effect".

Water placed over fire begins to boil. This is observed a thousand times, a million times, 20 billion times, and the mind tries to develop theories which explain this regularity. The more experience Man gathers, the better the chance of finding high correlations between events, the more compelling the impression that all processes of the universe are regular ones. Our sciences group around those segments of life which seem to show regularity. "Knowledge" is the neural reaction to those regular occurrences, while religion and art remain the interpretation of the individual, the unexpected, the unforeseen.

Consequently, there is a positive correlation between experience and knowledge in its forms of "control-knowledge." The knowledge-response increases, the symbolic response decreases as an individual or social group accumulates more experience.

In the meantime, however, these processes continuously change the mind itself; it needs an increasingly strong stimulus to break through the well-established patterns, but this stimulus is frequently furnished by the inner pressures of social groups, which continue to grow in size. The inventions of a highly developed civilization are not so much a direct response to Nature and environment as a response to the pressure of increasing groups for whom survival becomes a more complex process. They also, of course, presuppose a certain amount of experience, but it is experience and pressure which form the causative factor. [26]

Perhaps these observations are helpful in reconsidering more fully the various responses of the conscious mind. Once more, we will assume that the sensation of hunger occurs. There will be immediate reactions in the case of a child in which the social control response has not yet been developed. In a primitive, this response will be present as the result of being the member of a tightly knit small social group, but it will lack the cushioning by an interlinked, extensive system of technical control-knowledge. In his case the stimulus still penetrates the realm of abstract-imaginative reactions and the response might consist in the decision to go fishing, after an elaborate ritual in order to pacify the river gods. In a more highly developed civilization, the last factor might not be absent, but it tends to diminish in importance.

Returning to the organic basis of these processes, this would seem to mean that growing up — individually as well as culturally — consists in an increase in the complexity of our neural reactions so that the energy transfer within the organism and the transformation of energy received from the outside tends to an increase in the type of energy needed for these processes and a decrease in the other types.

This view occurs, for instance, in ancient Hinduism, in the theory of the three "gunas" or basic types of matter, which has also a modern ring although the augmentation of our factual knowledge has made it a far more intricate and complex matter. It occurs frequently, however, that ideas which are projected in early cultures via the imagination reoccur at a much later stage in the form of scientific theory. [27]

We know that bio-chemical, bio-physical, bio-mechanical and bio-electrical processes occur within the organism. There might be additional forms of energy which are as yet unknown to us. About transfers in terms of the first three, we possess considerable knowledge; of the fourth some aspects are known but are not quantitatively measurable; the more complex mental-spiritual processes cannot be made to fit into the picture to any satisfactory degree.

The first three could be considered to be of a comparable type and be labeled "physical" in the more general sense of the term. This leaves us with what we generally call "mental energy" and what could be termed "spiritual energy."

The transfer or possible change from one energy form into the other is reflected in our conscious mind, but only — and this seems to be a reasonable although speculative assumption — to the extent that these processes can be influenced by action.

It is also a point that may be assumed to be agreed upon, that the first idea which appears in the mind can be re-enforced or weakened by the conscious mind itself. In other words, the energy transfer and changes within the mind enable us to build up more complex reactions, thereby continuously changing the structure of the mind itself.

Reasoning from the findings of sociology and social anthropology, it appears that this building up of a structure follows definite rules. In the life of an individual as well as a social group, we find that life is first strongly imaginative. This would mean that the mental functions which we label imaginative are built up first, possibly because they are the most important means of survival under adverse and harsh conditions which they make more bearable by creating a projection into the future, a future which is either placed in a hereafter or on earth itself or in a combination of these attitudes. [28] Early imaginative reactions also furnish images of various ways to do things and in this way contribute to the development of magic. Much primitive magic is utterly fantastic but some of it, perhaps purely by the law of averages, contains useful notions which are later substantiated by forms of knowledge.

If the imaginative reaction, in terms of the energy which it uses, is the most complex one, we would have some explanation of the fact why in times of emergency it would also function as a reservoir of energy which can be drawn upon and which can be re-transferred into the "lower" forms of energy that are used within the organism.

It may cause controversy to use the terms "imaginative" or "spiritual" thinking as interchangeable since this may seem to imply that the spiritual reaction does not reflect "reality". But the conclusion is unwarranted because the relation between mind and reality is a completely different problem, and nothing has been stated so far which implies that either sense-perception, conceptual thinking, or symbolic thinking, either of the image or abstract type, conveys a picture of "reality". This matter will be reserved for some later reflections.

During the occupation of the Netherlands in World War II a spontaneous strike occurred which was met by the German occupation authorities with drastic measures, culminating at the end of a week in the threat of a death sentence for those who continued to strike.

Afterwards a map was drafted which showed the geographic distribution of the strike at various moments and also showed the political affiliations of the strikers. This analysis showed that, after the death threat, the strike only continued among small religious and leftist groups.

This would confirm the contention that the spiritual reaction is one which requires but also gives strength. Psychologically speaking, a purely rational or intellectual reaction could not have led to the same result, as a "felicific calculus" of the Bentham type, measuring pain versus pleasure, would not have resulted in an attitude of self-sacrifice.

Additional proof is furnished by the fact that the religious leader has been the strongest group-builder in history, in view to extension in time and space as well as to the intensity of feeling among the followers. The German sociologist Max Weber spoke of the "charismatic" leader, indicating "charisma", or visionary and inspired knowledge as a specific reaction. [29]

The philosopher Scheler distinguishes "salvation knowledge" from humanistic and utilitarian knowledge and attempts to prove that the first one is a completely different psychic reaction which has no direct relation to the other forms and occurs only in Man. [30] He also asserts that this reaction places Man in direct contact with the higher cosmic forces, but this point is a purely speculative one and does not enter into an attempt to analyze the various reaction forms of the human mind.

Historically speaking, it appears justifiable to assert that the early stages of a civilization show a greater intensity of religious thinking than later ones. An explanation of this phenomenon could be based upon several factors: first, an early civilization lacks experience so that it cannot react intensively in terms of knowledge-patterns; second, Nature seems to build up the symbolic patterns first as the most essential ones for survival, especially under more primitive conditions.

Greece furnishes a standard example of this process, although both

India and Western civilization supply also convincing arguments.

In the nomadic, pre-historic stage of Greece, we find a strong influence of nature deities; later on, after the Greeks had settled down,
ancestor cults and agricultural rites were added to their religion while
a fervent artistic imagination gradually blended the deities into a varied
and diversified pantheon. When the Greeks began to think more in
scientific terms, the interaction between religion and philosophy caused
the near-human deities to change into abstract principles, a transition
from image to abstract thinking which was very evident in the case
of the Greek upper class. [31]

The complexity of the Greek city-state and the difficulties of the
masses caused the growth of mystery religions in which the element of
personal salvation was much stronger than in the official civic religion.

The entire process shows clearly a change from religious to secular
thinking until reversals in the life of groups and ultimately of the
entire Greek community caused a return to religious attitudes, brought
about by frustration which in turn strengthened the capacity of projec-
ting into the future which the human mind possesses.

In other words, the symbolic reaction was strong in the beginning,
then weakened and was ultimately increased again by a less rewarding
response in terms of the human and natural environment when the
position of the Greeks in the world began to deteriorate.

This process was clearly visible in Greece because the absence of a
strong caste of professional priests made constant contact between religion, philosophy, art and science possible, so that there was no freezing
of the conflict into an antagonism between church and science such as
occurred in Western civilization. Greek society possessed great fluidity
and elasticity and still furnishes an excellent field of observation for all
possible psychic responses, except extreme ones, as Greek individualism
knew the one and supreme restraint of a sense of measure and harmony
which banned the unhealthy and the abnormal from their lives. It is
probably this same individualism, combined with this wise restriction,
which made them such superior artists, while the lack of mental pressure enabled them to see the life of "form" more perfectly than any
other nation ever did. Greece is the eternal and triumphant symbol of
the free mind and of an unparalleled love for beauty.

The dominance of the spiritual pattern in Greek life made them
reason in a way that is different from ours. To them, the idea came
first, and thinking in ideas meant the highest form of happiness, an indication of the strong stress which Nature places upon the development
of this type of reaction. It rewards the effort with emotional satisfaction
of a specific flavor, of a finer texture than our other pleasures, heigh-

tened by the feeling that it results from an effort of the individual, expressing more his innerself than any other form of activity. 32

To us observation comes first, the idea or concept afterwards. This is repeated in every textbook, but it is unfortunately only a partial truth. In the first place, it is an idea which determines in what direction our observations run, although the idea in turn may be a reflection of impulses, desires, needs or whatever term one chooses for these unformulated and non-specified organic forces. It seems that vision and imagination come first in life, observation second, and knowledge third as a reaction in between the two others and drawing from both of them, with the original impulse at the source of all three reaction patterns. Even science starts in the imaginative realm, with the notion that things are perhaps different from what they appear to be, with the dream that there are easier ways of doing things than painful and strenuous physical toil. But just observe and sit back and be surprised about the remarkable vacuum that will show itself in the human mind, and in some of our "scientific" efforts. Nature does not sacrifice its secrets easily, and the mind seems to respond only when there is a challenge, a condition of duress from which it seeks to escape. Otherwise it remains as placid as the world around it, even if this world is filled with facts and figures which do no more than repeat what we can already see with our own eyes. Of course, the complexity of our world gives a justification to the piling up of data, but it is purely relative; the gathering of bricks makes little sense unless we plan to build a house from them.

Perhaps the Greeks were closer to the truth: develop and stimulate the imagination as much as you can, and knowledge will result when life demands it. The Greek attitude was reborn in the Renaissance, the period which preceded and led to the era of explorations, inventions and discoveries. Of course, the Greeks were equally eager to develop the intellect and to learn about "cause and effect", but to them this world of mechanical causation was secondary to the world of spirit and beauty, the realm of teleological causation where purpose is more important than correlation.

Once more, Western Europe in the 17th and 18th century created philosophy and art, and ultimately a second wave of inventions followed in the 19th century. But the mind had to gain structure and shape first, establishing order within itself before it could transmit this order to the outer world.

The sequence: observation — hypothesis — science is a standardized version of what occurs in the human mind; it lacks life and beauty and does not see the mystery in us as well as around us. The Greeks knew better: it was amazement that was at the root of knowledge and philosophy, the capacity to marvel, to be surprised, to break through the world of sense perceptions to a clearer and simplified realm. Knowledge was a reward for effort and, in its ultimate form of abstract thought, the outcome of suffering and misery. Behind all that we have achieved lies the unhappiness of millions.

## CHAPTER III

# THE DIAMETER

Having equipped Man with a number of basic reaction forms, we have to ask ourselves what picture they give him of the world in which he lives and whether there are any possibilities of determining the relation between this picture and the outside world. The problem has been elaborated in thousands of different ways, but they are reducible to a few basic formulations.

It was again in Greece that this problem emerged first and was stated in its fundamental possibilities. In the early periods of Greek civilization, the Greeks were quite convinced that their deities were real, and it was not until philosophies from Asia Minor began to occupy the Greeks that it made them uneasy to have altogether too human Gods. In order to overcome this, they postulated abstract natural forces as the ultimate causes, but, in doing so, they merely substituted abstract thinking for image thinking, without making much progress otherwise. Their principles were still absolute ones, operating in the universe and known to Man, without any analysis or criticism of the ways in which Man acquired this knowledge.

The Sophists did not like absolutism, either in society or in thinking — the two frequently go together — and they developed the idea that knowledge in any general form was impossible because each individual mind was different in the first place, while, secondly, it received different stimuli from the outside world. Consequently, knowledge was no more than a semantic convention by which comparable values are attributed to individual meanings although they are basically different.

It is obvious that this view constituted a danger to the stability of Greek morals and Greek thought. Socrates, belonging to the aristocratic party, attempted to counteract this threat by asserting that the abstract forms of thinking are the same for each individual. Mathematics, with its concept of a line, a circle, a triangle, furnished him with his weapons of attack, but he extended his theory to moral ideas, thus laying the foundation for Plato's philosophy of ideas. [33]

Was Socrates right or wrong? The question is still problematic, and no satisfactory answer has emerged from centuries of discussion. There is no argument about the point that the mind can create general abstract mathematical ideas, but what is their relation to reality?

Those ideas originated, in all likelihood, from the observation of the heavenly bodies which seemed to follow regular patterns in their movements. These patterns could be seen in abstract form, and laws were discovered which appeared valid for these forms, quite apart from their relation to anything that was actually happening. If abstraction A is valid, abstraction B and abstraction C can be combined and integrated in any fashion which seems logical to the human mind. The initial abstraction A is not a direct outward reality, consequently the derived abstraction would be even less so. Yet it appears at times that by the process of abstract reasoning we re-approach reality at a higher level at which the derived abstractions are valid.

This would lead to the conclusion that the outer world operates according to the same laws as our mind, and this conclusion has been frequently drawn. However, it is not tenable. Since the history of science furnishes frequent examples of abstract theories, proved experimentally, which became untenable, there is no justification for assuming any simple relationship. It appears that the abstract superstructure can be changed to explain the same set of facts so that the relation between "reality"-observation—abstract concept is one about which more negative than positive statements can be made. On all various levels of operation, the mind takes a specifically focussed picture, the specific focus coming out of the condition of the organism, and, in spite of all religion and metaphysical philosophy, there is no evidence that there is any psychic realm in which the world outside us is reflected without an admixture of this organic slant. In fact, all our thinking takes place in terms that are related to our experiences, and there is not a single one that cannot be reduced to empirical factors.

Another and more important question is how these pictures which the mind takes differ and whether there is more "reality" on one level than upon another.

Philosophers, moralists and physicists have all agreed that our sense impressions give us pictures which are not "true", although 99 per cent of mankind lives by and acts in terms of this sense perception, which is at least reliable enough to keep them alive and in working order. In fact, at times they appear to furnish us with our most reliable guides, since they are at least immediate and general. It is frequently more the images with which we adorn our sense perceptions than the perceptions themselves which prove unreliable.

At any rate, we know enough about it to be able to say that they do not convey "reality" to us but only some of its attributes like extension, motion, duration, etc. They also separate some forms of existence from other ones which direct sense perceptions do not disclose to us.

We have another level of psychic approach to the world which enables us to see things in terms of interrelation, "cause and effect" relations, etc. As our technology improves, this level of approach also acquaints us with aspects of the physical world which, in earlier periods, remained outside our ken, and which have to be re-integrated into our systems of knowledge. Technology widens the field of observation but does not basically alter the relation between "fact" and "theory".

"Theory" lifts the regular occurrences out of the total stream of life, but it can do no more than stress some aspects of life that seem to take place in regular and re-occurring forms. Whether all of life does this remains a moot question, as even the greatest believer in science cannot sustain the view that human experience takes in all of life. It gives us only a segment, but what goes on outside this segment is pure speculation and phantasy. The segment which is given in our experience is not in itself regular, but we take the regular aspects out of the local of our experience because they are the occurrences over which we can gain some control.

As what goes on in the segment contained in our experience is influenced by events outside our experience (at least this seems a logical assumption) there is no absolute or reliable form of knowledge. Knowledge is a purely human and relative affair, a formulation of the regularities of past experience which have no bearing on the future, except as a purely humanly calculated probability of continuation or recurrence. The only positive aspect of the whole process is that the more extensive our field of experience, the more reliable can we make the calculations of our probabilities, although they also become more complex.

Knowledge, in the form of theories, has a probability of reflecting "real" occurrences and relationships, but it is no more than that. It possesses a higher degree of accuracy than is given by direct sense perceptions because it is based upon more general and farther reaching observations. It tells us that "reality" is not what is given by our sense perceptions but it does not tell us what it really is. It is a different picture, more accurate in some respects, less accurate in others because it brings out the typical and leaves out the atypical.

The tree is, as the poet sees it, a thing of beauty; as the scientist sees it, a structure of atoms; but neither view tells us what it really is. Knowledge is always the result of interaction between the human organism and his environment and it can never get beyond this limitation.

If knowledge C results from the interaction between individual A and environment B, it is clear that C is neither A nor B but a function of A and B, in which neither factor is stable. In fact, the knowledge C changes A into $A_1$, so that we get a new relation between $A_1$, and B in which B — even if it were stable — would not appear stable to us. On the other hand, the influence exerted by B on A must also change B so that it is logical to assume that both A and B change.

This interpretation is a long way from the Greeks and from the rationalists of the 17th and 18th century who were so firmly convinced that the human mind and the universe operate according to the same set of laws and that, once we find these laws, they become attuned to one another in perfect harmony. A beautiful belief, but there is no proof of it, and it belongs to the realm of hope more than to that of empirical knowledge. It was but another instance of the remarkable phenomenon that we need not only perception and knowledge but also a set of beliefs.

This phenomenon is distinctly unpleasant to the modern psychologist who likes to operate with the idea of the equality of human nature, and equality within one generation. He tries to solve the problem by talking vaguely about symbolic thinking, without asking why Man should have this quality and — this is even more important — how it affects him. Why there is so much more "symbolic" thinking in some cultural stages than in others is a problem that receives a far more satisfactory answer from cultural philosophy.

In the first place then, there is the empirical observation that Man seems to need a set of beliefs and general ideas which are not verifiable in terms of his experience. Perhaps they are the formulation of his subconscious fears, hopes and aspirations which, through the process of being taken into the realm of conscious thought, become subject to the controls which the conscious mind can exercise. In this way they become less threatening, less likely to create severe emotional disturbances, less ominous. They can be woven into a set of beliefs, and this very process diminishes their awesomeness: the vague feeling of impending disaster that is caused by unformulated emotions. At the same time they gain the possibility of interacting with the realms of direct experience as well as with ordered experience in terms of knowledge, thus becoming a part of that intricate system of interaction which exists in the conscious mind. Our experience may tend to change our beliefs because the logical imperative of our mind drives us to seek a certain consistency, to eliminate contradictions which become too obvious. On the other hand, the psychological weight seems to be on the side of belief as the reaction which makes life bearable when it has become rationally unacceptable. Since a great part of our life has been rationally unacceptable, it was a wise precaution of Nature to equip us with beliefs which enable us to live, even if life is a burden and a sequence of misery, despair and frustration.

The interaction between the two reactions is clearly visible: the more acceptable life becomes, the more our beliefs weaken, the less reason there is to project life into the future, either on earth or visualized in the hereafter. But if this quality of projection did not exist, survival would become almost impossible, as life would exhaust itself in the emotional satisfaction of one generation.

Perhaps this question of emotional satisfaction should never have been asked. There is no human happiness in terms of any simple need-fulfillment; Nature has entrusted us with a far more complex task, reaching across many generations, and our real reward lies in accomplishing our task in this gigantic drama. For millions of people, there has been destiny in death, misery and starvation, and we have as yet no definite proof that physical need-fulfillment alone would create a functioning world, although this assumption is frequently noticeable in much of modern thought.

On the other hand, one would hardly argue a return to asceticism, which fitted specific social stages but not ours. But equally wrong is the oversimplification that the satisfaction of needs creates happiness. It is simply a standard belief of no greater validity than the medieval idea that misery was a condition for spiritual growth. While the spiritual reaction is not all of life, it is equally wrong to assume that it can be neglected. Let us reexamine the evidence.

In our own generation, life has been uncertain, dangerous, catastrophic, in spite of all our knowledge and experience. From our store of knowledge we have derived little that helped us to cope with these situations, except some ideas of "cultural lag" and individual frustration which were helpful but not exactly conclusive.

It has been belief rather than knowledge with which Man meets the crises of his existence. These beliefs seem to center around the vague idea that, somehow or other, better things have emerged from conflicts.

The function of beliefs of this kind is quite different from that of traditional religious dogmas which attempt to create certainty in order to forestall doubt. But the intensity of belief is determined by psychological necessity, not by a transmission of ideas which can just as well result in doubt as in conviction. Once the basic necessity exists, beliefs might center around ideas which have been supplied by others, but the weight they receive remains a result of the psychic structure of the individual. His beliefs reflect his emotions more than his knowledge, which has been transmitted artificially to a greater extent. Much of our knowledge is felt as coming from without, as having no bearing upon the life of the individual, especially as knowledge is forced upon us in society more than belief. In our beliefs, we have more choice, more correspondence to our emotions, which are directly at the root of them.

The future is the most essential part of the mental life of most of us. It is hidden in ourselves and somehow reflected in that mysterious structure of ideas in which the non-real is more important than the real. The non-real in our ideas is this half-projection of the future, not merely our own individual one but some part of our function in regard to the whole of mankind.

Our mind becomes specific when mind and reality meet, but what remains hidden of reality in the future is mirrored in our religions and philosophies. We could not live if it were otherwise. If our mind would exhaust itself in the present, we would be lost in emotions that would demand rapid satisfaction, and any such behavior forms call forth mental rather than physical deterioration. Our mind warns against this because in itself it contains different dimensions: it is an instrument set for a performance which reaches far beyond the span of our individual lives.

The role which knowledge plays in this world of our ideas is relatively secondary. We are much more concerned with the intangible, with the subtle fluctuations that we cannot even formulate. They strive for form rather than content, carried by the rhythm of sound or word or color when the contents disappear into the realm of the irrelevant.

Our mind seeks strength in these subtle mirages as if they had no relation to the reality of life. And indeed, they are no photographic portrayals of what has happened but prophetic voices which speak to the stuff of which our spirit is made or the mind when it is as yet un-coarsened through the disillusion of the dream which has become reality, pale and empty like the holiday toward which we were looking forward.

The non-fulfillment of our desires is a part of our lives, the postponement of the realization of our dreams a necessity for further motion. An excessive degree of social communication weakens our minds because it breaks through the finer texture of our individuality.

It should be our goal to reserve a part of our untapped strength and not to wear out our elasticity by the vain efforts to translate all that seems desirable into a material reality. Instead we create useless needs which sap our strength and narrow our horizon to a mechanical world which has been robbed of rhythm and mystery. And instead of giving satisfaction, each additional material need means a moving away from the equilibrium toward which we should be striving.

But Nature itself calls a halt. Our mind possesses brakes which operate via emotional resistance and frustrations or by creating images which mirror a different world. We overstress the present and lack the capacity to think in terms of mankind as a whole over a period of hundreds or thousands of years. Haste has become the disease of modern life: a haste which is no more than nervousness caused by the strain of "getting and spending". We are loath to admit that Western civilization presents only one possible attitude towards life and equally reluctant to consider what the purpose of our excessive activity consists of.

It is harmony which creates human happiness, and harmony is essentially a condition of equilibrium. Why it should be thought that an equilibrium can be reached by spending more and more energy is an article of faith of modern Man for which there is little real support. There is somewhere a satisfactory equation between energy spent and energy received, and — although this equation may differ for various social stages — there is no reason to assume that *our* equation is *the* equation. If there was greater emotional happiness, there would be a desire for permanence rather than what has been called the "acceleration" of history.

Our needs definitely show a structure, and our ancestors wisely divided them into the necessary, the useful and the superfluous, with the goal of leaving adequate room for the emotional and the spiritual side of our nature. But we assume that need-satisfaction answers all questions, although the recurrent crises of modern life demonstrate clearly that expansion of needs does not create equilibrium because it does not correspond to our innate mental structure. Mental disease is the price which Western Man is paying for his achievements, but, since he refuses to admit his illness, it is hard to suggest a cure.

At the root of much of this are the illusions which rationalism created in the course of the last few centuries. We grow restive when the millennium of equality and prosperity remains forever around the corner, but how it could arise out of a world which shows increasing instead of diminishing complexity is a problem that is being studiously avoided. The increased stress on equality — human, political, racial, etc. — may be partly a compensatory mechanism that is of the greatest significance, since it aims at an equilibrium-condition. But it is not sought in a conscious or scientific version, although much of the compensatory factors are explained and fostered in pseudo-scientific language.

If we have the two factors: increasing functional complexity and compensation via socio-political channels, a scientific effort should be made to work out a ratio for these factors which ultimately reflects the semiautomatic seeking of a structural equilibrium. The prevailing sociopolitical trends show clearly that the need for compensation exists and that the dream of Man's gradual growth into a sort of state of equal rationality has no real foundation. If increasing structural complexity arises out of human nature, we must draw the conclusion that this differentiation is innate in human nature even though organized society overstresses it so that compensation sets in.

This leads to the conclusion that, if functional differentiation would be decreased, the function of the compensatory mechanism would also diminish. Thus, the choice seems to lie between a conscious decrease of functional differentiation with a concomitant weakening of the socio-political compensations or a continued increase in functional differentiation with the result of greater, and possibly uncontrollable, tensions between the technological and the socio-political level.

The choice — if there is one — does not seem hard to make, as the tension in question has twice already led to near catastrophes from which mankind has by no means recovered.

The question is whether the decrease of this tension would be brought about more easily in the technological or in the socio-political realm. At present, the reaction between the two is a cumulative one, although we can observe constant efforts to reverse the process. However, the illusion which has been created in the masses of a constantly increasing prosperity makes it hard to reduce political tensions because it would take great courage to revise this image to more normal proportions.

How change could occur via the technological realm is difficult to see because the technologist belongs to a social sub-group which cannot deviate from the pattern of the group as a whole, unless at the price of martyrdom. It is only the awareness of mankind as one interrelated social group which could reduce technology to a more functional status; yet this is hardly feasible so long as it is a major instrument of inter-group competition. If world society were to create — or is creating — a certain equilibrium out of itself, the same result might be reached by a gradual relaxation of tensions. Yet how this could come about while the rate of increase of the social sub-groups differs so greatly is hard to visualize. Unequal rates of increase are not necessarily the reason for intergroup tensions, but if the increase is accompanied by a rise in the technological level, there must ultimately follow a change in the power-structure. Technological improvement if not overcompensated by numerical increases would tend toward a reduction of social distance, but if population increases more rapidly, the goal of actual improvement is not sufficiently reached so that tensions toward other social groups result.

The idea of structure, although it does not lead to the concept of complete equality, nevertheless implies a workable degree of cohesion, and this cohesion cannot be achieved if social distance — either between the classes of one national society or between national or regional societies as sub-groups of global society — is neither too small or too large. It is perhaps a struggle between a sharper sense of reality which is also emerging in regard to our society and our desire to project in our minds a more perfect world. If "reality" comes into a sharper focus, we may be approaching a state of greater maturity which would involve "matter-of-fact" rather than ideological thinking.

We tend to agree about the basic attributes of Man as an individual, but our judgment deserts us if we form opinions about national groups. Then the individual no longer possesses the same degree of "goodness" or he is spoilt by "wicked leaders", who are, however, also individuals. The optical illusion of national ideologies makes it difficult to postulate an "abstract national group" in the same way as we postulated an abstract individual. The abstract individual never existed but the concept provided a certain possibility for objective judgment. In global society, however, our emotions are too strongly involved to make us realize that the national society is a structured social group which could be given the same degree of abstraction in order to provide a yardstick for existing societies. But while we emptied our concept of the individual of specific contents, we have not succeeded in doing this for the social group, although sociology and social anthropology have made great strides in that direction.

The abstract concept of the individual was a function of a desire for less social cohesion in order to evolve new social patterns, while what is needed now is an increase in cohesion in order to create a functioning world society which can retain its basic forms for a long period to come.

Our thinking is ultimately the reflection of our basic emotions, and it is no extravagant statement to say that we are at present more interested in stability and permanence — not of what is but of what can be within the limits of our present possibilities — than in a continuation of change, particularly in the technological realm.

Thus, the concept of structure, as an ethical postulate, means the limitation to what is humanly desirable rather than to what is humanly possible. As a theoretical postulate it represents the recognition that the rate of change of Western society of the last few centuries is not *the* rate of social change and that change is only meaningful if seen as motion toward a new state of equilibrium. Social change is not a goal in itself but is related to the purpose of adapting the largest possible social group to the best possible conditions. On the other hand, it is evident that the more complex groups which are now emerging are not moving toward an equalitarian society but toward a more highly differentiated one.

Since this means that social pressures on the individual are increasing, it is becoming more imperative to establish an emotional and spiritual realm in which the individual can refind his balance.

Our society has to solve a number of problems which are far more subtle than their presentation by the types of political-economic thinking which prevailed in recent decades. The more mature mankind becomes, the more the individual will insist upon his own free realm of living and thinking, and this basic need must be reconciled with his role in an increasingly complex society.

To ignore the problem is a method of the past which can have no lasting value in a world which is daily developing a more astute sense of reality but which is not deriving sufficient emotional satisfaction from the world which is unveiled before its eyes.

Reality is our dearest friend and our most dangerous enemy. It can destroy the finer texture of our mind unless we learn to understand that "reality" is not what seems desirable to us today or tomorrow but what corresponds to the deeper dictates of human nature "sub specie aeternitatis". [34]

## CHAPTER IV

# THE SPECIFIC ATTRIBUTE OF THE GREEKS

It is probably safe to say that more has been written about the Greeks in the course of the centuries than about any other nation. If we assume, as Kant believed, that Nature follows a definite plan it would seem that She wanted to bring the achievements of the intellect to an all-time high in order to furnish later generations in various cultures with a beacon or a sign-post.

Apart perhaps from painting and music, the Greeks reached a level which becomes all the more surprising if one realizes the smallness of their cities and their limited technological possibilities. But their intellect soared high, with a quality of permanence in their master works that is difficult to explain. Numerous generations of schoolboys have brightened when they were taken out of their own severe and unbending cultures in order to participate in the exploits of the Greek gods and heroes, who were so intensely human and so much more like what they wanted to be themselves. And yet also the sternest scholars would write long and labored books about Plato and Aristotle, proving that they actually said what the scholars were eager to state themselves. To make it more respectable, it had to be explained in terms of Greek philosophy.

The Greeks themselves were hardly as complex and "pesante" as they were sometimes made, and they were equally able of providing a source of inspiration to young people in many countries who were more interested in a way of living than in the worshipping of the correct accent in the correct place.

And this was perhaps more what it ultimately amounted to for the Greeks themselves: their philosophy was a way of living, a road to happiness and balance, not a blind accumulation of knowledge for the sake of knowledge.

To the Greeks, life had a purpose, and this purpose was perfection. Perfection of the individual, certainly, but this perfection could be reached only via an entire community. The alpha and omega of this perfection was harmony, a proper relation between the various attributes of Man; whether they be called body, mind and spirit or drives, intellect and reason remains ultimately immaterial.

The Greeks saw life as a process of motion but a motion that was dark, ominous and threatening unless it could be brought under control and given form. Nature around them seemed to possess this harmony, this rhythm, more than Man himself; so Nature became a thing of perfection, not an indifferent field of action and reaction as we see it. The Greeks clearly realized that Man was Nature's most restless animal, charged with a higher potency, full of danger but also capable of developing to a greater perfection. In fact, the potency was felt as too high for permanence and survival: there was an element of pessimism in life and, at any moment, the negative seemed to outweigh the positive.

Hence, the attempt to freeze life into the purity of forms: first came the more carefree world of the gods, who enjoyed greater liberty than the humans although under the supreme control of a sense of measure and dignity; later on, the abstract principles of the philosophers took the place of the all-too-human gods, but they were living forms to be visualized in ecstasy rather than arrived at intellectually, although the dialectic process was basically a logical one. But logic was a tool to reach the world of the perfect forms that were in last analysis the religious values translated into the abstract in order to reconcile science and religion.

The Greeks were curious but they were also afraid. Their practical and technical knowledge had to be imbedded firmly in a set of beliefs and values that gave structure to the mind, and this giving of structure was far more important than the practical knowledge itself.

Perhaps this is the key toward an explanation or rather an interpretation of the Greek mind. It was striving for a structure, for a body of principles and ideas that would give permanence, not to the world — about that the Greeks with a relatively static economy were not overly concerned — but to Man, who was groping his way from primitive imaginative thinking to the clarity of abstract and formal thought. It is Man himself who needs these ideas, though he all too readily assumes that his ideas also reflect the outside world. Man was seeking stability but not the world outside him which, now as then, follows its own impenetrable laws at which we keep forever guessing in the conceit of our own insecurity.

It is this need which explains the striving for word-perfect expression, the desire to create "noble words, and magnificent ones, in overflowing love for wisdom and beauty", as Plato put it. Or if one should wish to express it in a modern fashion: the mind itself seems to carve out more definite neural reaction-patterns as the individual or the group gains maturity. This formation of more permanent patterns may set energy free that is otherwise absorbed by the reaction of the mind as a whole while it gives at the same time greater strength to the mind by the creation of "re-enforced" reaction-channels.

In fact, by being philosophers, artists and thinkers the Greeks performed a pioneering task which later peoples and cultures imitated, owing them an eternal debt of gratitude. Once these patterns have been formed, the need for them diminishes, and it is perhaps quite natural that we are no longer seekers of truth and beauty. Our mind has already the structure and patterns which it needs, although it would be quite a valuable question to ask whether this is really so. But this question does not fit into the present argument and will be saved for a later occasion.

This striving for structure, this eagerness to develop the mind into a perfect instrument, seen as a goal in itself rather than a practical one, explains to some extent why modern thinking has less exalted notions about the role of ideas. The Greek idea, at least in Plato's thinking, had the attributes of a deity: [35] it was "real" — in the sense of supernatural, as the philosophers put it: transcendental reality; it was perfect and it furnished the goal for whatever existed in the imperfect physical world. In this sense, it was clearly a deity translated into abstract terms, yet also in this higher world there was a structure, a grading of value, a distinction of higher and lower, very much as in the Homeric Pantheon. We could say that the Greeks duplicated the world: the physical world and, beyond it, the supernatural world. Many of us still have this same idea but we do not make the supernatural such an exact, although more perfect, replica of the natural. Our beliefs about the supernatural world have become vague and indefinite, but to the Greeks the supernatural was more real than what we call "reality". To express it crudely, one could say that our thinking is 90 % in terms of the natural, 10 % in terms of the supernatural, while for the Greeks the relationship was almost the opposite, although this may be an exaggeration.

If we look at this in organic terms it could be said that the Greeks used a far greater amount of neural energy in order to build up imaginative and abstract thought-patterns. They needed such thought patterns in order to feel secure, and, because of this imperative need, they assumed a reality that was superior to that of immediate sense-perceptions.

To us, a chair is a physical object of which we get an image via our senses. In addition to that, and in order to communicate with others, we can develop the abstract concept "chair", taking those attributes which a hundred or a thousand chairs have or seem to have in common. In daily life, we are not too accurate about this process, so that we live in a state of perpetual semantic confusion. [36] This abstract chair to us is, however, purely a concept, a form of conceptual knowledge.

The Greeks, on the other hand, were so eager to learn to think in abstract forms that the abstract ideas became more important to them than the real things. In other words, their mental needs took a high priority over their physical wants.

In the hundred thousands of years of human evolution, we find minute physical change in the first half million years and almost imperceptible mental changes in the narrow span of 6000 years of civilization. But the mental changes, however hard to trace, are there.

In addition to this neural process of change, there are, of course, also some very fine philosophical points involved which emerge from this possibility of very gradual mental differentiation.

Those complexities lie in the question of the more general abstract ideas which still present us with the same difficulties that the Greeks had to cope with. If we talk in terms of the most general abstractions like God or Nature, we still are undecided whether we talk about realities outside ourselves or are expressing ideas emerging from our mind, whose relationship to the world outside us belongs to the category of the unknowable, as Herbert Spencer termed it. The third possibility is to assume that those abstract ideas give us certain aspects of reality but that the total reality remains unknown, so that there is at least a functioning parallelism between mind and reality.

Much of our scientific and abstract thinking is based upon the tacit assumptions that events which re-occur with great regularity "have to" re-occur. The weakness lies in the words "have to", because we have no way of knowing why re-occurrence would be a necessity. That we assume this may be purely the psychological necessity of thinking in terms of certain ultimate computation points. For long periods the human mind has looked for the regular because the regular becomes the controllable. As our survival depends upon the controllable part of Nature, our wish to survive makes us think that the regular is regular out of a divine or natural necessity. But we remain with these assumptions in the realm of speculation, although society and social survival would become utterly impossible if we began to doubt the bases of these regularities in our daily life. [37]

Consequently, these assumptions are basically beliefs, and, as beliefs, they are a psychological necessity. What we can observe is, however, that the more experience Man gathers, the wider the field becomes in which he can observe regularities so that his thinking takes place more and more in these terms. Both knowledge and belief are fundamental attributes of the human mind but the relation between them shifts into the direction of — what we like to call — "empirical knowledge". The reversal point is reached when the mind of an individual or social group is no longer elastic enough to envelop the increasingly complex reaction-patterns of knowledge so that an attitude of skepticism or a renewal of beliefs emerges, as in the regressive stages of social development. The problem of how far this process of greater neural complexity can go seems to be a moot question to which no justifiable answer is possible unless we could calculate an organic life-curve on which we could plot the stages of our own development. But from that we are far removed, and we can only operate in terms of vague and general analogies in relation to life-curves of known animal-species which completed their life-cycles, but since the life-cycle is determined by the interaction between organism and environment, no valid inferences can be drawn from this.

Reasoning from a philosophical basis, we can observe that Western society has shown a preference for regarding Man's growth in terms of evolution and progress as a linear development, while Antiquity saw life in terms of re-occuring cycles, although there are definite beginnings of evolutionary thinking in Aristotle. It can again be pointed out that our thought-patterns seem to be part of a total life-attitude: Western civilisation has been dynamic, and, as a consequence, it sees life as an upward movement; Antiquity, although far from static, was closer to Nature and interpreted life in terms of an eternal rhythm.

There is undoubtedly more to be said for the second view because, as life offers itself to our experience, it is a process of coming and going, of birth and death, of decay and renewal, but it is not imaginable as a one-time process which has a definite direction and, consequently, a beginning as well as an end.

Modern Western thinking has focussed on one aspect of reality, due to the positivism and optimism resulting from rapid growth, but the Eastern civilisations have continued to stress the eternity of life itself.

If life is seen in this fashion, it occurs in myriads of forms, but as each form results from a definite constellation of the whole universe, the structure of each form would be a relatively stable one which cannot merge into other forms. In other words, each form is dependent upon a combination of factors, and its life-span is determined by the continuation of these factors.

To put it less abstrusely: the life-form "Man" can only exist under certain conditions, and this implies a limitation of the structural attributes of Man. Consequently, it is logical to assume that Man cannot acquire any wholly new attributes but that his changes have to be explained in terms of the structural qualities of the organism.

This is what the Greeks assumed, and we may take Plato as their spokesman. Plato was by no means a static thinker: his philosophy had the goal of developing in Man the capacity for abstract thought. Abstract thought is the form in which we transmit the experiences of one generation, as it were, "empty" of their specific content, to the next one. Thus this quality is of the utmost importance to Man, while it has the added function of developing an essential part of the mind.

Plato, and a number of other Greek thinkers, possibly overstressed the general importance of this factor because it was important to them.

Greek thinking meant the transition from religious to philosophic rational thinking, involving a further concretization of the mind, a widening of the realm of the regular against the irregular which was seen as caused by whimsical and unpredictable deities. Philosophic thought-patterns in comparison to inspirational religious thinking means a reduction in the intensity of underlying emotions, a better equilibrium.

The Greeks, however, were aware that Man operates at all times in terms of emotions, intellect and symbolic thinking, but, when their philosophy reached its peak, Greece was nearing decline so that the symbolic reaction, as possessing a high survival-value, seemed the most essential one. It had been very strong in the early period of their culture so that it could be blended with their natural sciences into a philosophy when the occasion demanded it. This was, of course, much more true of Plato as an aristocratic patriot than it was of Aristotle, who was closer to our concept of a scientist.

Plato, as well as Aristotle, developed categories for the growth of the Greek mind or "the mind", as they saw it — in its psychological as well as in its socio-political stages. Pre-history was to them a golden stage in which Man had relatively few needs and lived under the religious-familial rule of the tribal leader. Thinking was largely in terms of the imagination; each phenomenon was seen as the activity of personal deities to whom an appeal had to be made in order to obtain favorable results. It should be pointed out, however, that in their nomadic stage the Greeks had nature-deities who were vague and general, and that strong personification set in only when they took up more permanent abodes and reached the agricultural stage.

Law, in this period, existed only in the form of divinely inspired judgments of the tribal leader for each specific case.

It is obvious that leadership could be acquired only by those who possessed a strong spiritual-imaginative reaction since this was the foundation of the life of the group.

In the early periods of group-life there is no question of meeting the problem of survival in terms of an individual pleasure-pain reaction in which the positive outweighs the negative. Life is dangerous, ominous, uncertain, and it can be coped with only because the imagination guides it by magnifying everything into bizarre proportions, but in the structural configuration of these often weird beliefs there is a strong element of protection and a groping for cause-effect relationships.

If a primitive tribe sees a thunderstorm as the action of an angry god, it strives to find a cause for this occurrence, while the appeal to a deity enables it to act off some of the anxiety which otherwise would reach a dangerous point of accumulation. Much later, when it is realized that the thunderstorms take place in recurring patterns, the anxiety diminishes, protective measures become more efficient, and there is a tendency to look for a "cause-effect" explanation in terms of the known regularities of accumulated experience.

If we witness a thunderstorm we have some vague ideas about electric charges, and we do not seek an immediate relation to the supernatural because we can deal with the phenomenon within the framework of our experience.

If, however — and this is important — the same thunderstorm would last for fourteen days and fourteen nights, it would transcend our previous experience and it would again lead to imaginative reactions in all possible variations, in order to find some causal explanation as well as — and this would be the more important aspect — to reduce tensions. People who had never worshipped would flock to churches, law-abiding husbands might attack their wives, etc.

In fact, the invasion from Mars was a case in point. [38] This proves that if the stimulus is strong enough, it causes the imaginative reaction, which breaks through the established and protective layer of habitual neural reaction-patterns.

### Figure I

A ————————— cortical layers
B ————————— sub-cortical layers
C ————————— thalamus

In the primitive mind, a stimulus of intensity $X$ reaches region A, because there is no strong structure in the intermediary region B. As the mind matures, definite neural channels are formed which reinforce the regions in which they occur.

### Figure II

A
B
C

After this development has taken place, a stimulus of the same intensity X only reaches region B because this region has been strengthened and given structure by reaction to normal occurrences. A stimulus of greater intensity Y would still reach region A.

This means that it would be possible to establish reaction-thresholds for each specific culture and the various stages of each culture. In the early stages reaction A dominates thinking which is largely in imaginative-metaphysical terms with a transition from image to abstract thinking. As a culture matures, reaction B becomes stronger with a transition from rational to empirical thinking.

In the period of decline, segment B can no longer cope with the vast amount of accumulated experience, and reaction A becomes again stronger but in terms of individual salvation — the escape from culture-pressure — rather than in terms of group-religion as in the early period.

In the case of the individual, the predominance of one reaction over the other depends upon the intensity of the stimulus which can be an outer or an inner one. In the case of organic frustration, reaction A would emerge, but it is a basic error of Freudian psychology to regard frustration as the *cause* of reaction A. Reaction A has the much wider function of survival under adverse conditions [39] — including those conditions under which accumulated experience is insufficient for rational living, and organic frustration is but one instance of a lack of rational equilibrium. It should be stressed also that reaction A always remains the reaction to the unknown and irregular part of life, and since the relation "Man-Environment" unfolds itself in terms of changes of both factors, there is always an unknown part of life so that reaction A is a basic, fundamental and permanent one. The only possibility lies in probability-patterns — in terms of religious beliefs, metaphysical theories, and mathematical calculations, but they all belong to realm A as they are reactions to the unknown and irregular part of life.

Reaction A may be the most complex neural reaction — requiring the greatest amount of neural energy — because it occurs under the most difficult conditions, namely those of the early social stages as well as under challenges of great severity. That the early social stages should be considered as offering a hard challenge is evident because there is no accumulated experience to draw upon.

The assumption that reaction A is a complex one of high neural intensity would explain why the leader in terms of the spiritual-imaginative reaction would be the founder of the most lasting and extensive social groups. The world religions are the largest and most durable social groups. If we interpret society as a field of forces, this gives us the following situation:

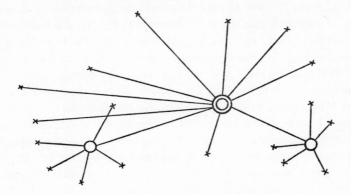

O  Charismatic leader with high A reaction

o  Sub-leaders

X  Followers

A second reason which would lead us to conclude that reaction A is the high energy reaction is that Nature has arranged things in such a way that this reaction is built up first as the most important and fundamental one. It is typical of the preliterate societies in general as well as of the early stages of each subsequent civilization. As civilizations go through a stage in which they borrow from one another, it is evident that the period in which this reaction dominates becomes less in relation to the progress of mankind as a whole, but it is a complicating factor that not all civilizations possess the same intensity. The greater the intensity, of course, the greater also reaction A, but also: the more mature the civilization, the less reaction A becomes, so that it has to be decided in the case of each civilization which factor — intensity and/or maturity — is the more important one, while it still remains necessary to establish a relation to each specific challenge which the civilization in question undergoes.

A civilization, like all forms of organic life, has a standard life-curve, [40] measured in terms of the energy which manifests itself outwardly:

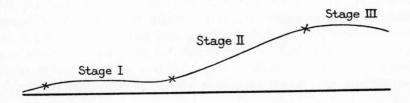

During stage I, there is no great outer manifestation of energy, and it must be assumed that the available energy is used for the building-up of mental structure: it is an introvert stage in which reaction A (the imaginative-symbolic one) predominates while there is little experience on which the rational-control reaction B can be based.

At a certain stage of history, and this often seems a rather sudden change, Man begins to break through the spiritual patterns which have been established by the exercising of the symbolic reaction and enters upon a more extrovert stage: developing more economic needs, a more complex social structure caused by the need for defense, etc. He becomes more dynamic and individualistic and is less concerned about inner problems, less dominated by fear and anxiety.

In this stage II the symbolic reaction is less frequently applied, and the stress is placed upon the development of rational control, or, in other words, reaction B gains in importance as the socialization of Man reaches a much higher level. Man also develops many more needs and for that reason is frequently termed "weak or decadent" by the representatives of the preceding harsher period. He is also constantly warned that he is doomed because he is neglecting the beliefs of his ancestors, while he is also frequently charged with "immorality" because the development of the intellect gives him a wider choice of action-patterns, and this same trend is stimulated by an increasingly complex social structure. It is, of course, obvious that the greater rewards which life offers to the individuals lead to a neglect of the symbolic reaction which may be needed again later; so the prophets of doom have a certain justification.

In the history of all civilizations, this stage re-occurs under the varying names of rationalism, progress, enlightenment, renaissance, liberalism, freedom, etc.

It seems that ultimately a stage is reached in which the neural system of a large number of people belonging to a specific social group can no longer cope with the increasing need for more and more complex reactions. The neural reaction channels are apparently no longer capable of carrying the required load, and definite signs of fatigue become visible: a society can no longer operate except in habitual patterns. As this prevents it from meeting successfully the new challenges from the human and social environment; the "followers" no longer admire their leaders, and the society begins to petrify through lack of communication between the various classes, and this very easily leads to a breakdown. The lack of communication and the inelasticity cause anxiety in the insufficiently large numbers who are aware of this process and they search for release via the symbolic system, either in the form of revivalistic religions or via philosophic systems which seek either mental control in order to diminish anxiety (like Stoicism) or advocate the short-term physical reaction as another although short-lived method to reduce mental tensions (the Eat-Drink-and-Be-Merry-philosophers in their assorted forms). [41] Consequently, the stage of stagnation, petrification, decay or breakdown leads to a reduction in technological development, a regression of the exact sciences, a lack of social control, and a spasmodic revival of the symbolic reaction in which salvation movements, frequently imported from other cultures, compete with the official churches, which are sometimes used to re-enforce the tottering political structure. The element of the "visionary leader" is re-introduced into social life, and it is certainly not accidental that the great visionary leaders arose when the reaction-patterns of great cultures began to show strong indications of impending breakdowns. Mankind, in those stages, becomes again antirational because the rational control-patterns have become petrified. Energy is released — otherwise used for the further growth of the control-patterns — which expresses itself either in direct emotionalism (frequently in the form of "pleasure-seeking") or in a renewal of symbolic patterns as a means of warding off extreme emotionalism and abandonment. Very frequently, we can also observe a hovering between those extremes. The absorption of energy by these two reaction-patterns (the short-term natural and the symbolic one) frequently create the impression of the existence of organic deficiency because the energy-division within the organism changes. Less energy is used for the building-up of neural energy so that the other organic energy-forms receive a larger share.

Man suddenly becomes aware that he has been "suppressed", and since there is a strong interaction between mental and sex life which seem to use comparable forms of energy, this "suppression" is mostly seen in terms of sexual frustration, although in reality a far more complex and intricate process is taking place. Partial proof of this is furnished by the fact that actual sexual abandonment does not reduce tensions but creates new ones by causing emotional frictions which in turn lead to an almost automatic re-establishment of social controls.

It is amazing to observe the existence of a sort of social feed-back system, as has been demonstrated psychologically by cybernetics. [42] It seems that, as long as there is enough energy to reach an equilibrium, Nature reaches this equilibrium, also in society, without any conscious action of the individuals involved. The individual, unwittingly, performs the commands of Nature, as Kant has pointed out in such a magnificent manner. [43]

Beyond the growth, maturity and decay of civilizations we have the history of mankind as a whole, which goes through the same stages, using the civilizations as stepping stones. In this process of growth of mankind as a whole, we have not seen any limit as yet to the reaching of more complex neural reaction-patterns, but it is rational to assume that mankind as a whole will show a life-curve comparable to that of the individual civilizations.

If the stage of development that a social group has reached could be measured in terms of the relation between its reaction-patterns, we could conclude that mankind is still in a relatively early stage, because 90 % of its reactions are in terms of the symbolic reaction rather than of those of the rational control-patterns. It would need entirely new sciences, however, arising out of a combination of the exact and the social disciplines, to give to such a question an answer that would possess some degree of scientific probability. Efforts in this direction are being made, however, and it is hoped that this discussion may occasionally furnish some useful idea, although the presentation in this form is purely meant to stimulate interest, as an individual can only guess at points whose adequate treatment would require a knowledge of all sciences.

The relation between psychological reaction levels and social stages was stressed strongly by Plato, but his interest in society had a definite ameliorative foundation which made him give excessive weight to the symbolic reaction in the form of "philosopher-Kings". He sought a static society because he wanted to ward off the decay of Greece, but he overlooked the fact that the relation Man $\rightleftarrows$ Social/Natural Environment is always a dynamic one, and that a static society is an impossibility. Even the most rigid caste-system has to leave room for social change or it will soon be overrun by more dynamic social groups.

Life itself consists of change, and however much our mind may grope for stability in order to cope with the challenge of the human and natural environment, no modern science can exist without making change in Man as well as in Nature its basic presupposition.

Plato's views of society were dominated by his philosophy of ideas, in which he tried to establish absolute values. There is no reason, however, to assume that the contents of the symbolic mind are absolutes. The existence of the symbolic reaction as such, just as of the rational and natural reactions, is perhaps — and that point is argued in this study — a permanent attribute of the human mind, but the contents of all these reaction forms are determined by human experience, although this experience is transmitted to the various psychological levels in a fashion which is basically unknown to us. We do not find agricultural deities among hunting tribes, but we cannot say with any degree of exactness what images may emerge from the minds of the hunters, since the most unusual combinations occur.

We may be justified in saying that there is nothing in the mind that has not entered through the senses — although even that is very doubtful, but we have no reliable knowledge of how the mind processes sense-perceptions in its various organic stages. We can draw only general conclusions in regard to the dominance of one or the other function and in regard to their interrelationship, the dominance of one always seems to mean a decline in the other.

A purely animalistic life — existent only in pathological cases — would not lead to the building up of control patterns; a completely regulated and rational life does not feed the imagination. In reverse, strong symbolic and imaginative activity disregards the requirements of formal control, while completely "socialized people" frown upon strong and uncontrolled emotional reactions. In other words, the available energy can be used to build up either the one pattern or the other but not both to the same extent, as they are to some degree contradictory, although they are also complementary in regard to the necessity of their co-existence.

This, of course, brings up the question again as to what extent our mental reactions can be influenced by conscious mental or physical behavior. We can tell ourselves or be told not to do this or that: in that case ideas on one mental level interact with those on another level, but the process leads to the building up of a different action-pattern only if the underlying emotions remain below a certain threshold. Overwhelming emotions wipe out all mental control patterns and lead to immediate action unless in a completely socialized individual who has a limited survival capacity. This proves that the structure of the mind is a fluid one which can change with tremendous speed if the proper energy is released under an extremely strong impulse.

In emergency situations we are guided completely by the imaginative reaction, which in a fraction of a second may create the image of a possible alley of escape. This would again lead to the conclusion that the imaginative-symbolic reaction is the superior one since it also seems capable of releasing energy which revitalizes the entire organism in an instant. Thus there would be good reason to assume that the energy A, underlying reaction A, is superior to those of reactions B and C, although the various energy forms draw upon one another within the structure of the organism.

The extreme vital importance of the imaginative-symbolic reaction is also evident in the phenomenon that practically all cultures, especially in their early and intermediary stages, develop specific techniques by which they seek to bring about this reaction in an artificial manner. We refer to the various methods of asceticism.

The assumption is: A, that the symbolic reaction is of the greatest importance to the social group, so that possession of it enhances one's social position; B, as a result, it becomes important to create this reaction artificially.

The reaction in question increases, because of its survival potency, under conditions of duress and of organic deficiency. Ergo: reverse this process: create the hardships and the deficiency purposely, and the symbolic reaction will come to the fore, enhancing one's prestige in the group.

These techniques can be observed among numerous pre-literate groups, for instance, the vision-techniques of the Plains Indians, as well as among the civilizations, most notably in the cultures of India and of medieval Europe. Why in these instances the symbolic reaction was particularly highly valued will be investigated later in the case of medieval Europe, while, for the others, mention may suffice.

These techniques have become so strongly identified with cultural stages which put extreme value on the symbolic reaction that we practically identify them as "ascetic stages", indicating a correlation between asceticism as an attitude and the specific mental reaction as the concomitant.

It is possible but not quite so convincing to relate the other basic reaction-patterns to life-attitudes. Plato did this when he distinguished the doric, the ionic and the lydian-phrygian attitudes [44] in which the first one is close to asceticism, although the Greeks never developed it in its more extreme version; the second one is conducive to the growth of control-knowledge; while the third one is an attitude of individualistic pleasure-seeking, more properly called hedonism. Thus, in the various civilizations we can also make a distinction according to attitudes into: doric or, if stronger, ascetic periods; stoic or rational periods, advocating all those forms of restraint which build up rational control-knowledge; and, finally, hedonistic periods, which are materialistic and tend toward decay. It is obvious then that the doric and ascetic periods correspond to predominance of the imaginative- symbolic reaction; stoic periods to predominance of the rational-control reaction; hedonistic periods to a combination of the latter and of the short term or natural reaction. We approach disintegration if the last one begins to dominate.

Thus, we get the general picture as shown on page 51-

## CIVILIZATIONAL STAGES

| | *Mental reaction* | *Attitude* |
|---|---|---|
| **STAGE OF EARLY GROWTH:** *Low rate of change.* | Strongly symbolic-imaginative. Little control knowledge. Strong emotional reactions curbed by symbolic control-patterns. | Doric or ascetic (asceticism being the indication of higher tensions or severer challenges). |
| **STAGE OF GRADUAL MATURITY:** *High rate of change.* | Weakening of the symbolic reaction. Concentration on technological and social control. Knowledge (econ. system, central. gov., defense, law, science, etc.) Art as survival of the symbolic reaction. Emotional life becomes rational. "Character" as expression of stability gets higher esteem than strong emotions and passions. | Rationalism in regard to econ. needs, family, religion, etc. A seeking of balance but not successful through neglect of the symbolic reaction. |
| **STAGE OF LATE MATURITY AND DECAY:** *Decrease of rate of change. High polit. tensions.* | Petrification of mental reactions. Habitualization of life. Little communication between classes as a result of lack of mental elasticity. Re-emergence of symbolic reaction. | Individualistic. Return to emotionalism. Escapist patterns. Materialism and extreme idealism. |

From this chart, some interesting conclusions can be drawn in regard to the inner structure of different cultures. 45

## CHAPTER V

# MENTAL REACTIONS AND SOCIAL STRUCTURE [46]

Two conflicting ideas have frequently obscured our thinking about the structure of society. Western society has operated, at least in its political approach, with the concept of the basic equality of all individuals making up society, supported to some extent by religious and some psychological ideas which regard the mind as an instrument moulded entirely by cultural factors. On the other hand, numerous thinkers have stressed that society is based not upon the equality but upon the inequality of men, and they undoubtedly have logic on their side.

It is quite obvious that, if the concept of equality is carried to its logical extreme, there could be no society, since completely equal units would neither attract nor repulse one another and no structural field could develop out of a pure agglomeration of individuals. Somewhat grudgingly it is at times admitted that there are, of course, age and sex groups but that at least all normally developed adult individuals should be regarded as potentially equal. They are so treated by a good many laws although not by all or perhaps not even by the majority of them.

This idea of "equality" is part of our symbolic system, and to determine its function and contents is a somewhat chilling undertaking since there is still an atmosphere of taboo around our basic symbols. Yet it might be necessary to perform this operation since great mental confusion results from the identification of symbolic concepts with realities that are covered by the same term.

If we say that A equals B (A and B are equal), most people know what is meant, namely that if we substitute B for A there wil be no difference. If we carry this formal concept into social relations, it becomes quite obvious that we cannot substitute the surgeon for the professional boxer without causing some minor upsets in both realms of activity. Consequently if we still want to say that they are equal, we must admit to ourselves that we are using the word in a specific manner, giving it the value of, for instance, political or human equality without stating this explicitly.

However, we have already reduced our statement to quite a different one, to wit that people are equal in some respects, namely, by rights or attributes which are granted to them by an outside source. If we say that people have equal political rights, we mean that they should either possess these rights — this is an opinion expressed as a general belief: they should — or the situation is that an agency of which the people in question are no part grants them equal rights, and this has no bearing upon the fact whether they are or are not really equal. In other words, if we use the term "equality", we do not talk about an actual quality of the people but about a quality which we attribute to them for specific reasons.

In order to enquire into these reasons, it might be commendable to look first at the opposite aspect of society. In reality people are different: they are young or old, male or female, weak or strong, smart or stupid, white or black, French or Chinese, skilled or unskilled, virtuous or vicious, etc., etc. This is the situation we find without paying any attention to the question whether this is as it "should be", which is an entirely different matter.

From these differences results the need for cooperation: the man needs the woman, the children need the parents, the old need the young to defend them, etc., etc.

The first human groups are based upon a relatively simple functional division: propagation of the species, protection and education of the very young, subsistence, clothes, defense, shelter, removal or reduction of anxiety by a religious system, communication, etc. As soon as a group has met the challenge of life successfully, it becomes convinced — Man is Nature's most conceited animal — that its ways are right. It develops the habit of transmitting its folkways and mores to the next generation, and this is obviously the only thing it can do whether the group is small or large, simple or complicated.

On the other hand, the challenge that each generation has to meet is different from that of preceding generations. The transmitted pattern is useful only in some respects; in others it becomes a retarding force. As a result, there is a constant need for change, correction, adaptation to new problems and new attitudes.

Let us use some examples. In a relatively static society, social position is frequently inherited according to familial status. If this society has to meet a strong challenge which necessitates technological innovation, it will soon become a slogan that people should be appointed according to ability, not according to the status of their families. The society in question would be eager to reduce the importance of kinship groups in order to survive.

In another case, the difference in wealth between the classes might become so great that the cohesion of the society is threatened because there is no cooperation between the very rich and the very poor. Those who become aware of this will press for a better distribution of income in order to save the group as a whole, and this would be done under whatever ideological presentation would be understandable to the group.

In a third case, entire classes of a society may reach higher mental maturity, and this may express itself in the insistence upon certain rights, like choosing leaders instead of having these functions performed by members of old families. In such a case, the slogan becomes political, and it is said that a group of people or all the members of a group should have political rights. These rights can be distributed equally or unequally. If they are distributed equally, the assumption is that all people have equally well founded political opinions. It is quite obvious that this is not the case, but the symbolic concept "equality" is used to replace an outworn social system by one which is closer to the actually existing power structure of the society in question.

Society, in order to survive, needs the performance of a number of functions. Theoretically, this is done upon the basis of ability, but never in reality, although society cannot wholly ignore ability, since the various functions have to be performed in order to insure survival. Consequently, a society tends toward a functional division from which it cannot remove itself too far. On the other hand, it never reaches it either, because there are always the elements of power, prejudice, bias, etc. as each leading social group tries to perpetuate itself by building up protective barriers that are tolerated by the rest of the group so long as the leadership function is carried out reasonably well or so long as the group has to meet only medium challenges.

The functional structure, however, is always the underlying basic one, and if we hear expressions like equality, inequality, social justice, freedom, liberty, etc., we deal with symbolic presentations which reflect the tensions in a society which either in one direction or the other has veered away from its functional moorings.

It must be remembered, of course, that this functional basis is not a constant, because it consists of human needs and human needs that differ although they fall into the three basic categories of physical, mental and symbolic-spiritual, corresponding to the basic attributes of Man which, although themselves functional constants, vary in their interrelationship.

If we realize that it is basically — as Sumner pointed out — the inequality of men and not his equality which explains society, we obtain a different view of its structure. Between units of different energy a relational field develops which is based upon need-fulfilment.

In the first place, we have the natural differences among people in terms of age, sex, physical, mental or spiritual strength, and in addition to that, each social group develops those qualities in Man which fit into its pattern. As each group has to meet a specific challenge, it also has a specific pattern, so that pressures are exerted in order to make people conform to this pattern. The pressure exerted by each pattern is in turn one of the causes of the formation of new patterns, in addition to the challenges which the outside world exerts. Generally speaking, each social group strives to replace the short-term natural reaction (immediate response to drives and emotions) by a rational social one, but this transition is completed successfully only by a number of people and by those the adaptation is, of course, related to organic stages. Each society presents a challenge to the individuals who belong to it, and those who adapt themselves most successfully are the ones who are capable of building-up more complex reaction-patterns. As this involves greater energy, we obtain the picture of society as a field of interlocked energy-groupings in which smaller or larger groups of people gravitate toward those who have the greatest possibility of adaptation.

On the other hand, each society has its own specific pattern, so that its challenge to its group-members is a specific and not a general one. As a result, an individual of greater strength may adapt less successfully than one of less energy, and in this way Nature builds a certain reserve. The pattern of each group is thus not a constant but a variable, and by keeping this reserve, the group as such has a stronger survival-potential, since the individuals who do not adapt themselves to pattern A may become very successful in relation to pattern B.

Although the challenge of each group is a specific one, it has nevertheless general attributes, namely those which are instrumental to survival. Group-survival needs an economic basis in the first place, although this does not mean and has not meant in the course of history that all members of the group have a survival basis. On the contrary, social groups can afford to let a certain percentage of their members die off, and this percentage varies again with the stage of development a group has reached. In the stage of maturity, there is a strong tendency to include the survival-rights of all group members in the goals of the group, although this goal is rarely 100 % realized.

Next to an economic basis, we find that division of labor, and consequently discipline, social conditioning and communication, is an absolute essential. Without language, for instance, no group, however small, can progress beyond bare existence. This need leads to the development of government, especially in its function of defense, to the further extension of technology, to practical science and to professional groupings.

The physical aspects of life, including economic needs, propagation of the kind and rudimentary education plus the more complex social needs which emerge from group-life as such are all concerned with the immediate and direct challenges which the group has to undergo. In addition, there is the need for a wider outlook on life, placing its problems not within the perspective of one generation but upon the long-term basis of many generations or of mankind as a whole. It is characterized by the phenomenon that energy has to be saved for future challenges of which the content is as yet unknown. This need explains the symbolic function which distils from our experience the concepts, values and beliefs for long-term use. These concepts contain the re-action to the uncontrolled and irregular part of our experience and assume the psychological form of belief rather than of knowledge, or at least empirical knowledge.

An individual may say: "I know this to be true", speaking of a belief, but this is the expression of the great psychological weight which the symbolic function possesses in terms of energy. Our beliefs can influence our knowledge, run contrary to it, or, conversely, knowledge can undermine belief, depending entirely upon the relation between these two basic reactions within the individual. Some individuals show a poor communication system between their mental reactions, and they are fully capable of holding beliefs which run contrary to their knowledge, without any great psychic discomfort. This can be explained partly from the fact that our educational and social systems tend to stress one or the other reaction, so that the individual uses habitually one mental "gear" and shifts into "first" or "third" without being aware of it, relapsing immediately into the habitual one if the stronger-than-average tension is removed. As this relative lack of mental elasticity increases, the more habitual the reactions of a culture-group become, involving, of course, the danger of a breakdown if a sudden strong challenge presents itself.

A strong imaginative symbolic reaction aids an individual or a group because the imagination projects many life-situations which do not have to be met at the time but which may arise later. This can be observed clearly in children, who through their imagination play the roles into which they may be put later, except of course those which hold no strong imaginative appeal. It is quite remarkable that this projection into the imagination differs considerably and that one child can be absorbed by acting out a part which has no appeal for the others. It should also be stressed, however, that the imagination is relatively detached from immediate experience and that the possibility of its combinations although emerging from experience-elements is practically limitless.

Generally speaking then, each social group has physical, mental (predominantly the need for co-, super- and subordination) and symbolic needs, and out of these needs arise the permanent institutions of all cultures: family, economic system, government, control-knowledge (social and technological), art, pure science and religious beliefs (the last three belonging predominantly to the symbolic realm, although established religions become social systems with their own government, social system, control-knowledge, etc.). There are, of course, many intermediary realms, like law, for instance. Law seen as the rules emanating from a government belongs to the realm of control-knowledge while concepts like justice, natural law, etc. are part of the symbolic realm which are used to support positive law with a long-term foundation.

It is evident that society can exist only because the individuals possess the basic needs and, behind them, the basic reactions to a varying extent and in a varying relationship so that they are complementary to one another. This is clearly visible in the division into classes which each society shows. Apart from original natural differences, on which little material is available, a basic difference results from the accumulated experience in terms of the challenge which each group meets.

All functions are always divided — whatever the organization might be — into simpler, intermediary, and complex ones, including foresight, planning, guidance and cooperation of less controllable factors. Thus, even if all people were equal at the start, they would no longer be so after a certain period because the various functions are met in terms of different reactions. The simple ones require mostly a short-term physical reaction, combined with a certain amount of control-knowledge; the intermediary ones mostly the rational-social control reaction, the leading ones the capacity to deal with the basic aspects of control-knowledge plus the capacity of long-term planning and the continuation of effort by developing and stressing a symbolic system.

Take, for instance, the symbols by which business organizations seek to perpetuate themselves and to stress their institutional continuity.

Thus, again assuming that things are equal at the start, after a period P a situation S is reached in which all individuals engaged in functions of type I show predominantly reaction C-B; those engaged in activities of type II, reaction B, those engaged in activities of type III, reaction B-A.

"Simpler" or "more complex" are relative concepts but they are contingent upon the fact that in all societies more people are engaged in type I, less in type II, still less of type III. Certain percentages have been determined by recent sociological investigations, most notably those of Lloyd Warner and his school.

If we grant again now that reaction A-B involves more energy than B, B more than C-B, it is clear that society is a field of forces which is determined by the law that:

X (the number of people in function I) $\times$ C B $+$ Y $\times$ B $<$ Z $\times$ B A (Y $=$ number of people in function II, Z number of people in function III).

If this were not so, the sub- and superordination which each society requires could not be explained. Hence, from the existence of society, we can draw this conclusion in regard to the energy-weight of the basic mental reactions. The question whether this difference in energy-weight is a qualitative or a quantitative one can only be decided by the exact sciences. It is known, however, that the organism shows bio-chemical and bio-electrical processes. Whether there are additional ones, and whether they are reflected in these mental reactions cannot be answered at the present time.

It is of some possible importance, however, to observe that the assumption that the symbolic reaction would take place in terms of a different type of energy might aid to explain some of the phenomena of super-sensory experience. In this case, it would be conceivable that this specific energy-form would reach the mind also from the outside, without participation of the known senses. The assumption of the symbolic reaction in the form of a higher energy type is also supported by the phenomenon that direct influence on the symbolic realm seems to be able to set the other reactions into motion within the limits of their interaction, dominated in turn by the survival-potential of each individual and his resistance to outside influence, which would have to be higher than his own to bring about a direct transmission.

If we put the foregoing observations into a diagram, we obtain the following result:

Mental reactions
predominantly:

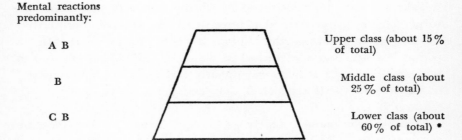

A B          Upper class (about 15% of total)

B            Middle class (about 25% of total)

C B          Lower class (about 60% of total) *

* These percentages vary considerably in sociological studies and are only used as an illustration. The diagrams are not drawn according to percentages but only to illustrate the class-structure.

However, in the life-history of a social group, we can observe a gradual lessening of the A-reactions until they recur in the late period. If we apply these two schemata to the development of Western civilization, the following diagrams emerge:

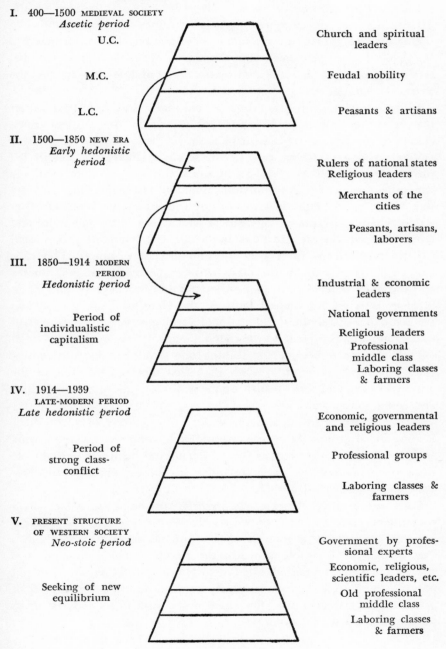

I. 400—1500 MEDIEVAL SOCIETY
    *Ascetic period*
        U.C.

        M.C.

        L.C.

Church and spiritual leaders

Feudal nobility

Peasants & artisans

II. 1500—1850 NEW ERA
    *Early hedonistic period*

Rulers of national states Religious leaders

Merchants of the cities

Peasants, artisans, laborers

III. 1850—1914 MODERN PERIOD
    *Hedonistic period*

Period of individualistic capitalism

Industrial & economic leaders

National governments

Religious leaders
Professional middle class
Laboring classes & farmers

IV. 1914—1939
    LATE-MODERN PERIOD
    *Late hedonistic period*

Period of strong class-conflict

Economic, governmental and religious leaders

Professional groups

Laboring classes & farmers

V. PRESENT STRUCTURE OF WESTERN SOCIETY
    *Neo-stoic period*

Seeking of new equilibrium

Government by professional experts

Economic, religious, scientific leaders, etc.

Old professional middle class

Laboring classes & farmers

It has been observed that the pattern of a social group changes in direct correlation to its experience. The emergence of new patterns frequently involves the coming to the fore of new social classes if those classes represent the type of experience which is needed for the new pattern of the group. When the universal spiritual culture of the Middle Ages no longer represented the attitudes that corresponded to the desire for national and economic consolidation, the power passed to the group that was instrumental in the process of the creation of national states, supported in this endeavor by the rising middle class, namely the national dynasties.

When, in turn, expansion became economic and industrial rather than territorial, a comparable shift took place from the national aristocracies to the large entrepreneur of the capitalistic period.

The attitude of seeing progress in terms of increasing wealth led ultimately to a sharp cleavage between the classes, from which a strengthening of the governmental function resulted. This function was, however, no longer in terms of government by the aristocracy but a new type of government emerged in which control became more and more centered via the executive branch in the hands of professional experts, representing the rise of the middle class to power. This class had been most aware of the clash between entrepreneur and worker and was able to develop, in its professional and bureaucratic jargon, an ideology which compromised between the views of those groups and the remnants of religious and national ideologies which, in turn, had undergone an adjustment to the economic age.

Each class as it became the leading one developed its own symbolism: the purely religious symbols were first replaced by those of the national states, and they in turn by those of economic internationalism and cosmopolitanism.

It is interesting to note that, except in the case of revolutions, leading social groups do not disappear but continue by making a compromise with the new patterns that have emerged, while, if resistance to these patterns develops, they are quick to make themselves the proponents of dissatisfied groups.

Each group clings, however, to its original symbolism, which, as a consequence, has frequently only a very loose connection with its present policies. For instance, a number of the churches adhere to a symbolism that belongs to a period in which the purely spiritual function was stronger than in our period, but this originally ascetic pattern does not prevent them from being completely modern in their dealings with the economic system, which they could never want to see reduced to its former subordinate function.

Another example is the use of the concept of sovereignty. This idea was part of the symbolic system of the national states, and, although at least many national states cannot be considered as self-determining, they nevertheless cling to the formalistic concept of sovereignty, filling it with those contents that the exigencies of the moment require.

We have also observed that the younger a group as such — quite apart from the physical attributes of the component individuals — the stronger its symbolic reaction, because the element of group-unity is of the utmost importance. In those periods, the symbolic function dominates the rational reaction, so that it is considered irrelevant if the contents of the symbolic reaction run contrary to those of empirical knowledge. The latter are shaped according to the former, to the horror of those who react mostly in terms of habitual, rational patterns. This was true in the early days of Christianity, when the upper class Romans were shocked by the superstitions and ignorance of the Christians, and, in the present time, we can find that in Communist countries — relatively recent social groups — the symbolic reaction is much stronger than the rational one, to the amazement and disgust of the more empirical Western world. The West overlooks, however, that its own symbolic system also does not stand in any logical relation to its knowledge, although isolated philosophers, theologians and scientists make occasional desperate attempts to establish such a relation. This is of no importance to the average person, who has a much sounder view of his symbolic notions, namely to leave them alone and not to ask the question of why and how.

Group-symbols emerge from the life of a culture-group, and, since life itself is far from logical, it is hardly rewarding to look for consistency in the realm of our symbolic thinking.

Group-symbols are simply a part of the life of the group, and they are not questioned so long as the group possesses strong cohesion and has not entered upon a predominantly rational period. For that reason it is also quite understandable that recently emerged social groups are extremely sensitive about their symbols and cannot tolerate to have them questioned or doubted, since they are only in the process of acquiring the cohesion which older groups are no longer even aware of possessing.

Thinking in terms of cultural stages is relatively rare, and we are much too apt to judge other cultures in terms of the pattern which we have reached. It is obviously impossible to understand other cultures in this fashion. Anthropologists are doing a marvellous job to overcome this bias, but they can claim only partial success, especially in regard to the more complex cultures.

Even the relatively simple notion that the relation symbolic function/ rational function is correlated to group-experience can be very helpful in order to gain an insight into other cultures.

In other words, to determine the pattern of a group in a general theoretical way we need two basic factors: the duration of the group up to the present time and the cultural pattern of the members at the time the group started. If we have these factors, and if we also know the pressure that is exerted on a group from the outside, we can calculate its pattern in a general way and draw certain conclusions as to the behavior of the members. Of course, the more data are given, the more complete the conclusions, but, at any rate, there is a general theoretical framework on which conclusions can be based.

If we look at the inner structure of a group, we can always observe that the functional division expresses itself, however impurely and indirectly, in the class structure. Within the group, each class sets a challenge for the other classes: the lower groups have to follow the pattern as formulated by the leaders but the leaders can carry out this formulation only in such a way that it really expresses the group-goals. If they choose other formulations, the group allegiance would disappear, and they would automatically lose their function.

The formulation of the group-pattern by the leaders expresses the tensions which exist in the group. As these tensions appear in a transmitted form in the rational and symbolic realm, it might be safer to attempt to gauge these tensions as they exist among the lower classes. The aggressiveness of a national group, for instance, can be measured less well from the utterances of leading statesmen who translate the tensions in an unknown way into symbolic utterances than from the aggressiveness of the average person who is the "cause" behind this verbal behavior. Aggression by a group should be seen obviously as a group-phenomenon, and such aggression is not possible unless sufficient tension exists in a sufficiently large group of people. Whether it would be possible to develop an instrument of measurement for such tensions is, of course, another matter, but there is no reason why it could not be done to some extent, although the absence of the final challenge which sets off the action is a severe handicap. It is also very important whether a group — according to its life-curve — is in the state of dynamic expansion or whether the dynamic part of the curve is levelling-off. The position on the life-curve determines the response to a challenge in its more fundamental aspect, so that, for instance, a quality like aggressiveness should be regarded as a variable and not as a constant.

The mechanism which sets the group as such into motion is the growth of the organism, which results in a different interrelationship between the basic reactions and the corresponding needs. If the organism is seen as operating within definite structural laws, it is clear that this motion takes place with a certain rhythm that corresponds to the life-curve. Thus, needs cannot be expanded ad infinitum but only inasfar as they correspond to organic growth. At a certain stage, people tire of further need-development and search for ascetic or stoic patterns in order to strengthen the symbolic reaction or to reduce the increasing complexity of society, as "the more needs, the more complex the society", so that the system of challenges and responses may threaten to outgrow the neural reaction-capacity of the individual.

If modern mankind is seen as one society — and this is the view to take because people live in a state of "consciousness of kind" in regard to all peoples, we are undoubtedly still in the dynamic stage, or we may not even have reached it, so that there is no reason to become alarmed about the levelling-off of need-development, but one day this process will set in according to the law of probability. There is as yet little of a control organization in relation to world society in terms of a world government — the attempts of the United Nations in that direction have not reached any definite stage — so that world society operates predominantly in the economic and the symbolic realm. This would mean that the history of world society as such has barely started, and many years hence, our period will probably be referred to, and correctly, as the stage of semi-civilization, since the rules of what we call "civilization" still do not prevail in international society in spite of a definite trend in that direction.

In the light of the present discussion a point comes to the fore that may deserve discussion. We can observe that the substitution of the rational-social reaction for the direct and more emotional one has taken place, in the course of history, in increasingly larger social groups. First the family was — what could be termed — the most effective social unit, namely that group which exercises the most far-reaching control over the activities of the individual; then the clan, the tribe, the confederacy of tribes, the loosely knitted empire, the city-state, the national state, and finally the super-state and the contemporary regional groupings of nations. Within the effective social group individual or group violence is forbidden by law and is considered antagonistic to the interests of the whole, so that self-control and rational behavior become the habitual behavior pattern of the majority of the people under normal conditions.

If this effective social unit widens into a larger group, this is only possible because the individuals become capable of building-up more complex reactions as societalization in terms of a larger culture-group involves — generally speaking — more complex behavior than that in smaller groups. Thus, the history of mankind clearly shows a pattern as a whole, namely the adjustment of the individual to increasingly complex situations, although this evolutionary growth is not a linear but a spiraling movement in which there are stages of regression.

Social groups go through a stage of culture-borrowing so that the effect is cumulative, since this borrowing presupposes a greater absorptive power of subsequent generations.

One factor which appears to contradict this is the observation that language, at least in structure, seems to have become frequently simpler instead of more complex. But language has two major functions: emotional expression and communication, and in the process of maturing of a civilization, the latter aspect takes precedence over the former, which may lead to a simplification of structure as the finer shadings of expression are lost.

The greater complexity of the reaction-patterns — and this is not to be overlooked — is in the realm of control-knowledge, not in that of spiritual or symbolic thinking or in relation to emotional life.

In these fields, there is indeed a loss which leads to compensation if the basic structural relationship between the basic reactions becomes disturbed. The prophets, crying in the wilderness, the strong emotions of the a- or the anti-social all have their own deeper meaning, and it is always again amazing to realize that Nature has a general magnificent pattern in which everything somehow seems to fall into its proper place. It is perhaps a part of this grandiose scheme that we can but rarely acquire this detached view of life, as we ourselves are all like mechanisms set to perform a function in the general pattern. The symbolic reaction gives us glimpses of this rhythmic flow of life's processes, reassuring us that also all misery and all suffering have a purpose and make a contribution to life which is superior to that of the successful and the contented.

If this view of life is needed for our survival and if it can only be acquired through suffering, this would mean that life operates under a set of iron laws from which our increasing mechanical controls will offer no escape, because they dull our sense of cosmic awareness instead of awakening it. Our inventions and controls only make life livable for more people but whether they change the basic aspects of life is at least doubtful.

We have bombs which can kill and maim a hundred thousand people but it takes the effort of somewhere near the same number of people to produce them. We may not have progressed beyond the savage who kills one enemy with his club.

The solution of life lies in ourselves and in our capacity to reach maturity, but of this process our technological development is only one aspect. We have increased the span of life of the individual, meaning that the group as such has a higher survival-potential, but real progress could only be made if mankind itself becomes the effective social unit so that group-survival is no longer under the threat of other, antagonistic groups.

The "law" of increasingly larger groups would indicate that we will automatically reach this goal, but the problem of our generation is whether it can be reached by evolution instead of by revolution. Awareness may give us a choice between these two possibilities but this awareness would require great courage of the individual.

The courage to have a conviction is becoming increasingly difficult to find as group-life controls the individual more and more, so that he has little opportunity to struggle through to an opinion of his own. Modern life has become increasingly clever in regard to distribution of energy, and the greater variety and comfort it offers lull the individual into convenient acceptance of slogans and of an uncritical applause for group symbols.

It falls to the intellectual to be more than an entertainer, a producer of the ego-image of his audience or a formulator of group-symbols. He needs the courage and integrity which make it possible to say "No", if that is the answer which critical and objective thinking requires. It is his task to forge the underlying forces of society into evolutionary ones before they burst into the fury of uncontrollable flames. It is also his task to live in isolation so that the submerged part of his nature, not yet formalized by the pattern of his culture, can come to the fore.

But Nature herself arranges all this, and perhaps all we need is to learn again to listen to the sound of the rains and the roaring of the winds and to observe the brightness of the stars:

"And behold the height of the stars. How high they are".

CHAPTER VI

# SYMBOLS AND THE INDIVIDUAL

EXCERPT FROM A CASE-STUDY

The first symbol I can remember is one of anxiety and fear, namely the image of an unseen fire which still returns in the form of roaring flames around a strangely cold and detached looking building as if it had no real part in the process of its destruction. This fire occurred when I was about 4 years old. When I woke up from the noise across the canal on which we lived I was told that nothing was the matter but I refused to believe this and, instinctively, many earlier fears coalescing into this one experience, I became terribly frightened so that, many years later, I could still see the flames very vividly although I had never seen them in reality.

The reason why this first symbol was a negative one kept on puzzling me for many years. Was it an indication that the negative already outweighed the positive, that, in spite of excellent care, the feeling of being unable to cope with life successfully loomed like a threat, or was it purely the insecurity of early life in which everything is frightening and of gigantic proportions?

I can also still remember that it was as if all things were separate. The sounds, especially those of approaching footsteps or the howling of the wind in that storm-blown seaport, the colors of darkness stood out by themselves without growing into a part of something larger. They were forces which were menacing like living people, while the people themselves again were very much like them: separate sounds and smells and colors, each playing a role of its own.

Only gradually this distinctness disappeared, merging into houses, peoples and animals, although the winds and the clear puddles of rain which reflected the wavering street-lights, the slight rippling of the canal as if it resisted the wind, remained things by themselves, lending a comfort that yet had a vague uneasiness about it. The sense of mysteriousness, of a fear that shifted from a pleasant tingling of the skin to the sensation of being strangled by an invisible hand corresponded strongly to the sequence of light and darkness. Every day anew the light dispersed the remnants of nightmarish dreams, of obsessions in which creatures of weird forms threatened an indefinite but all the more ominous disaster, leaving behind a feeling of insecurity which caused a groping for support from the adults, who had grown into unities, although as yet strongly connected with immediate perceptions. On rainy days they seemed to carry the hostile outside world into the protective cosiness of the lighted room, and they were at those times less able to dispel the fear that the figures in the wall-paper were really alive, unkind goblins who were kept in check but barely, so that any disturbance in the equilibrium would enable them to carry out their mischievous pranks.

Toward the evening the fears combined themselves into the concrete threat of a giant brown bear who was sitting on the couch of the darkened parlor, not an essentially evil animal, but somehow to approach him or to go into that darkened room was a mortal danger. When my parents would open the door so that the room became semi-lighted, the bear dissolved itself slowly, although I could never understand that my parents did not appear to notice him when his snout and the heavy brown fur were so clearly visible. At those moments he seemed almost friendly, as if he realized that he was there for me alone and there was a sort of a bond between us.

It was as if he approved of parts of me, but I was not to come near him. From a distance he gradually became a friendly and protective although whimsical god, but to approach him remained sheer madness although tantalizing as if it gave the power to end life if things would really become too bad.

But they never deteriorated completely, not even in the many days of sickness when the worried faces of the adults were seen through a haze of fever which carried with it a rhythm of throbbing and pain that resulted in strange and soothing images. To become sick was like a journey into strange lands, full of adventures and novelty. These interludes were also accompanied by the arrival of unusual delicacies and the vague realization that weakness carried a lot of privileges with it and that it was in some ways preferable to the harsher days of complete health.

This same sense of novelty was to be gained, although more perilously, by setting forth into the outside world, which was more solid and seemed to possess fewer dimensions, thus creating the feeling that life was not quite as dangerous as it had seemed before. But what attracted most were not the swans in the canal or the pretty flowers in the lawns that were pointed out to me but rather things that seemed to possess a life of their own, like the cracks in the rustic wooden bridge that were like roads leading into the bowels of a submerged world or little piles of dirt that grew into mountains through which channels had to be dug for the on-rushing waters.

For the first time life appeared in its real cold dimensions when the swans in the canal fought with each other. It was breath-taking, as if a mask had been torn from the make-believe world of sweet adult words, of something real that was far superior to the rows of neat houses and the scrupulously mowed lawns. I could feel the blood rushing through my veins, and became almost blind with hatred when the municipal attendants came with large nets or poles to separate the fighting animals.

Later on, I felt strangely ashamed of these strong emotions and attempted purposely to return to the now childish world of imagined dangers. Suddenly I knew that the bear had not been real, and at that moment I longed for him passionately, as if the world of the imagination was warmer and more varied, more protective than the outside that seemed to encroach brutally on what had belonged to me and stripped me of all possession. It became more essential to own things, since I had suddenly become aware that there was nothing in this outside world that could be regarded as safe.

The struggle between the real and the imagined world oppressed me, and the more the first one gained focus, the more desirable the second one became, in spite of the realization that its whisperings and advices were frequently strangely incongruous, as if compelling me to do things against which other parts of the mind warned imperatively. This stands out most strongly in the case of an overwhelming desire to fly: each time I descended the stairs from our second-floor apartment, I knew with penetrating clarity that I could fly, that all that was needed was to spread out my arms and I would float down gracefully and without effort. But with exactly equal clarity I knew that this was not so and that I would be at the foot of the stairs, covered with blood and moaning pitieously if I would let go off the bannisters to which I clung in perspiring desperation. That such a conflict of such extreme sharpness could exist left a feeling of unreality that never completely faded, and I still suppress the image of descending the stair case in my first parental home as soon as it presents itself as if I am still undecided as to how the issue is to be met.

This disturbing clash between reality and unreality made me turn more toward my father, who appeared as a victorious warrior in the struggle with the outside world, overwhelming and somewhat frightening but nevertheless showing a road out of the protective but false security of the peaceful livingroom. The more I turned to him, the more puzzling it became that the adult world seemed a mysterious territory, situated somewhere between what gradually had become real and the realm of phantasy.

The things which I had begun to take for granted were surrounded by puzzling rituals and uncomprehensible fables which appeared as a particular kind of meanness of the adults, a purposeless exercise of power in order to enslave the young in a permanent way whence there was no escape. The adult world was an in-between world of a particular coldness and without the appeal of the fight of the swans or the beckoning, yet dangerous allurement of the sounds or the limitless light of the starry evenings. It wanted to take hold of the body and divide it, in an utterly incomprehensible manner, into good and bad parts so that the latter became alluring and fascinating and seemed to unleash frightening sensations that became all the more interesting because they were in the realm of the forbidden. The more the danger of this territory was stressed, the more it re-appeared in images which had the appeal of a reality that was much sharper than the vague awards held out for "goodness" which seemed to consist entirely of a dull and unadventurous life stretching into the far distance.

But it was disturbing that a compulsion was exerted by this life so that there was only an escape in a mysterious bond with others who labored under this same suppression and wanted to build a world that imitated the adults but in a far more romantic way in which taboos of an entirely different nature, which emerged as by themselves, were valid. Only occasionally the dichotomy of good and bad suddenly penetrated into these games when generally unnoticed differences came sharply into focus, resulting in an alarming link with the images of the early night. Even then, however, they were more general and less specific than in the direct rulings of the grown-ups, who seemed to be in possession of a far more exact knowledge than fitted our own world of shadowy half-values or of direct unmistakable physical superiority in terms of blows and bloody noses.

There was a wholly mystifying relationship between the realm of the forbidden and what was presented to us under the term "religion". Everything that pressed like a heavy weight upon us and the strange hostility of the grown-ups towards our reality were condensed in the idea of a still more terrifying adult who seemed to rule not only their repulsive reality but even the sacred world of phantasy whose lightness and gracefulness became threatened by this superior force. The fact that this power was depicted as "Good" did not penetrate our consciousness, which operated in an entirely different set of values in which goodness was nothing but a restraint on what was real and adventurous. The distinction between good and bad became increasingly congruous to the difference between ugly and beautiful because all the "goodest" aunts and uncles were of a horrifying appearance, only slightly mitigated by the fact that they came like the Persians, carrying gifts.

The compromise between these two hostile and almost mutually exclusive worlds was epitomized in the ritual of the birthday party, when the superior forces unbent and supplied some of the things that were needed, although with a sugary and restraining sweetness of whose utter falsity we were fully aware.

But at those times we learned to pretend with the artfulness and the artificiality of the adults, who always acted like people upon a stage unless they quarrelled, and those quarrels possessed a sort of concentrated and repressed spitefulness which was magnified by their being so horribly unlike the warriors of our imagination, armed with swords and shields and engaging only in picturesque and noble battles.

Yet, in spite of our resistance, the adult world exerted the fascination of something that had to be coped with. That aspect of it we never questioned, and we were fully aware that our escapes were only temporary, and we were even jealous of those who had penetrated more into this hazardous realm, and those older ones could leave us suddenly with a horrible sense of inadequacy and inferiority so that our games were emptied instantaneously of their interest and appeared like senseless motions of which one became ashamed.

The winter and the full summer were the times when growing into the other world seemed more simple than in the spring or the fall. In winter, when there was ice on the canals, the two worlds suddenly blended and the grown-ups came to our realm, skating along the canals and generally behaving like completely understandable creatures, interested in achievement and adventure, and blending into the radiant brightness of the winter nights when a magic hand had turned everything into beauty and phantasy. Then, we were also aware again of those remote forces of Nature which seemed to gain a contact with this now more real "goodness" as a sort of blending of many elements into a harmony that possessed an understandable rhythm.

The same was true but not quite to the same degree of the summer vacations when forests and moors gave a setting into which we submerged completely, followed and somewhat restrained by our elders who were constantly warning us not to overdo things, unaware of the imperativeness of our exploits and the sense of intimacy which the forest gave us.

The end of the vacation always sent me into a fit of crying when I realized that once more this hostile urban world which was the incarnation of the superfluous was lying in wait for me. The only comfort was a very elaborate forest-ritual, carried out in great secrecy, in order to secure my return to the same place next year.

Already at that time I must have been aware that this dualism between a distorted, superfluous and disharmonious world and the simple delights of Nature was to continue with increasing oppressiveness. It ran through everything: in school there were on the one hand the delights of the classics and the pleasing knowledge of physics and chemistry; on the other, the boring grind of many other things which seemed superfluous and which only created more contempt for the adult world as wholly devoid of beauty and harmony. Then, more oppressive and apparently unescapable, there was the choice of a career, being held before one's nose, and as every adult activity seemed about as dull and monotonous like the other, utterly unacceptable in terms of the values of our own world.

Some gave in to parents as representing a world of overwhelming power, others flipped a coin as a reliable pagan ritual, and still others simply tormented themselves. There was no escape from this hateful world, except in new dreams which became sharper and more pressing, presenting the image of a girl, unencumbered by all that had become oppressive. She was a pagan goddess, wild, beautiful, whimsical and forever beckoning, although she was never captured in these dreams, which seemed to contain a warning, a line that whenever passed left a sense of misery and guilt.

It was of the utmost importance to hunt for her in reality, a secret to be shared by nobody, and somehow related to one's role in the various games or exploits. Forever she would seem to appear, sometimes in the form of the glimpse of a face in a crowd, a sudden brightening of eyes, or a flash of understanding like "I also like Homer", or it could be a form far away which was leaving for some unknown place, or some one, living in a mansion in England or a mountain cabin in the Alps, listening intently for something that might be coming. But these dreams, the contents of the writings of poets and novelists, also seemed to enter into the realm of the forbidden, making what now had become society appear in its utter cruelty, stupidity and loathsomeness, not even reluctant to reach with its soiled hands for what appeared as a sacred goal, far above the buying and selling that went on in the streets, horrid through their disgraceful ugliness.

There was no comfort in the realization that others appeared capable of accepting this world readily. This made it all the more frustrating, resulting in moods of abject self-rejecting as well as in a sense of cold and disdainful superiority. It was comforting, however, that there were also partners, those with whom a bond could be established and who also wanted to escape. Life became a search for those of the same spirit, with the image of the Girl hovering in the background as the unattainable, at least in this world which seemed to close in on one, so that any motion outside the prescribed realm began to acquire a courage that was not there and was even sinking lower and lower under the impact of increasingly hostile and burdensome challenges.

Escape was needed. It came unexpectedly.

At the end of my high school years I went with a friend to Austria to join a group of Austrian boys on a mountaineering trip. They all belonged to the youth movement and were convinced of the necessity to return to Nature and simple and harsh living. It proved to be a revelation.

On a rainy day we left the train at Zell am See and began our march toward the Gross Glockner. The low hanging clouds deepened the uncertainty I felt about this venture and my own awkwardness in regard to the carefree mountain climbers. Toward the evening we reached the snowfield, and suddenly when the clouds broke the majestic landscape of glaciers and rocky peaks was right in front of us. It was breathtaking, and I resolved then and there that this must be the world I had seen in my dreams. This finally was the realm of neither the real nor the unreal which had been missing, and the challenge of the mountains would generate the courage that had become quite imperative. Behind it all was a sort of a philosophy of power but an un-materialistic power, made of a superior stuff that promised freedom from the people in the cities below.

The first venture lasted only a few weeks, but the image remained. With the concentration of youth I acquired all that had been written about mountaineering, and at last there seemed to be the solution of something that was forbidden and that dwarfed the torments of the preceding period as not fitting into the life of a pioneer and an explorer. The substitution, which was really a sublimation, became almost complete: I developed a religion of mountain-worship which suppressed everything that had been insoluble. It was an ideal that was not so remote as the life in terms of an invisible world which had been held up to me without ever generating any warmth or conveying any tangible reality. In a vague way I probably had accepted it but as soon as it became concrete, it bore a relation to the dwarfed and strange life that many people led, guided by an imagination that no longer deserved the name and was no better than a set of frozen and petrified principles that were inhuman rather than human or only approved of by a frustrated and suffering humanity. There was no greater horror than this concretization of phantasy, entailing an irreparable loss of freedom and independence and preventing the recrudescence that was an inherent part of Nature. It included the right to be born and reborn, without being weighed down by the feeling that things done in this or that way had been wrong and had to be carried like an eternal burden, choking off one's right to feel and to live, and leaving nothing but the torture of gloom and self-reproach.

Ideas were needed, more desperately than bread, since that was available. Only the mountains offered an idea that could be translated into a reality, a perilous balance between life and death but for that reason all the more satisfying compared with the problems that were without dimensions, an eternal living in half-fear of sickness and decay, while these were only there because they were willed by minds that had lost the desire to be strong and healthy.

The songs, accompanied by a guitar, that told of soldiers and beautiful maidens, of battle and blood, sounded sweeter than the hymns about eternal life in the depressing churches of the crowded cities. They also sounded better than the political songs and the campaign speeches which generally created the image of a world in which the rhythm of Nature would be lost even more irrevocably. And they were mixed, at least in Germany and Austria, with the stench of beer and smoke that had become taboo to our rituals of snow and sun worship.

When we returned to the cities, we carried with us the plans for a following ascent, and the problems of daily living and our studies had become completely ephemeral to these goals, a compromise that we tried to ignore, the last weakness that was due to disappear when things became more favorable. We seemed to be waiting for something, for a transition that was translated by some into political goals; by others into a creative desire that rarely led to any real efforts, due to a constant state of exhaustion and to the vague conviction that the idea already set us apart and that there was no need to translate it into reality. But we argued endlessly about these matters, developing violently opposed factions and longing for the cloak and dagger that seemed to fit into the atmosphere. A natural result of the denial of the world of the "burghers".

This transition involved a shifting of value in regard to the Girl. She was less of a symbol but also less in the realm of the forbidden. Love had to be strong and passionate to gain approval; something to be postponed until perfection could be found. Even then it had to remain secondary in a world which belonged essentially to the male; occasional lapses of short-lived interests were met with silent disapproval as a sign of disloyalty, but they were not an issue that involved any very real values, apart from the aspect of stoic self-control and devotion to unspecified ideals of which we were nevertheless quite sharply aware.

It was clear that a rift had to develop between those who were capable of sustaining this semi-ascetic self-denial and those who could not. The first group made a gradual transition to extreme nationalism as a tangible group-goal, leading them back to the world whence there was no real escape, while the others, one by one, faded back, with a bashful smile, into the once-abhorred daily life. Only a few continued to see the mountains as a goal in itself, growing into solitary escapists who isolated themselves from all others and sometime sacrificed their lives to their fanaticism.

Once more the symbol seemed to lose in the same measure as it became a reality. At times the symbolic appeal of the mountains would fade out, and they would turn into hateful, forbidding lumps of stone and ice, against which some helpless little animal was battering in vain and without purpose.

But one thing remained. The physical courage which had been gained translated itself into the rebelliousness of a greater individualism, since there was no group whose goals permitted identification with them. They were too alien, too much within the orbit of a foreign life, so that the necessity of return began to loom larger, first seen almost as a kind of treason but then more as the renewal of a battle which almost had been lost. In a devious way the return to group-life could not be denied, but it had to be given a goal, the aim of transforming it into something different. But there was no starting point in the life of a settled country like Holland, where things went according to a pattern that suddenly seemed more normal than the abyss that was left behind. The dimensions which had been developed were incongruous, as if they had emerged purely from my own nature without relation to a tangible reality. The goal of some form of constructiveness appeared like a desire for frantic activity, out of proportion in regard to the slow and measured flow of life in which only the mentally unbalanced seemed to find serious flaws. But what about these rumblings that passed through Europe, the frightening explosions, the undercurrents that could be felt with physical clarity, the hatred between people. Where was either the sanity or the insanity, in seeing all this or in not seeing it? Or was the tiger saner who, even without hunger, jumped at his dumb-witted prey, inflicting upon it the penalty of Nature. Was it again necessary to look for the few who were aware of this, or were there none? Were people moving like tired puppets, unaware of the forces that moved them, going through their habitual motions with a minimum of consciousness, like sleepwalkers, afraid to wake up to the light of the breaking day?

Again there was no symbol, simply an amassing of anxieties which found no pivotal point, no possibility to gravitate even toward an imagined solution, regulating at least the tormenting mental cycles which went round and round threatening to increase to the speed of frantic despair or ultimate breakdown. For a brief moment, an old Chinese painting of a tiger became the symbol.

His eyes were half-closed, looking at the world in sleepy contempt, but behind it was the potential of ferocity, of avenging fury and of escape. The latter was essential; it was the problem of escape which still remained crucial as acquiescence had once more become impossible.

For the first time I went through a process of intellectual awareness, realizing that underneath all was this desire for freedom and self-expression, rejecting all controls and as yet unconscious of the fact that Nature automatically applies brakes when they are needed. The symbol of "self" became one of whimsical self-indulgence as a demonstration of independence, a protest against the mechanism of society whose wheels continued to turn in exactly the same indifferent and ignoring fashion. The animal struggling with the icy rocks had become a speck of dust upon a neatly polished machine, merely unheeded because of its unimportance. And yet the smaller I became, the more audible was the creaking, the more visible it was that the machine was heading toward a breakdown. The more comforting also the idea that I had no part in this process which was far from being as constructive as it pretended.

And again the same image returned, but its contents became more realistic, translated into a philosophy more than a vision, a process closer to that of other people, of ideas that could be argued and debated as to their reality and practical value. But the more concrete things became, the more they presented themselves as insoluble, tied to the problems of thousands and thousands of people, pushing one another in circles within the confines of a narrow prison. The lack of freedom was then a physical problem, rather than a mental or an imaginative one, and it was no longer sufficient to create a phantasy world in which time and space were manipulated to fit the desire of the moment. It involved a hardening, as if the turning away from the idea was a loss and a form of treason, so that there remained an urge to find once more a goal that was translatable into a vision albeit a more concrete one.

The image which emerged was one of space and physical strength: no longer of inaccessible mountains but of rolling hills with wide vistas and with an activity that was free of the staccato and the cacophony of the European city. Something also fundamental and direct in its thinking, without the trappings of involved and tortuous ideologies, expressing ultimately only the power struggles of different groups.

Once more it was an accidental occurrence which gave content to the image. Some American students appeared at the German university at which I held a small job. They were like creatures from a different world: carefree, living independently as if nothing much bothered them, natural without being aware of it. They seemed to rise above the others, to possess the freedom that was studied in those who were so proud of it.

Was it simply greater strength that exerted this fascination? A moving away from the realm of conflict, clothed in the tiresome tirades of the professors, who so rarely were capable of rising above their limited little topics which they nursed with almost pathological devotion into weird and monstrous structures that became like endless chess games, played without logic or rules, purely dominated by the mood of the moment or the state of their digestion? Or was it the greater simplicity, the artless faculty of the Americans to see the mind as an instrument to be used when needed, not as something that had to be coerced into acrobatics, draining the organism of its vitality and the spirit of its light and effortless phantasies?

Or was it rather the absence of these undercurrents of sadism and cruelty, the habit to seek a natural equilibrium, without being forced by being crowded in by thousands of people to built up a defense or an attack that forced the individual to draw upon his last resources so that he became mad with exhaustion and fear, longing to punish others — almost anybody who could be attacked — in order to diminish these unbearable tensions? The most nightmarish aspect was the effort to cure the diseased mind by the pretense of physical strength, a desperate effort at conscious regeneration, an effort that carried to the utmost depths of cruelty and meanness since it was bound to misfire. Exhaustion cannot be cured by exhaustion of a different type which merely taxes the organism more heavily so that the mind only gains the power to translate into action what has become an obsessive merry-go-round. But there is but brief relaxation in the commitment of evil, which reverberates and is magnified by the suffering of others until it is finally met by those who can rise above it in a dream in which there is no room for revenge. A dream which once more gives proportion to these quarrels which feed upon each other with maddening velocity.

But there were no such dreams in this German life in which no one looked beyond his own immediate interests or those of fanatic groups which preached the brotherhood of hatred.

There was no escape but flight from this wheel of disorder that was moved by forces over which no one seemed to possess any control. People tottered toward a disaster which blinded them with a light that obscured their sense of inferiority and frustration by presenting their selfishness as a noble goal and their lack of balance as a sign of force. Like the madman who dances through the morning crowd of the sober workers, not even causing them to smile, these people frantically raced to and fro, believing that they were impressing a world that had gone to the other extreme of studied and artificial indifference, not certain that a glance toward the madman would not make them break out into the same apocalyptic dance.

The more ineffable these conflicts became, the greater the admiration for the orator who appealed to the crudest emotions, which conjured this same image of strength before the tired brains of the masses. Strength was the content of the image, that is not to be doubted; but what is strength? The excessive activity which is not accompanied by joy but merely tends to impress others? The disdainful withdrawal? The flight into liquor and sex?

The frenzied attack upon the weak that leaves one with a sense of shame and self-contempt? Or is it rather the brightness and purity of the Acropolis, the sense of balance which avoids the "either" and the "or" but sees everything within the shifting hues of light and darkness? The quality which makes life diaphanous because it is seen as the marvelous balance which Nature herself produces, helped perhaps somewhat by the brightness of the mind that watches this stupendous process with awe, gaining an effortless attitude, a moving with the rhythm that is inescapable?

But perhaps this balance was tied to external factors, perhaps it needed a certain amount of space to come to fruition, an absence of other people or an attitude on their part which removed the undermining sense of anxiety. It could be that only some individuals could reach this at rare moments when they could merge into the flow of life which itself had become broad and majestic. But the turbulence of the waters at other times would press upon the individual particle, making it rise to the same pitch of tension as those around him, rising in the foam and spray that was lost in the mad rush of the stream toward the ocean of death. So there was no escape but to dream of this ocean, to long for the final release when the tensions which were inherent in life itself would fade out into this dreamless quietude, this final merging into the subdued rhythm of ultimate rest.

However, there was the contradiction of will, the possibility of consciously bringing about the conditions that would create a better balance. Why would it be impossible for the individual or for Man, once he realized the causes of his tensions, to change them, to dam the river in its more violent parts so that there would no longer be the endless accumulation of misery and suffering, the same pattern of brainless living until Nature was forced into putting her harsh laws into operation because Man, although the capacity had been given to him, continued in the blindness of his own stupidity?

Was Man Nature's most stupid animal because he was the most conceited one, refusing to see on account of his blind pride? And it seemed all so simple: space, tolerance and individuality, those three would weave life into a ever-changing texture that would not wear or be torn, that could derive all that is needed from its own harmony and beauty, a world closed within itself and held firmly within the capacities of Man if only he could cross the threshold from disequilibrium to equilibrium, pass from obsession to clear thought, change from the conceit of self-righteousness to the tolerance of intelligent living. Why was this so much that it seemed impossible, or would it be gained only after another nightmare would leave Man with the realization that the world of the morning was not half so bad as that of his own mind? Man was his own worst enemy in a world which demonstrates the laws of Nature from dawn to dusk for all who care to see and to listen in silence until the rising and falling becomes clearly audible.

Was it true then that the image could be translated into a reality or at least into a vagueness that would be indicative of the reaching of happiness when time and space lose their urgency and limitation, so that dream and reality merge into the timeless rhythm of the ocean on a windless day?

The realization was sharp and painful that also this is a dream amidst the din of battle and the compulsive motions of myriads of machines, grinding the human mind into a lifeless mechanism so that he cannot escape into the simple world outside. Yet they are creatures of his will, whose revolt might be controlled so that they will serve instead of rule. They represent power, but in them the power is bound to a structure. They repeat the laws of Nature within narrowed confines, repeating what needs to be heard.

The image and reality are but two sides of the same world, and the distance between them is the measure of our own maturity. We do not dream of things beyond us but of things within ourselves, of things that are yet to come and that will narrow this margin that has driven us through endless centuries of misery and suffering toward a goal that has come within our vision. As the mountaintop may seem close to the exhausted climber but still holds its gravest challenge, so we may be able to see the harmony that once more may slip from our grasp. But if it does, it is our own responsibility: yours and mine, because Nature seems to show her intentions so clearly, that it would be the price of our own blindness which we would have to pay.

# PART II

# APPLICATION OF THE BASIC APPROACH TO WESTERN CIVILIZATION

## CHAPTER VII

## THE MEDIEVAL ATTITUDE 47

It is the purpose of this and the following chapters to apply the "theory" of the preceding section. In a twofold manner, however, some reservations must be made: in the first place, the word "theory" might be overambitious as it is more a classificatory scheme which has been presented that emerged out of a tentatively formulated philosophy for which no convincing proof can be furnished at this stage. Secondly, it is not the intention to give a historical presentation of this general theory but rather to demonstrate it again — and at greater length and with more detail — by relating it to the reality of Western civilization which has, of necessity, unfolded itself in time. It is also not implied that the social philosophy which has emerged in this analysis is readily applicable to other civilisations although their stages of growth show similarities but, on the other hand, social developments are cumulative so that they show simultaneously the limitations of Man's basic structure and the innovations which are concomitant with the concept of growth.

Growth — organic growth — means motion within limits, and, as far as social life is concerned, these limits can be read out of history in a general and vague manner which defies concretization. Concretization is given by the past, unclearly unfolded by the present, but unknown in relation to the future. The only decisive factor is that Man changes in accordance with his experiences which he can never transmit entirely so that only comparable stages of growth absorb the results of comparable experiences.

For this reason, in spirit the Middle Ages have become alien to us because we can only vaguely recapture the overwhelming anxiety which overwhelmed Man of this period. It is a period of youth, in regard to the Germanic tribes which became its chief carriers but it also inherited the decay of the Graeco-Roman civilization and the wider basis which had been given to the Western world by the emergence of Christianity.

It is noteworthy that the great religious leaders of the world — Christ, Buddha and Mohammed — arose when the leading world-civilisations tended to disintegrate into smaller dynastic, tribal or national units. A general human appeal was needed, directed at all of mankind although in reality the influence of these religious leaders remained limited to their respective civilizations, at least in the initial stages.

A general human appeal requires the inspired, intensely human leader who translates the anxieties of Man into religious beliefs which are accessible to all and which transcend the prevailing dogmatic religions, the spirit of caste and class, as well as all forms of tribal, national, racial or economic prejudice. In addition, the religious leader shows the need for restraint which is essential in periods of disintegration and of excessive materialism.

It could be added that Christianity, for the first time in history, presented an individualized system of ethics, indicative perhaps of the beginnings of a more dynamic civilization which had to set off a realm for the individual, in order to guarantee the possibility of development. It was only natural that this was done in religious terms — by the concept of grace — because religious thinking is not only Man's most general mental faculty but also because Christianity marked the beginnings of a new civilization which had not as yet gained enough control or experience to create more rational thought-patterns.

The religious zeal of early Christianity was so intense that it would have brushed aside rational thinking, as indeed it lost many of the achievements of the Graeco-Roman civilization. On the other hand, it could not have achieved its organizational forms if it had not been able to build upon the remnants of the Roman Empire.

The younger a civilization, the higher its vitality, the more dominant becomes the need to project its life into the future so that the present becomes relatively unimportant and is seen merely as a preparation for things to come. This attitude enables Man not only to reach out over a period of many generations but it also enables him to endure the hardships which are innate in the early stages of a dynamic period when the need for social cohesion runs far ahead of immediate material needs.

Both these factors dominate the Middle Ages: the need for a universal philosophy, responding to the requirement of restraint of young and vital peoples who dimly feel the need for greater unity and the revitalisation of the remnants of a more ancient civilization of which the patterns of social and economic control can come to life anew if placed under a more general human perspective, beyond the confines of national power.

Man is always new, and it is only possible afterwards to read a meaning into the happenings of many centuries ago when it seems as if Nature unveils its plans to create this greater unity among Man, of which only the greatest and most inspired leaders are aware, at the cost of suffering and self-sacrifice. Sacrifice points the way beyond the narrow span of one or a few generations, and it is the expression of one of Man's deepest and most fundamental impulses: the desire for the continuity of life.

Desire is indeed too weak a word for this overwhelming emotion which emerges from the subconscious in a symbolic guise, appealing to Man's most innermost passions so that its presentation is held as sacred, inviolable, eternal — beyond the realm of doubt and of intellectual curiosity. It is the expression of the survival will of tremendous groups over long periods, within which dynasties, economic systems, political beliefs come and go while the symbolic superstructure endures in a most amazing and awe-inspiring manner.

This need, first predominantly emotional and carried by the sufferings of those to whom only sacrifice holds rewards, gradually became institutionalized in the Middle Ages, losing at times its inward glow, which was always rekindled, however, by the saints and thinkers and the nameless masses who labored at the great architectural monuments of the Middle Ages: its cathedrals in which the emotions of the beginning translated themselves into a corresponding style only at a much later date.

The desire for cohesion was uppermost in the mind of the Middle Ages: a cohesion which was gradually transferred from the spiritual to the secular realm, but when the latter power became victorious, the Middle Ages were drawing to a close and its universality was lost in the more tightly knit social group of the national state. The pre-eminence of the spiritual does not bear transmittal into concretization: its concretization is a threat to its underlying emotions, to its religious fervor and the inwardness of its life.

The Middle Ages was the introvert stage of Western civilization in which the Western mind gained its most essential human foundations, which could not have emerged if the psychic energy of Man had turned too early to the acquisition of power over the natural and social environment.

We can no longer understand the tremendous desire for the spiritual values which, in our mind, since ages have been translated into other forms of control and achievement, hiding the anxiety which may still lie submerged in our minds but which is no longer channelled into constructive efforts although it might be partially responsible for the violent outbreaks which, time and again, shake our rational structures and bring them to the verge of disaster.

But also in the Middle Ages the struggle for those values was strong, violent and incongruous. Social cohesion was a postulate and not a reality; the Middle Ages was a period of deeply religious life, of ruthless wars, of poor economic and social conditions and, at the same time, with the undeniable artistic appeal of a period with a much more natural rhythm. It showed a starting admixture of religion, superstition, great philosophic and theological learning as well as of gross ignorance. Consequently, the geniuses of the Middle Ages were of gigantic proportions: Augustine, Thomas Aquinas, Dante, Charles the Great, Palestrina.

Only the mind of young peoples could produce this bizarre mixture of imagination, simplicity and daring that was given cohesion by the guidance of the Roman Catholic Church, which had retained some of the elements of Roman statesmanship and its cleverness in giving unity to diverse elements.

The Church stabilized the teachings of Christianity, which thereby perhaps lost much of their original depth and sincerity. The self-surrender and renunciation which the Christians demanded was less convincing in a Church which grew into a dominant social structure. Consequently, the ascetic attitude, characteristic of the early Church, lost much of its original meaning when it became an official attitude. Almost every religion has ascetic tendencies since there is no doubt that the mind must sublimate basic emotions and desires in order to develop a strong symbolic reaction.

Monasticism is another phenomenon peculiar to the Moyen Age although it developed from Jewish and Greek beginnings. Stoic philosophy as well as Gnosticism had already tried to find a refuge in a monasticism of their own pattern. The Stylites, or pillar saints, of Syria, and the Baskoi furnished examples which were taken over by Christianity, although in the beginning merely by individuals. It was not until Benedict of Nursia promulgated his famous Rule about 529 that religious orders grew into social institutions. The simplicity which they all proclaimed sometimes proved hard to maintain and often became purely nominal. [48]

The difficulties which the orders experienced in the adherence to the Christian ideals of simplicity and poverty, led to several new orders like the Franciscans as well as to the wandering friars of the late Middle Ages who attempted to solve this problem individually. The more standardized the Christian pattern became, the more the danger of dissension and revolution grew.

Already in the first centuries of Christianity the Roman Church had a hard struggle to reach and maintain its position, which was threatened by the more liberal tendencies of Arianism and other groups as well as by the increasing independence of the Eastern Church. The victory of the sterner philosophy over the more liberal tendencies has to be explained as a reaction against the Roman pattern of life. The relativism of the late Roman civilization was the ultimate cause of a renewal of monotheism, in the same way as we have witnessed in our period cases of a return to a one-man leadership after a period of division and uncertainty, although of course the present change is on the political and not on the religious level.

Polytheism seems to be the original form of religion, since primitive man is more imaginative than systematic. He does not know the desire to deduce everything from one principle, although this tendency is undoubtedly latent in many primitive, polytheistic religions. The desire for a strictly systematic philosophy develops usually after a period of social pressure. The pressure exercised by the Romans over their subject nations was an important factor in the formation of Christianity. Self-denial and renunciation are characteristic of an attitude which is a reaction against excessive materialism as well as a form of the desire for symbolic experience. Medieval Christianity cannot be understood except as a reaction against the classical world, which, although highly civilized, began to lack those human qualities which are essential for national survival, namely unity and understanding for the material and spiritual troubles of the lower classes.

The idea of grace introduced a concept which, although — or perhaps just because — it was irrational, introduced a new element into life that gave hope to the downtrodden and the oppressed. According to medieval philosophy, belief was prior to knowledge, which serves to illustrate the weight of the symbolic reaction in an early culture period. Gradually the irrational element in Christianity was superseded by dogmatic beliefs, but it was never entirely lost. Even when the Church stabilized the forms of belief, Christian mysticism still found a way for an immediate and irrational expression of religious experience, although often only after serious conflicts with the Church. When the Roman Catholic Church began to lack the vitality to absorb changes, it saw its hegemony threatened by the Reformation, which meant the beginning of a more active philosophy, more inclined to tolerate individualism and to attempt to find new ways of life.

There is a definite trend of development in medieval life which stretches over an unusually long period. The most significant factor is the survival of the Roman Catholic Church during the destruction of the Roman Empire. This showed that the typical Christian elements in the Church were stronger than its absorption of Roman culture. The foundation of Christianity had remained un-Roman even though the ailing late Empire, further proving its deterioration, accepted it. The breakdown of the West-Roman Empire under the assault of the Germanic tribes set the forces of Christianity free, in contrast with the East-Roman Empire which maintained itself until the fall of Constantinople in 1453, but which lacked the deeper vitality of the West.

The cultural elements of the Roman Empire, which survived, were not the institutions created by Rome but the originally hostile Christian philosophy which had profited from the organization and culture of the Romans. Christianity was not destroyed by the invading barbarians but conquered them through its superior social forces and its high idealism which fascinated the unspoilt Germanic nations. The primitive virtues of morality, courage and loyalty, which these tribes possessed, were the qualities which Christianity needed to build its structure to outlast most other social formations. The Church, on the other hand, retained much of the Roman Empire that otherwise would have been lost. The Christian bishops took over many tasks from the Roman civil servants and endeavored to give shape to a world which would have been hopelessly chaotic. Especially in Spain and France important elements of Roman culture remained which gradually became amalgamated with the primitive forms of Germanic life. The conversion of the East Goths was the most important victory of Christianity, since it undermined the influence of Arianism and gradually led to its defeat. The superiority of Christianity in its Roman Catholic form over the forms of Germanic culture was as evident in the political as in the religious realm. If the first period of the Middle Ages is characterized by the spiritual victory of Christianity, the second one is defined by the struggle between sacerdotium and imperium in which the Church became the ultimate victor. The relation between Pope and Emperor dominated the Middle Ages as much as the relation between heaven and earth, God and Nature, or between good and bad. This peculiarly Moyen Age dualism appears in all those relationships in a sharp contrast which our modern world, recognizing only economic and rational conflicts, has lost. The spiritual force of the earlier time gave depth and proportion to its struggles beyond the mere solution of economic problems.

In the early Middle Ages the connection between state and church was very close. In the East Gothic Empire, which was so important for the preservation of Latin culture, the church laws are at the same time the laws of the empire, the synods have the function of national assemblies and the bishops are appointed by the king. This same development was carried on by the East Goths after Spain succumbed to the invasions of the Arabs. In the Holy Roman Empire, however, the influence of national Germanic elements was considerably greater. In some instances the landowner was the proprietor of the church, built on his estate. This innovation was based upon Germanic legal thought but meant a considerable departure from the early Christian system. Also the duty, according to Germanic conceptions, to carry arms for every free-born man led to the difficulty that the clergy had to be classed among the unfree. The power of the Franconian kings to appoint bishops and to summon synods meant equally a victory for the worldly element. In the beginning of the domination of the Franks the pagan influence on life remained important while Christian thought was partially submerged.

The survival of paganism was undoubtedly one of the causes which strengthened the ascetic tendencies of the Church. Although asceticism is an essential element of all religious or even idealistic movements, it increases as well as a reaction against excessive materialism of the ruling classes, as in the case of early Christianity, or as a measure to subdue the excessive vitality of young or primitive peoples. The latter happened in the medieval period. The anti-materialistic attitude of Christianity must be explained partly from religious and partly from social reasons. The function of restraining material impulses is common to all religions and makes them into the powerful ally of the state which — although to a lesser extent — has the same aim of restraining or at least controlling human emotions.

The degree to which this control must be applied is the eternal source of conflict between the state and the church as we can also witness in our own time. In the Middle Ages, since the general attitude toward life was pre-eminently religious, the Church found such powerful support among the people that it could become the leading social agency and the state was relegated to the second place. Already early Christianity had preached obedience to the state — even the pagan state — because political revolution could never be a tenet of a philosophy which abhorred violence. The ultimate goal of Christianity was to transform the state into a Christian state. This aim, never completely reached during Antiquity, was the task which was fulfilled during the Middle Ages.

The fact that the fall of the Roman Empire had caused widespread disorganization aided the Church in establishing new social patterns as the old Germanic ideals had given way to disorder and moral laxity. The relapses into paganism, or perhaps it would be better to say into the bad features of paganism, remains one of the most interesting phenomena. The negation of Roman civilization fitted the nationalism of the Franks often better than the strict application of Christian ideals which must have seemed unnatural to their materialistic spirit.

The difficulty of keeping Christian ideals led to the establishment of religious orders which could devote themselves to missionary work and the strict maintenance of these ideals.

The Church needed the firm structure of the Carlovingian Empire for its survival, and, in the early Middle Ages, the main power rested undoubtedly with the emperor. Unjustly Charlemagne has been accused of caesaro-popism but it was undoubtedly necessary for him to organize fields which later were considered as within the rightful domain of the Church. The establishment of a political and social order was a necessity for the further development of the Church, which saw theology reach a new peak at the court of Charlemagne. Medieval theology originated in Ireland, but its representatives were active in the Carlovingian Empire. In this period, however, religious life was a privilege of the few while the masses remained ignorant of the more complicated theological problems. This was not true of the later Middle Ages. In the dark period of the 9th and 10th century the power of the emperors as well as the spiritual leadership of the Church sank to a very low level. Sensualism and hedonism were unchecked until the famous convent of Cluny caused a revival of religious fervor. In this period the popes were dethroned at will by emperors but the influence of wordly rulers was on the whole beneficial because it forced the Church to consolidate its forces. The conflict between sacerdotium and imperium reached its climax in the days of Gregor VII and Henry IV when the investiture problem became acute. The prohibition of the lay investiture by Gregor VII was a source of conflict in the Holy Roman Empire as it meant an intrusion upon traditional rights. The emperor retaliated against this violation of his rights by refusing to recognize the pope, who answered by excommunicating the emperor. It is known how the emperor lost this struggle, but the conflict was not so one-sided as earlier historians would have one believe. In 1080 the conflict broke out anew and ended with the ultimate defeat of Gregor, one of the strongest characters among the popes even though he could not break the greater temporal power of the emperor. It was yet too early for the victory of the spiritual power of the Church.

Gradually the weight shifted to the side of the Church which saw the emperor Barbarossa recognize the papal power in 1177. The crusades intensified the close connection between sacerdotium and imperium, and finally in the 13th century Innocentius III succeeded in establishing firmly the Church as the highest power. However, the struggle was renewed shortly afterwards until the final downfall of the house of Hohenstaufen.

The doctrine of the Church as the highest power on earth found its most adequate expression in the papal Bulla "Unum sanctum" which developed the famous theory of the spiritual and the temporal sword, of which the latter is secondary to the former. This superior power of the Church was perhaps nothing more than an idea that was never realized. But even as a principle it aided in keeping the Christian countries together and giving them a unity in their struggle against the Mohammedans.

The fact that the ideals of the Middle Ages were far beyond the capacities of the average human being caused the continuous struggle against the pagan forces of sensualism and worldly lust for power. The Christian attitude possessed a certain social element which constantly endangered its stability as a social force. The denial of the world, the concentration on the supernatural, the sacrifice of material gain are demands which make it difficult to maintain a solid social organization. It was perhaps the resistance of the Germanic empire which forced the Church to consolidate its forces as a power to which all dissatisfied elements could flee.

Even when the Christian ideals penetrated the entirety of life to a degree which is difficult for us moderns to understand, we still find the violent relapses into paganism and debauchery which are typical of the entire Middle Ages. It was therefore essential that medieval life centered in the convents, which offered the possibility of conserving Christian ideals in their purity although they often sadly failed. The ascetic ideal was too severe to be reached in the world and could only thrive in seclusion. The abnormality to which the ascetic ideals often led, has been frequently stressed in modern writings. Although it must be admitted that asceticism possesses certain dangers, it is on the other hand of the greatest social importance to stress the value of emotional control and of the desirability of developing the higher powers of the human mind. If such ideals are absent, life slips back into unrestrained emotionalism and materialism with all the dangers of social, moral and physical deterioration. The forces of Christianity were responsible for the continuation of Western culture, which otherwise would have exhausted itself in senseless and endless wars. Today we can observe how the absence of well defined and high ideals threatened to destroy our entire civilization. Symbolic thinking gives a cohesion to human thinking which has been diminished by the mechanistic aspects of modern civilization.

The so-called "enlightened" ideas about religion which have become the fashion frequently overlook its social aspects. Christianity, unfortunately, often limited its humane principles to Christians and was not free from narrow-mindedness and bigotry in its treatment of the "unfaithful", but it at least checked the selfishness of national groups. Materialism can become a danger if it includes the admission of extreme individualism and hedonism. Even animals possess the instinct to preserve their energy wisely while man too often indulges in giving free rein to his impulses and desires. The spiritual demands of the Middle

Ages were the indication of the strong wish for survival of young nations who, instinctively, feel the need of strong restraint.

One of the purest expressions of this tendency is found in Francis of Assisi who renounced the pleasures of a wealthy youth to fight moral decay and suffering. Francis of Assisi had the strength of spirit to love "both man and bird and beast", to free himself from all temporal cares and to devote his entire superior personality to the development of a predominantly symbolic attitude.

Outside the religious orders Christianity was never able to combat the corruption and greed of its officials with complete success. The ascetic ideal did not penetrate the broad masses of the people until the 12th and 13th century, when the cult of world-denial and self-sacrifice reached its greatest intensity. Unfortunately this spread of very stricts ideals led also to great intolerance and to the institution of the inquisition. The systematization of religion led to a higher cultural level but also to greater regimentation. This explains why in the 12th century we find the beginnings of the later forms of heresy (Arnold of Brescia). This preacher was burned for his protest against the wealth and worldly power of the Church. From then on the conflict between the simple and ascetic Christian ideals and the power and luxury of the Church always returned. Best-known of these stringent minded groups are the Waldensians, who were followers of the Lyonese merchant Petrus Waldes, who preached the return to apostolic times. The gnosticism of the ancient period was revived by the sect of the Albigensians who advocated a simplified and direct form of Christianity. The pompous attitude of the official Church did not succeed in curbing these movements to which the common people felt affinity.

Inside the Church there was no longer a place for the uncomplicated form of Christian life. Francis of Assisi was the only reformer who maintained the apostolic ideals without getting into conflict with the Church, and even his activities were viewed with suspicion.

As the Church felt that its authority was gradually being undermined, it turned to the inquisition to enforce by fear what it could not maintain through inner conviction. In the later Middle Ages Christianity became "official", and the Christian attitude which could only spring from understanding and simplicity became inflexibly intolerant.

As a social institution the Church had perhaps the right to enforce discipline and obedience as the natural consequence of the Christian hierarchy exemplified in the Church. To deny this would mean to reject the Church as a social organization, an attitude which later became predominant. In the Middle Ages the power of the Church was not felt as a burden by the majority of the people, and its position as the sole interpreter of Christian doctrine remained unchallenged over a long period even though the Church could not enforce its rule strictly or consistently.

The consolidation of the Church as a temporal power naturally led to a more rigid application of its rules with a resulting loss of much of their meaning as the contrast between ideal life and reality became of necessity clearcut. The inhumanity of the inquisition was a sign of the breakdown. Christianity, with the Golden Rule emblazoned on all her churches, devised in the inquisition the violation of her own principles. We must not forget, however, that the great, half pagan masses of the people were not so horrified by these proceedings as historians of later, more humane periods might expect. Unfortunately the masochism inherent in the ascetic attitude changes easily to sadistic cruelty. The inquisition was a phenomenon which indicated that the ascetic attitude of the Middle Ages had begun to break down, and as such was the counterpart to the increasing hedonism of the official representatives of the Church.

More perhaps than in the life of the individual, we can observe that the dusk of a culture period approaches swiftly after the peak has been reached. Why these changes take place is as difficult to understand as an individual's loss of vitality. We can analyze the immediate causes of the breakdown of medieval culture but we cannot analyze why it should not have continued forever unless we admit a process of natural growth in the history of mankind. Somehow the Middle Ages became the period of youth of Western culture, which grew into a more moderate, more realist and more materialist attitude toward life. Gradually the Western mind matured, losing its emotional and spiritual ardor but also its lack of balance, its superstitions and irrationalism.

The economic changes at the end of the Middle Ages demanded larger units of cooperation than the medieval, self-sufficient feudal economy. On the other hand, the spiritual ties which had united the entire Western world over long periods lost their predominance, giving way to reasons of an etatistic nature. Christianity began to disintegrate into national states in which economic interests took precedence over religious motives.

The dissolution of the connection between pope and emperor was the first sign of coming transition. The struggle of Louis of Bavaria with the popes of the Avignon period is the practical expression of the change which found its philosophic counterpart when the German kings and princes insisted that the imperial crown was not dependent upon the inauguration by the pope. Although the pope was first victorious in this conflict, the very king he had crowned announced in 1356 that

the election of the German emperor by the kings and princes was
entirely valid without papal sanction. This secularization and nationalization of the German empire meant the denial of the medieval hierarchy. This situation was accentuated by the dependence of the pope
upon the king of France whose prisoner he virtually became. From 1305
until 1378 the popes remained in Avignon under the immediate influence of the French kings. The writings of this period reflect the
change of attitude: the Dominican Quidort of Paris (1306) and the
jurist Pierre Dubois claimed the independence of the temporal powers,
which are derived directly from God in the same way as the Church.
Finally even the divine power of the Church was denied. Marsiglio of
Padua and John of Jandun claimed that the Christian community was
the source of all power and that the priesthood had no other task than
spreading Christian doctrine and administering the Christian sacraments.

An almost "political" attitude is taken by William of Occam who
represents purely opportunist views. He held that in times of danger
the king could dethrone the pope just as the pope could dethrone the
king. He insisted that infallibility is not a necessary attribute of the
papacy. The well-being of the Church in its entirety is the supreme
principle, not the well-being of its official organs. Here we find natural
law as an argument against the Church instead of the earlier idea that
the Church expresses natural law. These tenets are a natural reaction
against the unlimited absolutism of the Church. A further reason for the
decay of the papal power was the loss of the territory of the Church
state, which was annexed by the neighboring republics of Italy. This
was followed by the period of the schism in the Church, when both
Avignon and Rome became the seat of a pope. After the loss of unity
between sacerdotium and imperium, even the Church itself presented
a picture of dissolution and decay. The election of a new pope at the
concilium of Pisa (1409) only aggravated matters because the other
popes refused to withdraw. Christianity was then ruled by three different popes, all three claiming to be the representatives of God and
invested with the attribute of infallibility.

Even the concilia abandoned their traditional principles when they
introduced the procedure of voting according to nations instead of
according to principles. The principle of the superiority of the concilium over the papacy was also defended — an almost democratic
principle in flagrant contradiction with the hierarchy of the Middle
Ages.

We find already the principle of nationality as a dominating factor
which was going to shape the future for centuries to come. The voting

power at the concilia was extended considerably beyond the official representatives of the Church: at the concilium of Basle (1433) even doctors of theology and canon law were granted the right to vote. Also this concilium split into two different groups which continued their meetings independent of one another. In France the nationalization of the Pragmatic Sanction introduced a number of the principles of the concilium of Basle which denied the primary power of the pope.

It was not only the official side of the Church which showed dissolution and decay; also the inner form of Christianity was rapidly losing its positive force. The religious orders were gradually degraded into institutions to which the wealthy and the noble looked for economic security and safety. Together with this spiritual decay moral degeneration increased rapidly. The vow of celibacy was widely ignored; high positions in the Church were given to the sons of princes or noblemen without any regard for ability or morality. A "reformatio ecclesiae in capite et in membris" became an absolute necessity.

The ascetic attitude had lost its always precarious contact with the masses completely and continued merely as an artificial belief which had to be enforced by cruelty and oppression. The Catholic Church no longer represented the inviolate, sturdy Christianity of an earlier age but a twisted and warped cloak of misunderstood beliefs.

In scholastic philosophy the decay of medieval thought became evident in the extreme nominalism of William of Occam, who regarded the ideas as mere names instead of separate entities. Also in architecture we can observe an overwhelming multitude of superfluous decorations of a bizarre and fantastic type, of a loss of the functional interrelation of architectural elements.

In Germany the influence of medieval life lasted much longer than in France or England, which formed much earlier into the national states that meant the end of the universalist, spiritual, ascetic culture of the Middle Ages and the arrival of a more critical, realist and hedonist attitude toward life. This change did not find its first expression in new creations but in an attempt to imitate Antiquity, which personifies the attitudes for which the Renaissance culture felt an affinity. This process of imitation is a very interesting social phenomenon: when an attitude which has dominated a social group for a long time begins to lose its general validity, the opposing forces look for cultural patterns which represented similar ideas in the past. The Renaissance must be understood not only as the first strong reaction against medieval culture but as a reaction, which had not yet succeeded in creating entirely new forms of life. The interest in Antiquity sprang from a desire for the greater fullness of Graeco-Roman life, from admiration for the higher development of the arts and sciences, from a desire for mastery of economic and legal matters. In this process the Catholic Church was the link between ancient culture and the Renaissance. The Church had preserved a great part of Greek and Roman thought: in canon law it had maintained Roman law so that the reception of the 15th century did not have to start anew but found the ground prepared. However, in economic matters, the teachings of the Church reflected too much the system of a rural, feudal economy to be of use as an ideology for the growth of the economic system. This the New Era was to learn. Therefore it is especially in the economic field that we have to look for new ideas and new developments.

## CHAPTER VIII

## THE BEGINNINGS OF HEDONISM [49]

The beginnings of the hedonistic period can no more be fixed in time than the period of asceticism. We only attempt to distinguish these periods in the development of Western culture. No attention is paid to their existence in similar or adjacent periods in other civilizations. However, there have been opportunities to point out that the trend away from medieval universalism and a primitive economy began in the late medieval city, which gradually developed a fruitful and varied life. In some respects the late medieval city deserves the term "hedonistic" more than the later sterner types of economic growth under the guidance of Protestantism. There was undoubtedly a strong pagan element in the civilization of the Renaissance which was partially subdued when the revolution against medieval Catholicism had achieved its end of breaking up a dominant universal philosophy.

The Renaissance meant the actual denial of medieval philosophy, while the Reformation was the formal and final beginning of a new period of thinking. The Middle Ages and the New Era are frequently contrasted as universalist and individualist periods. This is in some respects a better characterization than "ascetic" and "hedonistic", yet, why should an individualist period mean a turn toward materialism? Individualism in its highest forms includes the mystic community with supernatural powers and is in this form asocial.

From a sociological point of view, we speak about an individualist period if we wish to indicate that the individual enjoys relative freedom from group pressure. If we exclude the few individuals who from their own will turn toward purely symbolic aims, it might well be that individualism in general leads toward a materialist trend. The stricter control of collectivist periods involves a restriction of the immediate satisfaction of wants as the individual is made subservient to aims like national power, conquest, glory, honor and similar concepts. The great social significance of religion is that it induces control over needs and restriction of their immediate satisfaction without an immediate materialist goal in view.

If we can use the word "normal" in relation to civilizations and social attitudes, it could be said that individualist periods are more "normal" than universalist or collectivist, since the last two offer less satisfaction to the individual. Life has attained some of its highest forms in ancient Greece, in Western Europe of the 17th—19th century and in North

America of the 20th century. In all three cases we must term these civilizations as individualist, yet they required long periods of preparation of a collectivist type. Human energy was first strictly organized for a symbolic aim and for the founding of material security.

The hedonist period which began in the end of the 16th century did not preach indulgence in material pleasures. The term "hedonist", as used in this study, is not meant to convey "pleasure-seeking" in the sensual meaning of the word but a positive attitude toward life as we find it: it implies a keen desire for expansion, for adventure, discovery, without any aversion toward spiritual problems but a disinclination to accept a prescribed formal belief, calculated to permeate one's existence. The New Era is less systematic, less logical than the Middle Ages, but it possessed more normal energy. Philosophically it vacillates between materialism and idealism: two poles between which it can never decide because it is not willing to sacrifice an active life for one of contemplation but neither to lose the broader aspects and outlooks inherent in an earlier cultural period. Idealism and materialism can both be built into consistent systems but their ultimate principles, the "idea" or the "substance" both evade an accurate definition. The contrast between these two schools can never be explained from an abstract point of view. All our thinking is socially conditioned, and in the end the struggle between idealism and materialism is always a struggle between classes at the same time. A static thinking upper class is easily opposed to a lower class which thinks in dynamic and pragmatic terms.

In the course of history this conflict expresses itself in a thousand different forms, with numerous additional factors, but it always repeats itself from the struggle between the Sophists and Socrates until the days of Marx and Kant, or of power versus law, to use one of the more recent versions.

Since substance seems to have dissolved itself into energy and as, according to the idealists, the idea also means force, there seems little reason for the struggle to continue. It does so, nevertheless, because it is fundamentally a social struggle, not very different from those about which tribe had the real image of its Deity. Only the ideological interpretation of the struggle changes: medieval conflicts were religious wars, while the wars of the New Era were colonial and commercial conflicts. The modern war is for living space; that means it aims at materials and labor, with the same disregard for individual human happiness as the common denominator of all human actions.

"Hedonism" as a mental attitude is a complex phenomenon which developed gradually, reached its peak in the 17th and 18th century and decayed in the 19th and 20th century. Its rise parallels the rise of capitalism in many respects but the term "hedonism" is broader than capitalism, which designates a type of economic enterprise and cannot be regarded as strictly logical. Capitalism is a term which had a magic appeal for a time but which still awaits an exact definition. The necessity of capital for economic expansion is typical of a period of development from a low standard of living economy to a higher one.

For this change the individual as well as the social group needs additional resources. If a carpenter wants to enlarge his workshop into a small factory, he needs buildings, equipment, tools, labor, etc. An individual is only capable of carrying out such a change if he has what we term "capital". For a society this process is far more complicated. It is ultimately based upon invention: the creative ability of an individual to think out ways and means to affect such a change. An isolated individual on a deserted island could only reach a higher standard of living if he discovered a way of storing sufficient products for his immediate use to free his energy for more important tasks.

In the earlier period of hedonism the rise in the standard of living was due to greater skills in the crafts, an extension of trade and commerce, a better division of labor and a certain technological improvement. The production of more luxury goods unbalanced the natural economy just as the present mass production may cause over-expansion.

In an ideal economy we would have a sufficient production of necessities, a reasonable production of useful goods and a restricted production of luxury goods. If, for instance, too many luxury goods are produced, a relative scarcity is given to the necessities of life which places them on a higher price level. The interrelation of the various types of goods is one of the most complicated economic problems. If we think in quantitative terms only, we can never approach this problem adequately.

The calculation that, if a given quantity of goods and a given number of people exist, a simple division is sufficient to ascertain the amount of goods which, theoretically, should be available for every person, is not correct.

If a group of thousand people produce goods to the value of $ 1.000.000.— it would be simple to say that the average income should be $ 1.000.— and that this would mean a living income for everybody. Whether this would be actually correct would depend entirely upon the amount of goods produced in each category. If, for instance, too many automobiles are produced in relation to foodstuffs, the price of cars might be so low and the price of foodstuffs so high that there would not be a state of real prosperity.

According to classical economic theory this would be readjusted automatically because the higher price for food would induce more people to devote themselves to its production. This supposition is only a half truth because there are more natural restrictions upon the production of some categories of goods than upon others. Besides these natural restrictions we have also to take into account the social forces which prevent these economic tendencies from fulfilling their functions.

An ascendant social group can check the production of necessities if it is more interested in the production of luxury goods.

The existence of poverty is not an economic but a moral problem. When small countries are often admired for the absence of poverty and a fair division of wealth, we must not forget that this is largely due to the fact that people in these countries know one another better and have more moral restraint against exploitation of fellow-beings than people in larger countries. A lot of time and effort are wasted on the solution of economic problems when we should in reality try to solve social problems.

Again we must repeat that many medieval theories were relatively sound, not because they were built on a religious basis but because they were the result of social ideals. On the other hand, ideals are often the outcome of preceding or contemporary unfavorable conditions, and thus a moderate idealism seems the soundest social attitude.

To a certain extent the hedonist period possessed this moderate form of idealism, although such a long period cannot be characterized without many reservations. If the attempt to reach a higher standard of living is prevalent in an entire social group, it can very well be accompanied by an ethical attitude. If the higher level is reached by a small group at the cost of the great masses of the people, it is merely tyranny and extortion. In reality the two forces are interwoven, and, unfortunately, a period of expansion offers some people the excuse to regard their private gain as a public benefit. Always, when an expansionist movement takes place, we hear the complaint that many of its adherents are recruited from the less worthy elements.

In this connection it is interesting to observe that, after the severe moral and ideological force of the Middle Ages lost its cogency, Renaissance philosophers became infatuated with the anti-social hero, who was from a medieval point of view nothing more than a criminal.

Machiavelli's "Il Principe" was a notorious attempt to free the individual from all social and metaphysical ties.

There are a great many intermediary forms between collectivism and individualism. In the Middle Ages the spiritual rule of the Church embraced the whole of civilized mankind while the economic unit was small and decentralized. This fact accounts perhaps partly for the dualism of that period which witnessed an independent economic development running contrary to the philosophy of asceticism.

In the hedonistic period the unit of economic, political and social life gradually grew into the national state while spiritual life became a matter of the individual, who, in that respect, was free from the restrictions of the Middle Ages.

The hedonistic period concentrated its energy upon the development of economic life while political restrictions tapered off until the modern form of the democratic liberal state was reached. Why this last form ultimately led to a regulation of economic life is a matter which will be investigated later.

In the early period of hedonism in the 16th and 17th centuries we can observe a struggle between the rising middle class, frequently aided by the king, and the feudal classes which were opposed to economic progress and greater individual freedom. Only in England, with its system of wisely balanced social groups, both agriculture and industry progressed in the same way.

In France the efforts of Physiocratism to aid agriculture came too late to stem the rising tide of political dissatisfaction, which was largely caused by the lack of understanding of the landowners for their social task.

The transition from a metaphysical outlook to a positivist philosophy was a very slow and gradual process. The individualization of religion did not mean a decrease in intensity, although the tendency toward a secluded life became less pronounced. Religion lost its most extreme expressions and tried to become an elastic social factor instead of an inflexible one.

As a social agency the Church had lost its position to the state, which did not recognize any worldly power beyond itself. The moral influence of the various religious groups remained high throughout the New Era and surpassed considerably the present influence of the Church on social matters. Early Protestantism in its various forms of Lutheranism, Calvinism, etc. was a sincere effort to reach a real community life which had been missing in the last, formalistic period of the Middle Ages.

The personal attitude toward work, which had grown in the Middle Ages, maintained itself for a long time, and it is not until the 18th and 19th century that modern labor problems began to develop and the class conflict overshadowed the old division of society in functional groups.

Psychologically, hedonism can be compared to the stage of an individual who is eager to lead a full normal life but who is willing to admit a considerable number of standards and principles which, according to his philosophy, ensure his success over a longer period. But always again there are relapses, not to such extremes as in the Middle Ages, but there is still a considerable distance between good and evil, honorable and dishonorable, rich and poor, cultured and uncultured. It is a period which shows a decreased mental tension but still a tension which is considerably stronger than the one which prevails in our own period.

If we dare to interpret this concept of mental tension, we would say that the human mind, as the instrument set to guide the human race through life, has entered a stage which is less indicative of long range achievement.

Compared with the Moyen Age, the aims of mankind have become less remote. Life after death still plays a considerable role, but it does not permeate all human actions in the same way as it did in the Middle Ages. The goal of life has become more direct: the mastering of life, as shown in the development of the exact sciences, and the turn toward a rationalist philosophy. Also in interhuman relations, the idea that the body should be ignored in order to save the soul begins to be abhorred by the more advanced thinkers.

In the early Middle Ages the occupation with metaphysical problems may have been natural to mankind, or, at least to its leaders. In the later Middle Ages this attitude had to be maintained artificially while in the New Era a rationalist attitude began to develop.

Throughout the New Era we can observe a tendency towards rationalism which gradually becomes stronger, although it continues to hover between the extreme poles of idealism and materialism, universalism and individualism. We can clearly distinguish, however, that the idealist and universalist element gradually diminishes until the modern period sets in which shows a return to a greater community spirit.

This development can be traced in the various fields of human activity. It is most obvious in the realm of religion.

Although it is almost impossible to bring back all religious movements which are generally grouped together under the name of Protestantism to one common denominator, we can nevertheless note such characteristics as the right of private judgment in matters of belief and conscience and the principle of voluntary association.

Protestantism is definitely a phase in modern Western civilization which accounts to a considerable extent for the development of modern industry and modern democracy. Its role changed in various periods from a more progressive to a more conservative one, and at times it was more a promotor of, at other times more a check on, movements like nationalism or capitalism.

There can be no doubt, however, that compared with Catholicism, Protestantism has a strong dynamic element, mainly because it only partly became institutionalized. The dominant position of the Bible as the Word of God left more room for the individual and reflected a very significant social change compared with the Middle Ages. Many of these trends had been prepared by the sectarian movements of the late Middle Ages but not to the same extent and with the same consistency.

Another important aspect was the much greater role which was allotted to the reason and conscience of the individual.

Psychologically this is a highly significant fact. It is almost impossible to determine the actual hold of a group over an individual, since a very substantial part of this is based upon early childhood experiences, social conditioning, etc. which gradually submerge into the subconscious. If a group considers the adherence of its members as an absolute principle with which the will of the individual has nothing to do, this hold becomes particularly strong. As soon as the fact of belonging to a group, or the interpretation of what one's allegiance consists of, is a matter which can at least be discussed by the individual, we take a very significant step forward.

As soon as the hold of a group over an individual eases, the individual witnesses a lessening of mental tension. In fact the person who has the most relaxed state of mind is the one who enjoys the greatest independence.

In this way it becomes natural that in early cultural stages collectivistic systems prevail. The process of culture is in reality a process of individualisation although with strong relapses. It is the tragedy of culture that greater mental independence causes greater material dependence. This creates an eternal conflict which apparently cannot be solved.

Yet it might be possible to acknowledge that an influence over the higher centers of the mind as, for instance, exercised by religion constitutes a much stronger influence on the life of the individual than the fact that an individual has to perform a certain number of economic functions in order to gain a livelihood.

Therefore it is of the greatest importance to realize the significance of the greater amount of liberty that Protestantism granted compared with Catholicism. Some Protestant sects of the extreme left even developed a contract theory of religious institutions. They made individual inspiration the basis of religious life. Even more rigid and institutionalized forms of Protestantism like Lutheranism and Calvinism had to allow a certain amount of freedom to the individual, as he was entitled to interpret the Bible as the ultimate authority in his own way.

The same tendency toward greater freedom is evident in the pluralism of Protestantism. There was a great variety of expression and it was never the goal of Protestantism to establish universal uniformity. The only issue which has played quite a role is the uniformity within a nation.

There is no common Protestant creed, and, even in matters of organization, considerable influence has been given to local custom and common sense.

Protestantism means individualism in accordance with the authority of the Bible. It is obvious that this resulted in a great diversity. Later on the institutional elements in the main Protestant churches became stronger but never to the same extent as within the Catholic Church.

One of the most important differences was that Protestantism in the form of Lutheranism favored the idea of the prince as the head of the state church. This led to a greater influence of temporal matters than would ever have been possible in the Catholic Church. It is one of the strongest arguments in favor of the "Diesseitigkeit" of Protestantism.

Modern sociology has clearly established that Protestantism was to a large extent responsible for the creation of the modern economic system. This is due to two factors: in the first place Protestantism set free the energy of the individual, which naturally tended toward the direction of increased economic activity and greater worldly power; in the second place its philosophy placed greater value upon an active life than Catholicism and thereby led indirectly to the same result.

We can make similar observations for England. Although the Church of England resembled in many respects the Roman Catholic Church, it nevertheless contained a much stronger temporal element. The English king was the supreme head of the Church, the sacraments were gradually reduced, the vernacular took the place of Latin and the marriage of priests became permissible.

Gradually the dependence of the Church upon the state developed even more strongly when parliament became the actual head of the Church instead of the king.

Puritanism, on the other hand, was even more pronounced in its individualism but retained a stronger element of the ascetic, which may have given it greater driving power than the other forms of Protestantism. We have tried to show the various approaches to life as differences in mental tension that may express the growth of mankind. In this respect we must consider Puritanism as the philosophy of a group of comparatively higher vitality and persistence, which has expressed itself in its economic role. The greater asceticism of Puritanism means the capacity of a long term philosophy and the ability to disregard immediate discomforts in order to maintain greater mental intensity.

This very tendency is evident in the term "Puritanism", "the pure or stainless religion". Most of its adherents came from the middle classes, which played such a large role in the building of the world as we know it today. The virtues of that class were the typical virtues of Puritanism. The Puritans maintained — at least under Thomas Cartwright — that the spiritual society was different from the civil. This view, also adopted to a large extent by the Presbyterians, proved a source of strength in a period when Erastianism, i.e. the control of the spiritual society by the civil, had a deadening effect on religious life.

"Whatever deductions and reservations we may make, it [the eighteenth century] was, broadly speaking, for the Church of England a time of spiritual deadness and coldness, of servility and legalism, of low ideals and materialistic standards. 'Enthusiasm', even in the more modern sense of the word, is repressed or discouraged; the voice of the church is silenced; the bishops are more like State officials than fathers in God; the inferior clergy imitate the worldliness of their superiors; 'the hungry sheep look yp and are not fet', and steal away in consequence to other sheep folds. There is an absence of vision and of high aims. Religion tends to sink into good citizenship, or cold morality, or stiff orthodoxy, or latitudinarian indifference". 50

Thus we can observe that the development of Protestantism towards greater individualism and a more democratic spirit has been a process with many setbacks. But the ardor of the early Protestants was not maintained. In the sixteenth century religion dominated the secular interests in men's lives, and tens of thousands were willing to die for their faith. Later on, the worldly aspects became far greater in importance, and Protestantism has even led to a considerable extent to nationalism. Religious liberty led often to the decay of religion and to its being used as a cloak for material pursuits. In the hedonistic period we make the same observation as in others, namely, that there is greater sincerity and intensity in the beginning while in the later stages the principles tend to become formalistic and to show less real power.

Let us consider whether similar observations can be made in the field of philosophy. Philosophy as a social force cannot be compared to religion and frequently it has been more an indicator of trends and developments than an active force. It is the merit of philosophy to express or to attempt to express what lives in a given period but if it is seen purely as an effort to arrive at absolute truth, it remains an eternal sequence of argument and counter-argument. It is much more deeply rooted in social conditions than is generally assumed and is to a large extent the expression of political, social or economic aims on the level of abstract thinking. In a very general way we can say that in periods of a social hierarchy we are apt to find philosophical systems which base an entire structure upon an absolute principle.

In periods of greater individual liberty and of more democratic trends philosophy develops a more rationalist trend and places greater value on experience and the world of reality. The entire period from the sixteenth until the twentieth century is dominated by a struggle between these two principles, the one a remnant of the Middle Ages, the other — at least to a certain extent — the principle of the future.

Catholicism is based upon the idea of authority, an authority based upon supernatural divine revelation which is organized in the Church as the continuation of the divine incarnation. When this unity disappears and with it the psychological tie which it establishes, a multitude of opinions appear that derive their veracity from logic and final assumption. Decisions are no longer pronounced with absolute but only with limited authority. The only basis to which general appeal is possible is reason, but there is no possibility to avoid a divergence in the various ways in which reason is expressed. Infallibility is no longer a prerequisite, and there is no desire to establish an authoritative opinion. Relativity and tolerance take the place of authority and mean, psychologically speaking, that the group-tie has become looser because there is no longer a generally recognized group-pattern.

Thus came the enormously increased importance of scientific thought, which supposedly is based upon logical procedure or, as in the case of the exact sciences, can prove its point through experiment and its mastery over Nature. Reason was the means to understand the processes of Nature. Thus the individual had become capable of acquiring knowledge through himself, and the individual mind had the opportunity to develop an inner structure which did not need outside confirmation. Philosophy in the form of rationalism and the natural sciences took the place of theology and religion, although there remained an interrelation which only gradually led to greater independence of thought. If the individualization of knowledge led often to relativism, it was at the same time a liberation of great forces and potentialities.

This liberation meant that mankind had outgrown the stage of needing a centralized spiritual control which performed the function of keeping metaphysical fear in check. When the human mind was more capable of building up a rational approach to life, this need became obviously less. Perhaps also the scale of human emotions lacked its former high and low and moved in a more moderate realm. The boundaries of the rational mind were by no means permanent and showed considerable fluctuations in the various periods, while there were frequently currents of thought which attempted to go beyond the boundaries of reason.

The elements of the New Era are of unusual complexity; they combine Antiquity and Catholicism, the growth of the national states and their political ideas, the rise of capitalism and industry, the expansion of our physical world, Protestantism, the modern arts and sciences, into a colorful although far from consistent whole. The co-existence of these various factors was only possible because the entire period was dominated by a spirit of expansion and growth which did not require and even would have been hindered by a strict pattern. The continuation of the existence of anti-rationalistic patterns merely served to develop the new modes of life more sharply and more consistently. Nevertheless also the anti-rationalistic elements had strong personal and individual roots compared with the universalism of the Middle Ages.

Within rationalism itself there developed considerable changes in the course of the seventeenth and eighteenth century. In the former period the foundation of rationalism was mathematics, which tempted the philosophers to find a system of "universal" mathematics. This became the foundation of the systems of Galilei, Descartes, Spinoza and Leibnitz. In the political and social field, the state became the instrument of reason which curbed individual instincts and individual arbitrariness but in an absolute way. Law retained an absolute aspect as the expression of reason and was embodied in the ruler. Only later the idea developed that the individuals themselves should express their will in the state, and that law was the common denominator of the individual wills rather than a superimposed instrument of order and regulation. Also in this respect we can observe a steady increase of individualization and a tendency away from the establishment of absolute values. This was the quintessence of enlightenment and its tenet that the human mind is capable of understanding the world and therefore to master it. At the root of this philosophy remains the idea that there is nothing arbitrary or accidental in Nature and that everything is ruled by laws which can be perceived by the human mind. Experience in itself is too complex to be fully analyzed as such, but by reducing it to its fundamental factors we can arrive at a system of cause-effect relationships which led to understanding as well as technical mastering of Nature. The greatest achievements of this approach were celebrated in the exact sciences: Descartes' discovery of analytical geometry, Newton's calculus and Leibnitz's infinite.

In the political sciences the success was far more limited, due perhaps to the much more complicated nature of the observed phenomena. It was not sufficiently realized that reason means an abstraction from reality and a state of mind which is only capable of understanding certain parts of life. The law that rationalism seeks is the order the human mind needs and which is read into the existing world. This finally led to the conflict between the world as it exists in the human mind and the real world, a problem which a mind believing in abstraction can never overcome, as was evidenced by the unfortunate dualism of that entire period. The desire to master life led to the capacity to control and regulate certain natural processes, but it remains entirely debatable whether this should be regarded as proof of their occurrence in reality in the same way as the human mind perceives them. The human being has only been successful in repeating certain natural processes under certain conditions, but by eliminating a number of factors he cannot control or which he cannot understand.

The entire period should be seen as a closer approach to reality than the Middle Ages had achieved but an undecided and indefinite one which has not been able to overcome dualistic thinking until our present period.

## CHAPTER IX

## REASON AND EMOTION

A CASE-STUDY, BASED UPON *MICHAEL KOHLHAAS*, A STORY
BY HEINRICH VON KLEIST

The principles by which Man lives change in content as well as intensity. As these principles arise from his need to gain a certain stability, they also differ in psychological weight for each individual although they are expressed in identical terms. Great confusion results from the fact that we cannot measure the weight of psychological values and that we can only determine their changing intensity by analyzing their relative weight in different cultural systems. It is to some extent the structure of each cultural system which determines the weight of values, in addition to the emotional tensions of each individual which is the other determining factor.

As a consequence, general judgments in regard to this problem are of relatively small merit, and it seems more feasible to attempt an approach by means of case-studies which bring out both the individual and the cultural elements. It was decided to use a short story as the basis of a case-analysis since it demonstrates well how a general concept can gain a terrific emotional impact if it becomes the crystallizing point of a number of pent-up emotions.

Justice is a concept that is used by many and was one of the dominant ideas of many periods which were striving for balance, for a setting-off of a realm for the individual in which he could develop his personality upon the basis of respect that was given as well as asked. This seeking for an autonomous sphere is all the more imperative in periods of cultural change when the dividing lines from the past re-emerge in human consciousness to be tested and examined and re-evaluated in the light of changed circumstances.

When the unified world of the Middle Ages began to disappear and the national states of the New Era emerged, the individual felt uncertain toward these new power-bearers and wanted to be assured of a realm of his own that was not purely spiritual or moral but also legal, giving him a familial and economic territory into which penetration was possible only under certain conditions. The legal concept of "do ut des" became more significant than the Christian concept of mercy, which presupposes the very strong and the very weak but does not know the pride of the solid burgher who wants to give and receive under conditions of equity. The burgher was emerging from the peasantry and had to re-assert himself against the nobility which had to adjust itself to a society in which the nobleman could maintain his social status if he realized that new groups and new rights were appearing. As the society was in a period of strong and rapid change, the idea of justice was a fluid one, not yet crystallized into definite legal rules and regulations. It was the strength of the individual which defined whether this realm was wider or narrower, his own fighting spirit as well as his own determination. But justice meant that he had a realm not regulated by the benevolence or mercy of others but based upon an inalienable right, the recognition of the end of the relation of master and slave, lord and peon. The individual had grown in stature by gaining enough self-control to regulate his own life. He needed knowledge rather than belief, although ultimate principles were essential to keep his new-won self-confidence from growing into pride and arrogance.

This subtle balancing of right and wrong, this striving for an equilibrium in which the weight was more evenly distributed than before, was a delicate moral problem for the individual, who had to temper the precepts of reason with the principles of religion. It was not only the here and now but the then and later which had to be taken into account, the individual as a link between those before him as well as those coming after. It was religion which dealt with the larger dimension while reason focussed sharply and coldly on the present, where passions ran deeply so that the machinery of control had to be impersonal and efficient. As conscience had become individual instead of collective, the problem was an inner one, instead of being regulated by a system of outer, formal precepts.

When Michael Kohlhaas * set forth on his trip to sell horses in Saxony, nothing was on his mind except the rational game of comparing profits and losses, a pleasing pastime to the successful in life. And Michael Kohlhaas was successful in life: a prosperous horse-dealer and property-owner, a loyal husband, a devoted father. In a few words, the example of an "upright citizen", if this rather empty cliché is permissible.

A slight ripple in his calm was caused by a barrier on the road which had not been there before and where a few pennies were required for passing. A new feudal privilege as he was told, while they should be really decreasing in a time which was beginning to believe in progress. But the ripple grew into waves of displeasure when he learned that also a pass was needed which had to be acquired beforehand. This

---

* The story takes place around the middle of the 16th century.

seemed not only incredible, contrary to the more liberal spirit of the times but a downright imposition which his sense of justice began to question suspiciously. If there were any such regulations, why had he not heard about it as this was a fairly frequently travelled road. Or was he being made a fool of by the arrogant baron who had appeared upon the scene? There was little to do but leave some of his horses behind as a guarantee that he would still acquire the needed pass.

But a chain of thoughts had been set into motion, revolving around the question whether the demand had been justified. For Kohlhaas this was the only question, not the loss of time or money or the annoyance at the arrogant behavior of the baron and his crew, but purely the matter of justice, of a legal right to which he wanted to submit himself as a citizen, aware of the demands of an increasingly complex society.

But in Dresden he learned that the matter of the pass was no more than a fairly poor joke of the baron, who apparently had been in need of amusement.

A source of annoyance, but still not a really crucial matter to Kohlhaas, who did not mind too much to have been made the butt of a poor practical joke. The arrogance of the baron stung him perhaps in his burgher-pride, but also that could be overlooked as one of the frequent, petty annoyances of life.

So he rode back in a fairly good mood, after some very successful business deals. But the small cloud of his annoyance was to grow into a tempest when he arrived at the castle. His horses were but shadows of their former selves, thin, miserable, obviously ill-fed, and having been used for heavy field-work for which they were unfit. His servant who was to have looked after them had been chased away for his "arrogance", as Kohlhaas was told by the sarcastic and hostile major-domo.

Hot anger arose in Kohlhaas' veins, but he still suppressed his desire to throw the arrogant warden into the dirt. Perhaps his servant had actually misbehaved, perhaps there was some justification in the attitude of the others, although there was no explanation for their animosity but their own feeling of guilt. Briefly he refused to accept the horses in their present condition, and threatening to ask indemnity if the servant was without guilt, he returned home in a bitter and angry mood. His sense of justice, his dignity as a burgher and trader had been outraged, and the fine and intricate fabric of his balanced world had been roughly torn into shreds.

In his mind there was a churning of ideas, revolving faster and faster and breaking hard against the walls of his sense of justice. This was the core of everything, the computation point of the existence for which he had striven so hard, the chain which had tied down his fierce and uncontrollable passions. Now this dearly-bought control was in danger, and he himself was horrified at the fierceness of his anger, his desire for revenge and the pleasure he would feel in destroying those who had wronged him.

But there would be redress. The law was on his side, and he had complete faith in the incorruptibility of the laws and courts of his land. It was this which made him superior to a savage or a barbarian: this sense of being firmly embedded in a social structure in which each was to receive his due. And in this case there could be no doubt about the legal aspect. The law had to be on his side: his rights had been trampled upon, although it all still hinged upon the matter of the servant. His anxiety about this spurred him on to ride faster and faster toward his native village. He still hoped perhaps that his servant had been wrong so that this fierceness in his inside would let up and be submerged in the calm of a newly gained equilibrium. Then there would at least be peace again, and the brightly-lit world would be there anew, regained at the small cost of the loss of his two horses. The idea that all this might have been but a short and evil dream cheered him. It was already as if it had not happened at all, the more he approached the familiar atmosphere of his own native village.

The trees along the road and the houses in the distance were as friendly and re-assuring as ever. The sun, breaking through a fleece of white clouds, gave a warm, golden hue, and in such a world there could not really be any strife or error. It was an ordered and predetermined world, running according to the laws of Nature in an almost motionless majesty. The fierceness of his soul was but his own, his being out of step with a world that was tranquil and serene, a clear mirror in which his inner tempests were reflected in their smallness and insignificance.

Kohlhaas rode slowly, aware of the harmonious motion of his horse, and almost certain now that the rhythm of his own life was to be rewon shortly and without any great effort. Maybe a brief law-suit and matters would be righted again.

When he entered the living-room, the paleness of his wife and her obvious anxiety immediately dispelled these illusions.

There was no need to ask although the details had to be filled in. The servant had been brutally beaten and chased away when he had protested the use of the horses for heavy field-work.

Kohlhaas' suddenly magnified and sharpened anger froze into a firm resolve. The Law would give him justice. In its full majesty it would punish the arrogant trespassers and restore things to the proportions that, to him, were the only possible ones. In his mind, there still was this strongly carved order, standing out more visible even under the impact of his powerful emotion. He almost felt the existence of this strong structure in his mind, the nerves drawn taut under this pressure that threatened to break them. To himself he was almost the personification of this rational structure in its general form, it was embedded more deeply in him than in anybody else, although he was convinced that those above him adhered to the same principles but hardly with the same intensity. In others it could not be of the same physical immediacy, not burning like a passion whose excessive heat would appear as outer coldness. The idea of justice itself aroused this deep love in him which made actual people pale in comparison to this vision, like a star that stood out in great brightness in his own mind. Its brilliancy hypnotized him into insensitivity in regard to human weakness, as if it were an insult to this fierce god who loved, but with passion rather than with wisdom or mercy.

Now there was no longer the desire to return to quietude and equilibrium. The idea of ordered relations had faded in comparison to a justice that was a personal avenger, a holy sword aimed at one particular traitor. The rest of the world was cut off as by a heavy snowfall but, in the middle of the snow-covered, graying forest, there was a clearing, full of an intense light, in the middle of which the Baron of Tronka stood laughing loudly and derisively. But he was unaware of the firm step which resounded through the darkness of the silenced forest as if it stood by in anticipation of the things to come. He did not hear because he was too arrogant and full of self-love to hear much of anything, standing as a coarse and deaf-mute animal amidst creatures of far greater sensitivity who could listen to the vibrations of the soundless night.

The steps were still distant and circumspect. They would not come near at once but first be directed to the doors of those who were paid professionals in the service of the fierce goddess. But Kohlhaas already knew what would happen, as a blow whose impact he felt before it was even delivered. There would be motions and gestures, much shuffling of papers and endless talk, but nothing would happen. The sign of evil was already too clearly visible and the once seemingly firm structure of society was nothing but a formless mass of putrid human flesh.

This inadequacy was perhaps even welcome, a simplification, as if numerous rapid torrents were merging into one stream of overwhelming force, moving, guided almost by knowledge, toward a definite goal. The goal had been there before, but its coming into focus once more gave structure to this burning passion, impersonalizing it into something that was general rather than private.

It was a debt that Kohlhaas owed to a world that was rapidly losing its beacons, a scene obscured by selfishness, lascivity and easy compromise. There was a need for a flame to arise and to stand out singly before it broke into a conflagration that would destroy the world rather than see it decay. And the price of all this was two horses, still standing in the Baron's stables, feeble and miserable as if they knew that their well-being depended upon their redemption as a token of justice. But the slow and sequenced procession was moving.

The legal steps of Kohlhaas had no success since the Baron's clique managed to suppress the investigation. As a final move, his wife attempted to hand a petition to the Prince-Elect but was roughly thrown back by a soldier. A few days later she died from her wounds.

Things were then ready for Kohlhaas. He sold his possessions, purchased arms and equipped the small band of servants who swore loyalty to him.

Kohlhaas was on his own. Once more he was riding along the same road he had been on a few months earlier. No peaceful calculations of profits and losses this time but something that was much more his real self. A sereneness, resulting from inner freedom, was pervading him, and he felt no lonesomeness, because of his being apart from other people. Life in general was a mission, a task to be completed but instead of something vague and nondescript, to be worried about in terms of uncertain principles, his goal was clear and sharp.

This time he felt no incongruity with the world around him. Nature too seemed to carry a menace, to be full of hidden forces which penetrated the tranquillity of its outer appearance. Perhaps it even added strength to the decision in him; it made him more sharply aware of the narrow margin between life and death and the world beyond into which his intentions seemed to reach as if they were in harmony with it. This world was his justification, the confirmation of the order which it expressed more purely than Nature below.

Kohlhaas' inspiration was direct, a command that had come to him without the possibility of a doubt. It placed him outside human society, which had become a mockery of the order it was supposed to express. He himself was the human incarnation of that order, and those who felt it as intensely as he did would be on his side. The wronged, the rejected, those in whom a sense of justice was burning were his allies. They would come toward him as a deliverer, the prophet of a righteous world which had to come because it was the only one that could survive. The other, formal world was tainted with the smell of death; it was dying while it believed itself to be alive. But its life was that of conscious motion, the distorted movements of puppets that can no longer achieve harmony because their fears have made them rigid. They reach out for a reality that is no longer theirs.

Kohlhaas had left this realm of twilight behind, and the more they rode on, the more he reached out for this starlike clarity that needed neither question nor answer. Perhaps he was feeling genuinely happy for the first time in his life, having cut himself loose from his earthly ties and ready to submerge into the flames that he was to set himself. The destruction that was neither desired, nor avoided, like a renewal of life that was hardly a matter of his own choosing, but part of a much wider scheme whose ultimate meaning had been divulged to him with great lucidity.

What was needed now was not a climax, but precision: the coordination that seemed to come without effort with the greatness of his purpose.

There was to be no fumbling or errors: the process had needs to be like the closing of a steel-trap when the moment of revenge was at hand. But even in this revitalization of the organism by a great passion, tempered by a controlled and strong mind, the coordination was not to be perfect. The howling wind, the shying horse, the plaintive voice of a child were to break even through this rigidity into the casual rhythm of an unconcerned Nature. Perhaps the dynamic force which underlies human life consists of its being out of step with the rest of Nature, and this variance of energy-rhythms gives human life its greater intensity and variety.

But to Kohlhaas, any error was his and not due to Nature, in which there might not be the plan of which he was so firmly convinced.

Was even this idea of justice then purely an illusion, the product of an overwrought mind and of fierce emotions? Are there in reality no absolute ideas, and is there nothing but the great and oppressive silence of a universe about which we know absolutely nothing, except the contents of our own fearful guesses?

The point is quite defensible. Take Kohlhaas as a man of an extremely ferocious temper who had learned to control his impulses through his position in the social hierarchy and his equally strong desire to be successful and respected. The desire for this position in his own mind took on the form of a right, protected by a general principle — to make it all the more forceful — called "justice". When he felt the technical approach to this position threatened, namely an involved legal system of rights and duties, his control broke and the underlying fierceness of his character led him to kill and burn. Is it really significant that this latter process still stood under the dominance of an abstract principle instead of being simply killing for the sake of killing, and did he remain superior to a man who would act first and rationalize afterwards in order to protect himself against the impact of organized social revenge?

The answer is difficult. Kohlhaas possessed very strong social awareness. He never saw himself purely as an individual but first as a citizen, moving within the universe of an ordered society; later on, as an avenger and the creator of a new and better world. In other words, at all times his reaction was a strongly symbolic one, presupposing a quality of group-leadership and the capacity for imaginative projection of group-problems into a form of image-thinking. To some extent, Kohlhaas was right: if the corruption which he saw was as far-reaching and basic as he thought, society was on the road toward decay. But in his mind everything was magnified to a pathological degree. The corruption was there but it was not all-pervading, and it is the marvellous inner consistency of the story that he had to perish in the end but remained a hero instead of a lunatic because he himself finally understood that he had to lose for the sake of the idea under whose banner he had waged his battle.

True, there had been a small injustice, but he had committed much greater injustice as a revenge, so that ultimately his own God slew him with the sword which he had so precipitately handled himself.

Perhaps, at this point, the facts of the story should be interjected briefly: when Kohlhaas reached the castle, a wild attack was launched on everything and everybody while the castle was set on fire. During the mêlée, the Baron himself escaped, reputedly to a convent. When Kohlhaas and his band reached this convent, the Baron had left there. Kohlhaas almost set the torch to it, only stopped by a sudden impulse of mercy. As the Baron was rumored to be hiding in the town of Wittenberg, Kohlhaas' band, now swollen by dissatisfied and rapacious elements, marched on this town, giving it the choice between surrendering the Baron or being sacked. The town was set on fire three times while Kohlhaas, in the meantime, by clever manoeuvering and "total warfare"-technique defeated regular army units which had been sent out against him.

Finally, with an army of over 500 men, he conceived the idea of marching on the town of Leipsic but first stopped in order to regroup his forces at the Castle of Lützen. There, he issued proclamations which he signed as "Provisional Ruler of the World", asserting the justice of his cause and requesting the support of all and sundry who were dissatisfied with the prevailing state of affairs.

Martin Luther, the moral guiding star of the Germany of that day, made an announcement, at about the same time, in which he accused Kohlhaas of having broken all divine as well as human laws in his mad search for revenge. This announcement was also posted on a column of the castle at which Kohlhaas resided.

"He had just returned, while the people moved aside timidly on both sides, in the manner which had become customary since his last proclamation, from the place where he had held court. A large cherub sword, upon a red-leather cushion, adorned with gold tassels, was carried ahead of him while twelve servants, with flaming torches, followed. In this moment the two men *, their sword under their arm, stepped around the column, to which the announcement was attached, in such a manner to attract his attention. Kohlhaas, his hands crossed behind his back, deep in thought, came under the portal, raised his eyes and appeared taken aback. The two servants, at his appearance, moved back respectfully. Glancing at them distractedly, he moved, with a few rapid steps, close to the column. Who can describe what passed in his soul when he noticed the sheet of paper, whose contents accused him of injustice, signed by the dearest and most venerable name he knew, by the name of Martin Luther. His face flushed; taking off his helmet, he read the document twice from beginning to end. Then he returned, with uncertain steps to his henchmen, as if he intended to say something but he remained silent. He detached the sheet from the wall and reread it again . . ." *

Suddenly the idea of justice had been lifted from the contents of his own mind into a realm that he had to recognize as objectively valid. Luther was the man who had formulated his beliefs, and now this man rejected him and called him an outcast. Again something crumbled in Kohlhaas' mind: his order was then not the incarnation of justice, or was Luther wrong? This was the only possibility that would redeem him, and Kohlhaas had to find out.

The sudden realization that there might be two realms of justice overwhelmed and frightened him. His intensity had given him a power of abstraction that to him appeared as divinely inspired, as being directly and mysteriously in contact with something that was not himself. It was as if he had seen himself from a distance, as an instrument of God, not purely the toy of towering passions that now lacked a central point and were like forces that pulled him now to the left, then to the right, with a perturbing swiftness of change that placed him below rather than above his fellow-beings.

---

\* Who had attempted previously to draw his attention to Luther's announcement.

\* Author's translation from the German original.

This anxiety drove him, disguised as a peasant, forward through the night to find Luther and to ask him this question which threatened to overpower him. Was there no justice in his cause, then he would be worse than the darkest sinner, a wanton murderer, an arsonist who was committing these crimes to indulge in a self that was so painfully overstrained that there was no place for him in the society of Man.

He did not doubt for a single instant Luther's capacity as the representative of God. This man knew above all other men; from his word there was neither recourse, nor appeal since it was he who had shaped the foundations of his life.

Luther's initial refusal to listen to him was too trivial a hindrance to stop Kohlhaas. Pulling out his pistols, he threatened to commit suicide unless given a chance to clear himself from the accusations that were contained in Luther's announcement.

What laws had he broken? Human laws indeed, but they held no validity for him since the refusal of justice had placed him outside the pale of ordinary law. "I give so that you give" had been denied to him by the brutal arbitrariness of the Baron's behavior.

It had not been his desire to be put outside human society, but since it had happened, how could any law be invoked against him that had been denied to him first.

"Restore my basic rights that were violated, and I shall return to my home town and live as before".

These words spoken to Luther had an appeal of which Luther became increasingly aware. This was his own belief. Human law had to be founded upon divine law in order to be valid. If the two ran contrary to one another, there was some justification in following the dictates of one's conscience.

Luther was perhaps also a practical statesman. This strange and frightful man had created quite a following and had stirred up an unrest that was spreading through the nation. If it was possible to pacify him by punishing the Baron and restoring the two horses, there was a simple way out of a lot of trouble. And, of course, it might be wise to demonstrate that justice reigned in the Teutonic lands.

In the semi-dark study, with the wavering candle-light, there had come about, between these two men, some kind of understanding, hovering about uneasily but nevertheless noticeable as if there were some affinity that Luther nevertheless was reluctant to admit. Luther had grown into a solid pillar of society, and it almost seemed inconceivable that he should feel this sympathy for an outcast who had committed all the crimes that Luther's cautious soul abhorred. But beneath his respect for authority there was something deeper and stronger, a remnant from his own rebellious days that formed a bridge to the man across from him who had also refused to yield.

Luther remained silent, but in his soul grew the awareness that he was not going to refuse to help this rebel. It had become an impossibility as if it would be a violation of his own being, a disloyalty to himself of which he was incapable.

He finally promised Kohlhaas to request the Prince-Elect to grant Kohlhaas immunity and to bring the original case to court as should have been done in the first place.

Kohlhaas felt strangely elated. His hero had not failed him, and things once more fell back into their original order. It was this order within his own mind that really mattered to Kohlhaas, far above the question of wealth and poverty, even of life and death. He was only afraid of the dark chasms within him, of the gaping abyss that held a horror which could not be matched by torture or prison. It was as if within himself the world was present, but it had gained a frightening dimension, a power to destroy that the outside world seemed to lack and that only became dormant when the reflection of this world was not bent by the violence of his passion.

Yet this same world aroused the passions, and it was this incongruity that Kohlhaas could only overcome in this imagined realm in which the outside world had been reduced to a formal one. A stage upon which the puppets moved by divine ordination, going through the motions that fitted into the world of Kohlhaas' narrow justice. It could never dawn on him that this reduced world was not a really human one because in himself humaneness had been burned up by the blue flame of his justice, the creator of a world of progress and prosperity but not the whole world, since it knew not the slower rhythm of the days when Man's ambitions do not rise to fierce proportions but are content with the wind and the sky and the stars.

Perhaps it was for this same reason that Kohlhaas' desire to live was almost secondary, his downfall the logical outcome of a nature that strove so hard that life grew into a tight-fitting garment, an obsession rather than a dream, a sacrifice that Nature bought at the cost of one individual or millions of individuals. So that the others may live, balanced precariously between sin and virtue, health and disease, because they can watch those who cross the lines and then are heard no more.

This stupendous mechanism of society that surrenders the few to the many so that the beast may live in its own carefree and ignorant way, but not too carefree, not too ignorant. The sense of measure of the Greeks was lacking in these latter-day Germans who stood at the threshold of a world that was saying farewell for ever to this more natural world of the Greeks.

But Kohlhaas knew all this. He felt himself as the victim of something so overwhelming that it was an honor to be torn apart by it. Like the oak that is broken by the storm which merely bends the leaves of grass. Would it have been different in other times?

Other cultures, other pains. Or does society always sacrifice the required number to the deity of its own blindness? A tragic comedy that repeats itself like the rising and the setting of the sun from which we never learn to guess the coming of another day.

Who knows, and more: who cares to know? If wisdom is but the virtue of the aged, who but the fool should wish for the end of his days? Is it not better and more courageous to see Nature in its whimsical majesty, a rise and fall that needs no justification but the soothing pattern of its own rhythm?

Who would pity the leaves that fall if we know that they rise to a new life but a fleeting instant later? Coming from nowhere and going nowhere, can we not march to the sound of our own steps along this road that leads back to its own beginning?

Did Kohlhaas feel all this? Was he aware that his life was like that of the others, only set at a different pace? Was society like a mechanism in which some wheels run faster, and somehow or other put the other parts into their slow and measured motion?

Can we find those beforehand whose lives roll off at greater speed and who suffer where the others raise their eyebrows. Are not these tensions somehow noticeable so that we can make this mechanism run more smoothly, without the creaking of human cruelty and senseless waste? Is all this bitterness needed to bring out those who can turn it into a healing balm as if it had been meant to be like that all along?

Or is blindness one of the conditions of our life? Perhaps we cannot move in more light, but should not maturity lead us from semidarkness into the dawn of our partial knowledge?

Perhaps matters would have been different if Kohlhaas had lived in another period. The higher the rate of change of society, the stronger the emotions of the individuals who compose that society. Their emotions are but the energy that sets the mechanism into motion.

In a more static period, the life of a Kohlhaas would have unfolded itself with a slower rhythm. There would not have been this clash of wills, neither this pent-up energy that had to break forth into an orgy of violence and killing.

And how did it all end? Well, it ended, of course, in quite an orderly fashion, since Western civilization was to settle down to a long life to come and could only stand as much disorder as was conducive to its own growth.

A Brandenburg Court condemned the Baron to restore the horses to their former condition and to pay Kohlhaas the indemnity he requested. Then the Emperor prosecuted Kohlhaas for having broken the peace of the Empire and he was properly executed, a hero in the eyes of the people.

He himself was satisfied. The deity "Justice" had been restored to its throne, and so great was the weight of his mind over his body that the loss of his life seemed but a trivial matter to him.

Once more there was order in his universe, and order was the great and overwhelming passion of this life that had been so well and so ill spent, unless one believes as fervently as Kohlhaas did in the living power of an idea.

## CHAPTER X

## POLITICAL ECONOMY MAKES ITS APPEARANCE [51]

Perhaps it is no exaggeration to say that economics is the science of the hedonistic period: it developed in its beginnings and lasted as a leading science until the system of a controlled economy began to make headway and delegated the findings of pure economic theory to second rank. Economics, its growth, peak and decay, is typically indicative of the changes which occur in the human mind, although they may take place over a long period under the same label and may penetrate only superficially into the outside world. It could form a standard example for sociology of knowledge which tries to find the deeper psychological and social factors which underlie many of our social and economic changes. There again we find the same problem, viz. the real weight of a certain body of knowledge is analyzed by a relatively new science, sociology, instead of philosophy, or rather its branch epistemology, which supposedly analyzes knowledge. This again implies a change in emphasis: a psychological belief rather than a tested presupposition that many of the changes in thinking are due to social factors rather than to economic ones or, as philosophy would like to believe, to mental changes which are either stimulated by the outside world or are due to inherent processes for which no further explanation is needed.

It is interesting to observe how a science develops, holds a sort of magic appeal for a period of centuries and then fades out into a purely academic discipline. Only a short time ago it was possible that a book on economics would have the following adagio on the front page: 'Economics is not a theory of business activities but a theory of life". This hold of economic thinking on the human mind has been broken to a considerable extent, and what concerns us here most is how it came to develop and how it ultimately led to its own defeat.

Many of the writings of Antiquity have been considered to be of an economic nature although they centered more around the economy of the home and around some general observations about money, interest and taxation. Also in this respect the achievement of Antiquity was lost in the early Middle Ages, and it is not until the thirteenth and fourteenth centuries that we again find writings of an economic nature.

The Church fathers, especially St. Thomas Aquinas, deal with subjects like usury, interest and fair price, but they view the economic system as of an entirely secondary nature, a means to provide the strictly necessary goods for a life devoted to worship and religious contemplation. As long as economic thinking remained of a moralistic nature, it was more a negation of economic developments than a stimulus. Although the late Middle Ages knew already highly developed city economies with a considerable monetary system, the actual relationships found no reflection in theoretical thinking, since these activities ran contrary to the tenets of the Church. Only when the larger national countries like France, Spain, Portugal and England began to develop in the New Era, and when the feudalistic system of the Middle Ages had to make room for the centralistic rule of absolutistic states, there began to be an opportunity for economic thinking. The existence of larger economic units, viz. the national states, gave a sudden impetus to the role of commerce and money. The institution of professional armies, paid civil servants, etc., placed the economy on a money instead of on a barter basis. The increased significance of money was further stimulated by the increase in gold and silver after the discovery of the Americas, which led to a tremendous rise in prices. All these factors combined led to the concept that the possession of money was fundamental to the prosperity of a nation.

This idea became the basis of the first economic system, Mercantilism, which advocated the promotion of commerce in order to achieve a favorable balance of trade which, in turn, led to the acquisition of money. We can observe in the case very decidedly how economic needs created a theory, while, on the other hand, in its turn the theory stimulated the economic developments which the times demanded.

The decrease in energy devoted to spiritual matters led to an increase in mental energy which brought about a greater awareness of physical and economic processes. This greater awareness caused new experiments which were again the source of new discoveries.

Thus, the economic significance of commerce was overestimated because commerce was the most essential factor in the creation of larger economic units. In a process of growth the mind focusses on those things which are most essential for the aims which are only incompletely realized. The development of the mind itself leads to distorted views of reality which are necessary to bring about the next phase of its own growth.

In this long and weary process of bringing about a more complete mastery over the physical world than Antiquity or the Middle Ages had known, the creation of a more highly developed economic system was one of the most essential factors. We can trace the growth of the economic system as well as of economic thinking throughout the entire period which we are discussing.

It is a somewhat academic question what comes first in life: theory or practical application. The fundamental factor is the shift in focus of the human mind. Once this process has taken place, the actual idea of an innovation is a flash-like process which may be developed further either theoretically or practically or, as probably always happens in reality, in both ways.

As the increase of commerce was the first necessity in a period of widening economic ideas, it is clear that this factor would dominate economic thinking for a certain period. It is equally obvious that a trend toward a more highly developed economic system would lead to theories which stressed the importance of the other factors of our economy. The overestimation of the role of money led to a sharp increase in prices, which weighed most heavily on the poorer classes and placed the necessities of life beyond their reach. It is therefore entirely logical that a more organic system of economic theory, viz. physiocracy, developed which gave first place to agriculture as the provider of our basic needs. In this case again, the necessity of such a theory led to overemphasis: agriculture was raised to the function of the sole real producer of goods while industry or the crafts were supposed only to add value to already existing goods.

Physiocracy was created by François Quesnay, the son of a farm laborer near Versailles. Due to his unusual gifts he became in 1749 the house physician of La Pompadour and of Louis XV. His writings in the field of economics and government exercised great influence and led to the formation of a school of which Turgot was one of the outstanding members.

Quesnay ranks high because his economic thinking was part of an original philosophical system which was based consistently upon the idea of the individual. Quesnay applied the ideas of the Enlightenment logically to economics and created a theory of the individual as the basic unit of our society.

It is here not the place to discuss how far theories are "true or not true". This work aims at analyzing changes in thinking as indicative of certain trends of life, and whether the human mind can achieve a relatively correct picture of reality is a philosophical problem which was briefly discussed. It concerns us here in the first place in how far a theory fits into the pattern of change which we have outlined in the beginning of this study.

The individualistic thinking of the Enlightenment represents an effort to loosen the spiritual and mental ties of preceding centuries. The interpretation of society as dependent upon the consensus of the individual merely indicates that the individual is striving for greater liberties; as an interpretation of reality it would be a monstrosity, since all our progress in reality has been based upon combined efforts, efforts of groups from which certain individuals who realize the aims of the group come forward as intellectual or spiritual leaders. The individual of the Enlightenment who enters society of his own free will because he realizes that it is to his own advantage is a pure abstraction, an abstraction created to foster the goals of certain groups in society in a certain period.

According to Quesnay the "natural order" as contrasted with the "positive order" of human society is that of independent individuals who are guided by their own interest. It was the first time that a social theory was developed which abandoned all moral concepts.

The concept of the independent individual led to the idea that the tilling of the soil is the first basic economic activity. "L'agriculture est la source de toutes les richesses de l'Etat".

Agriculture, according to Quesnay, is the only activity which produces new goods; all other activities merely change the original products or transfer them to other places. Commerce, industry and transportation are dependent upon agriculture. Quesnay, on the basis of these ideas, designated the farmers as the productive class, while the landowners were called the distributive class, which devoted itself to administrative and political tasks. Merchants and artisans were loopholed as the "sterile class" while the workers were considered as economically passive. The idea of the fundamental importance of agriculture caused the demand that agricultural prices should be kept as high as possible through the reduction or abolishment of export duties. The underlying concept of the system was clearly to counteract the excessive stress on commerce and money of Mercantilism and to underline the significance of the production of goods instead of the largely fictitious wealth of money.

To achieve this higher production of goods, the Physiocrats demanded individual freedom, freedom in economic pursuits, freedom in consumption as well as abandonment of restrictions of residence and private property.

Government functions should be limited as much as possible: "Laissez faire, laissez aller, le monde va de lui même". The natural law theory of the inalienable rights of the individual formed the philosophical foundation of Quesnay's system.

There are many interesting ideas in physiocratic thinking. It created a picture which, apart from the excessive stress on agriculture, stressed the interrelation of the various branches of production and underlined the value of productive capacity instead of the accumulation of available goods. In spite of its goal to be entirely individualistic and atomistic, the concept of value played a significant role in the evaluation of the function of various categories of goods. This is an important point which since has been overlooked pretty consistently by economic thinking. There is no truth in the belief that only agricultural production creates value, but if we admit a structure of human needs in ratio to their importance instead of a formless demand, we obtain a concept which is based upon a more accurate knowledge of human nature than later economic thinking has sometimes achieved.

In a planned economy this problem of the structure of human needs will ultimately have to be analyzed very closely and may do away with the erroneous idea that, in a free economy, the individual actually receives what he wants most. An individual can choose on the basis of his needs but only in relation to existing prices, and the solution would ultimately have to be to adjust the price-structure to a carefully analyzed demand-structure, which never happens under a so-called "free economy".

The interesting aspect of Quesnay's thinking is that he stood on the threshold between a collectivistic and an individualistic period, advocating consciously the latter trend but with much subconscious influence of collectivistic thinking.

The next step in economic thinking was taken in England, which has always distinguished itself by a more harmonious development than the continental countries. It was never dominated so much by philosophic systems and was given to empiricism when the other countries were still struggling with metaphysical thinking.

It was also the first country to develop a free economy, and from the very beginning a series of inventions, viz. of the spinning machine, the steam engine and the mechanical loom, led to great significance of industry in its economic structure. It took the steps toward an individualistic economy consistently and created the theoretical system which dominated this development for several centuries and in many countries.

Adam Smith was the builder of an imposing economic theory which was based upon his moral philosophy. Under the influence of Hume he considered every action "moral" which would be considered justified by an impartial observer. This justification is possible because "sympathy" enables the individual to realize the feelings of his fellow-beings. As a basic quality this concept of sympathy is purely subjective and individualistic, especially since Smith tests the value of an emotion also by its social results, thus by its utilitarian value. This means that a psychological impulse does not originate from an abstract spiritual principle but from a vague awareness of the existence of other human beings. The restrained egotism of the individual leads to a natural harmony or a natural purposiveness in the world order which without excessive controls is achieved by the individuals themselves. This same principle leads to economic individualism, to the principle that little or no government interference with economic activities is necessary.

According to Smith, the foundation of the national economy is the annual labor of a nation, which constitutes the fund of all commodities that are necessary for consumption and further production. Smith limits this labor to the production of physical goods, showing an influence of the Physiocrats. Statesmen, scientists, etc., are not considered economically productive. It is obvious that the productivity of labor is highly significant for Smith's theory, and this caused him to develop very strongly the principle of the division of labor.

As under an advanced system of division of labor, nobody produces for himself, exchange value and price become the crucial points of the economic system. The quantity of goods produced determines also the wealth and power of a nation. Most other concepts of recent economic thinking are contained in the theories of Adam Smith but they remained largely undeveloped, while his labor theory of value was incorrect.

The production of goods according to Smith is largely guided by market prices, and this constitutes a strongly dynamic element in his thinking. Under a changing free economy, prices dominate the trend of development of the economic system and give it a somewhat haphazard structure.

According to Smith's fundamentally optimistic philosophy, this free interplay of forces leads to a favorable result. This idea is clearly an outcome of the conditions of his time, which still suffered under too many restrictions, like remnants of the guild system, tariff barriers, production regulations, etc. His fundamental idea of the beneficial influence of greater freedom is emotional, not analytical thinking. His belief in the basic morality of human nature is not based upon observation; it is an assumption he had to put forward to make his system work.

In the sequence of economic thinking, Smith took one of the most important steps towards a higher-standard-of-living economy by stressing the significance of the increase of production based upon division of labor. Mercantilism had prepared the way for greater economic regions and increase in commerce. Physiocratism stressed the value of basic agricultural production while Smith fostered the growth of industry and crafts. We are still in the stage when only the positive aspects of a higher-standard-of-living economy are visible. Competition is a purely constructive force which compels the individual to strain his forces to the utmost. Smith sees the economy in the first place as an exchange and market process and prepared the way for the later types of purely capitalist economies.

His method was entirely deductive and abstract. It has long been customary in the social sciences to make a sharp distinction between deductive and inductive processes. In the first case a few general principles are used to build up an entire system. If the principles are correct and the reasoning logical, the resulting system is supposed to give an adequate picture of reality. Induction proceeds on the basis of continued observation of facts and will arrive at some general conclusions conditioned by many ifs and whens. As it is very difficult in the social sciences to reason from a few principles, because the scientist is continuously influenced by his own knowledge of social matters, which tends to confuse the reasoning process, the argument about method has been quite violent in these sciences.

In economics, we can observe a continuous sequence of abstract and realistic or "historical" schools. It is quite obvious that the building of abstract theories as a means of creating patterns occurs especially in dynamic periods when things are in flux while the need to revise the pattern is felt strongly in static periods when the pattern is easily taken too literally and tends to become oppressive. In the early period of economic thinking we can observe a strong tendency to create systems, viz. Mercantilism, Physiocratism, the theories of Smith, Ricardo and Malthus, while later on the reverse trend manifests itself in the historical schools. In the beginning political economy, as a new science, needed a strong framework to maintain itself as well as to provide sharply defined theories which could guide actual developments. At the same time it needed an optimistic undertone, as it was based upon the firm belief that the abolishing of existing ties was a necessary step for the progress of mankind. Its individualism was an expression of the freedom needed by the rising middle classes in order to make economic developments possible.

Its concentration on the acquisition of material wealth required an individualistic system of ethics to supersede a collectivistic philosophy which would have kept economic activities within designated limits.

The first signs that the development of a capitalistic free economy was not so harmonious as Adam Smith and his school believed, came from the side of Malthus and Ricardo. Their more pessimistic views of the results of free competition and free enterprise did not lead to a denial of this system, such as was made by the later socialistic schools. They attempted to present the negative features as a result of natural laws which could be understood but not changed and which had a detrimental effect on a system of whose general excellency they were still convinced.

The fact that, in spite of the tremendous increases in production, the conditions of the working classes still remained deplorable, was explained by Malthus with the theory that the population has a tendency to increase at a much faster rate than the means of subsistence, so that the working class can never rise above a minimum subsistence level. As soon as it does, the increase in population will drive it back to the lowest possible minimum.

This rather naive theory received a semblance of truth from the conditions which existed in the early days of capitalism. Under a system of free competition, the employers attempted to keep wages as low as possible, and, if there was more labor than necessary to meet the demand, the workers were left to charity or starvation. However, all the basic assumptions of Malthus' theory are wrong: there is no reason to support his idea of a geometric ratio of increase of the population combined with an arithmetic ratio of increase for the means of subsistence; there is also no foundation in his belief that wages can never rise above the subsistence level.

Malthus attempted to defend the system of free competition and to present its dark sides as unavoidable natural occurrences. Similar tendencies were present in the works of David Ricardo, one of the sharpest minds who occupied themselves with economic problems.

He was also a typical representative of the classical school which attempted to create laws: laws which had a certain validity but only under conditions such as the author visualized. Economics created a human being which does not exist in reality, but by doing so it provided a pattern which made certain developments possible. There is no consistency in economic thinking, and, if the same ideas had been proclaimed in another period, they would have passed unnoticed.

Ricardo's theory centers around the concept of exchange value. He believes that it is determined by the quantity of labor contained in a product provided this product can be reproduced at will. If it cannot be reproduced at will, the element of rarity plays a role in the determination of the exchange value. The actual market price is determined by supply and demand but fluctuates toward the labor costs, as production will automatically tend toward the products which yield the highest profits. Labor gets paid its reproduction costs while the residue forms the profit. This makes the economic system into a rush for production which is led by the desire for profit. This supposedly produces ultimately the greatest benefit for the greatest number, although in this typical middle class thinking the worker never gets more than the means of subsistence. The spectre of the class conflict is already visible in this flat and inhuman philosophy.

At present theories like those of Smith and Ricardo have only an historical value as expressions of the desires of the rising middle class, and this explains their success. As abstract systems they are only interesting as an indication of the changes in the philosophy of that period.

The abstractions which they use are never pure abstractions but have a limited heuristic value under given conditions. As an abstraction the statement that labor is the cause of value is absolutely meaningless. It may determine the value which an individual attaches to a good he has produced, but it does not influence the evaluation of the potential purchaser. Under an already developed economic system the labor contained in a product undoubtedly is an element of the price, but it is the weakness of the classical system that it reasons on the basis of abstractions of limited validity and then continues its reasoning under the influence of actual or desired conditions.

Spiritual, ethical and economic individualism can be understood only, as has been said before repeatedly, as a reaction against existing spiritual and feudal ties. The desire for a lessening of existing bonds is the expression of a change in mentality which must be interpreted in terms of various stages of development of the human mind. The desire to create a more abundant life is a phenomenon which cannot be evaluated. It is neither good nor bad: it exists as at a given moment a tree begins to grow branches.

This desire caused the breakdown of institutions which placed too much weight on spiritual and not enough on material values; it led to an individualistic approach in ethics because allegiance to small social units was a hindrance on this road, while economic freedom was proclaimed to reach the higher production which, under a system of closed small social economic units, would have been impossible.

The explanation which was given for these trends was, to a certain extent, meaningless if one wishes to argue about the truth or untruth of a theory. As long as a theory is the expression of the goal of a social group, its effectiveness can be measured in terms of the success which it achieves. Its absolute validity can only be discussed if its social purpose is fully realized and if it is seen under the limitations of this purpose. For instance, economic theory has undoubtedly aided in creating a picture of economic conditions in our mind, in focussing our attention on subjects which were essential for the goal of a higher standard of living economy. Insofar as economics has operated with the pretence of finding laws, it has never reached more than a few generalizations of limited validity.

In the process of thinking, the human being struggles with the classification of his own aims. He forms patterns — or rather, intellectual
leaders create patterns — which express more or less clearly the aims of
a certain social group. There is rarely one undisputed leader, although
it may sometimes appear that way in retrospect. The intellectual leaders
dispute among themselves, and through this interaction the pattern of
thought of a group or a period develops. It is a rather fruitless although
interesting occupation to look for consistency in a social theory as long
as it is set to perform a definite social function. Whether objective
social science can exist is a problem we need not discuss here, as it certainly is not relevant for the early development of economics, a typical
example of a science with a goal which only penetrated university class
rooms at a much later stage.

The imagination of the rising middle class of the New Era was completely hypnotized by the idea of wealth, although the use of this wealth
was still subject to a number of ethical and religious restrictions. There
were few reflections in the countries which spearheaded this trend, viz.
France and England, about the subordination of this goal to other
aims. It was a quantitative and mechanistic idea which existed entirely
as an aim in itself.

Resistance to this middle class dream came in the first place from
Germany, where society had not yet shed its feudal bonds and where
thinking continued in the first place along national lines; this resistance
was kindled by a romantic spirit which was hostile to purely materialistic
considerations.

This negation of the Western European spirit by Germany was to be
a concomitant of the development of Europe until our present day. It
should not be regarded as a purely negative attitude, as we see later
that the modification and, partly, the denial of the Western European
spirit was a source of modern development. The non-acceptance of
18th and 19th century Europe was the origin of Americanism as well
as of communism as it has developed in Russia. Both attitudes had their
root in Europe, and both refuted the hedonistic spirit, although this
term is used here only for lack of a better word.

The trends of German thinking in the 18th and 19th centuries were
in the first place anti-individualistic and idealistic, perhaps because
Germany had not yet reached the stage of a unified national state and
had no group which proclaimed or had to proclaim the ideas of liberalism and freedom. It is obvious that the criticisms which the Germans
levelled at individualistic thinking were, in many cases, true. This
explains the great persistence of this form of collectivistic thinking
which was by no means new and claimed the great philosophic systems

of Plato and Aristotle as its predecessors. Fichte was the philosopher who overcame the thinking of natural law and of the contract theory. The idea of the absolute, self-sufficient individual was unacceptable, and, in going a step beyond Kant's system, he replaced it by the concept of the "ego who determines the non-ego" and the "non-ego who determines the ego". Epistemologically Fichte conceived the individual as part of a community instead of as a solitary individual. He regarded social life as the "conditio sine qua non" of our existence while he believed that its elements were subordination and coordination as the expression of the freedom of the individual but a freedom which could only realize itself in community with others as "lumen de lumine". As Fichte expressed it: "If there are to be human beings at all, there must be several". The ego does not exist until it has affirmed itself, and it can only do so through contact with others. All individual egos spring from the absolute ego which determines itself. This absolute ego was defined by Fichte as the infinite moral will of the universe, God, the absolute life which is expressed in all individual lives.

Similar ideas as developed by Schelling, Baader, Schleiermacher and others thoroughly influenced the social thinking of that period, which found its origin for a considerable part in the romanticist spirit of those days. Romanticism was by no means a purely Germanic movement as it developed also in other countries as a protest against rationalism, but in Germany it grew into an all-embracing philosophy, a poetic, religious and psychological revolt against the middle class philosophy of the Enlightenment. Its strong subjectivism was harnessed to religious experience and reconfirmed by an organic concept of state and society. It was wider, more profound, more extreme, more uncontrolled than the preceding trends of rationalist thought. The contact with the entire universe was its aim, in contrast to the attempts to make human life an interchange between individuals who were guided by utilitarian motives.

It was a natural reaction which in many ways took a step backward but a step which may have led the human mind once more closer to the fundamental aspects of life from which progress often means a deviation.

The refutation of individualistic social thinking was most consistently achieved by Adam Müller, who considered the state as "the totality of all human relations, their combination into an organic entity".

Although this sounds like, and was politically, a reactionary trend, it contains nevertheless many interesting philosophical ideas which had considerable influence and reached into our present times. Adam Müller expresses ideas similar to Fichte's: "The human being cannot be conceived outside a community"; he only finds his moral destination in community with others, etc. Adam Müller like many other of the romanticists found the realization of his ideas in the conditions of the Middle Ages.

Philosophically the denial by German idealism of rationalism and enlightenment contained many elements of value; socially and economically its return to the Middle Ages made it a reactionary movement which only had value as posing an antithesis of which our present times are showing but the initial stages. In the social and economic field, however, it was undoubtedly a merit that Adam Müller did not regard wealth and property as aims in themselves but as means for the higher goals of society. Adam Müller overlooked entirely, however, that a broader material basis was needed for a higher type of civilization and his constant praise of the guild and feudal system of the Middle Ages is a clear indication that he entirely misunderstood the period in which he was living. His theory has some value for a stabilized economy, and it is not amazing that, at a much later date, his ideas were once more adopted. On the whole, German economic thinking, especially in the case of Thünen and List, remained anti-individualistic in tendency, largely because Germany was lagging behind the other Western European countries in development and needed assistance by the government to overcome the gap which was already too large to be overcome by private initiative.

The realization that the increase in wealth in Western Europe in the 18th and 19th centuries benefitted only relatively small groups caused the growth of a number of systems of social thought which are generally grouped together under the name of Socialism. Socialism is by no means a modern phenomenon: it played a considerable role in ancient Greece and Rome, and only its presentation by Marx as a scientific system is a distinctly modern feature. Socialism is largely an ethical system which, operating on a materialistic basis, tried to bring happiness and prosperity to the large masses which had received no advantage from the increase of productive capacity and lived in a squalor and misery that contrasted sharply with the luxurious life of the upper classes.

The earlier idealistic but contradictory and confused systems of Socialism were given a definite and consistent shape by Marx, who combined a talent for scientific method with a deep compassion for the conditions in which the working classes found themselves.

Marx' economic thinking is founded upon Ricardo's theory of value, but he purified it, leaving no room for scarcity and utility as elements of value. Value, according to Marx, is congealed labor, not the actual labor involved but the "average socially necessary labor" needed to produce a certain commodity. Thus, value becomes a purely quantitative measurable matter, solely produced by physical labor, while all other elements in production are regarded as unessential, in fact as a form of robbery. Interest on capital, the profit of the entrepeneur and land rent are paid as surplus-value out of the work of the laboring classes.

Marx operated with purely ideological concepts which were highly effective in organizing the struggle for a better standard of living of the working classes and which deserve great credit for that reason, but which were too exclusively materialistic to present a balanced picture of human society and its intricate processes.

The idea that the mode of production in material life determines the social, political and spiritual processes of life is very one-sided. The famous sentence: "It is not the consciousness of men that determines their existence but, on the contrary, their social existence determines their consciousness" still awaits a satisfactory explanation. If we consider society in a static condition the statement has an appealing ring of truth but it cannot explain social change since it admits no force which would set this change into motion, unless we were to grant that material changes, occurring independently from human action, penetrate our consciousness and thus bring about a change in thinking. This would mean that electricity began to exist only when it was invented which nobody could seriously maintain and which could be easily proved to be erroneous.

If we take the statement as true, no social change could occur, although it comes about because new forms of production originate in human consciousness, and Marx does really no more than give sole validity to economic ideas while he regards religious, philosophical or moral ideas as sterile. He regards them himself ultimately as motivated by economic forces and thus being finally of economic purport themselves. However, it was a necessity for him with his dialectic method to see history in the form of a class struggle which would ultimately be overcome by a classless society, yet a classless society, if developed consistently, would mean the negation of all society. Society is a structure of coordination and subordination which has its own structural laws. If these laws would lose their validity, society as such would no longer exist.

Marx's idea that all spiritual forces of society, law, religion, philosophy, etc. are only a superstructure developed by the productive forces of society holds true in certain historical periods when antiquated forms of society hinder progressive developments.

However, it would be hard to maintain that the underdeveloped economy of the Middle Ages was the cause of their spiritual and idealistic outlook.

The greater material knowledge of Antiquity was lost in the early Middle Ages through intensive occupation with spiritual problems as well as through the more primitive mentality of new peoples which had to find first a common social foundation in spiritual values before they could commence to construct a more integrated society. It was, however, a change in consciousness which gradually led to greater occupation with material values but not vice versa.

The Marxian system is hard to understand because it contains individualistic and collectivistic elements. Its interpretation of society in the form of a class struggle is strongly individualistic, but its ultimate ideal of a classless, non-profit society is collectivistic and anti-hedonistic in tendency. The tremendous significance of Marxism and its preceding systems lies in its practical achievement of great improvement in the conditions of the working classes, but also in its function of being the first social system to overcome definitely the ideology of hedonist society. Many of its tenets are colored by its practical aims, but it would never have achieved its enormous significance if it had merely tried to gain the materialistic privileges of the upper classes for society as a whole. It had to deny the profit idea to do this, or it would have reduced society to a meaningless conglomeration of trading merchants. It created the image of a new society in which the forces of production will be properly coordinated, although it presented this under the erroneous term of a "classless" society.

This could only be true if the term "class" refers to the opposing groups of a hedonistic society but not if it were to mean the functional groups which, of necessity, exist in any given social structure. This same ideological bias colored the interpretation of physical labor as the only element capable of creating value. In fact, the change in productive forces which is so significant in Marxism, can only be achieved by mental or intellectual labor. The denial of symbolic force as an active social factor is an indication of the process of becoming more intellectually conscious which is typical of our modern world. If it were argued that symbolic force is a higher form of psychological energy than mental force, this increasing awareness would become a social process which has its negative as well as its positive aspects.

As it is the trend of this study to interpret social changes as an expression of the development of the human mind, no evaluation can be placed on any change except an evaluation which would be indicative of a certain stage in a process of growth and, consequently, also ultimate decay.

The negation of symbolic force, according to such an interpretation, would merely convey that the occupation with a realizable happiness in human society has gained precedence over the idea of balancing existing unhappiness with the expectation of life in a future world. This, sociologically speaking, would mean a shorter psychological range than the one which operates with metaphysical values. Again it must be stressed that the existence in reality of our ideas is not investigated but only the relative psychological implication of the changes in our mental structure. We are concerned with the change of the concept "free" in our mind, not with the problem whether this concept conforms to reality or whether reality is only partly accessible to our cognition or not at all. The concepts of religion, for instance, are investigated as indicative of psychological change, not in regard to their possibly existing absolute value.

Socialism performed also a highly important function by pointing out the relative value of capital in the economic structure, although it entirely overlooked its role in an expanding economy. To bring the economic system from a lower to a higher level, capital is the conditio sine qua non, and thus automatically the owner of capital is placed in a privileged position. The weight which was placed upon capital and which made capitalists a privileged class caused the tendency to develop those branches of production where the return on capital investment was largest without any regard for the basic needs of mankind. This accumulation of capital in the most profitable industries aggravated the lack of balance of the free capitalist economy which made it an excellent target for socialist attacks, although it must be stressed that, in the long run, a certain balancing influence was exercised by the structure of demand, which is only partly flexible.

It is not astounding that the final defense of free capitalist economy came from the side of the concepts of value of the consumer. It was the last anchor which individualism could find for a system whose supposed liberty was not leading anywhere near the harmony that it was intended to create. If the manifold human needs could be proved to find a reasonable satisfaction under a free economy, there was still a possibility to accept it as a workable system. Profiting from the obvious error of the Marxian concept of value as derived from the labor contained in a given product, the marginal utility school took the logical psychological step by explaining value from human needs. It cleverly circumvented the apparent existing relationship between value and labor in a developed economy by operating with the concept of an isolated individual who measures the value of a good in terms of the need he has for it.

Psychologically it was readily acceptable that on a lonely island a pail of water has considerably more value than an automobile, notwithstanding the vast amount of labor which is contained in the latter. This "marginal utility" school explained price in terms of utility and held that cost was derived from price and not vice versa. The basic concept of the new approach consisted of the realization that commodities are not valued according to their general significance but according to the merits of a given supply. As any unit can take the place of another one, value is determined by the least important employment which determines the value of the other units. This explains readily why the value of water is small on account of the abundant supply while that of gold is high because it exists only in small quantities. If they were available in the same quantities, the value of water would be immeasurably higher, since it fulfills a much more essential need. Older schools of economics had already operated with the concept of utility of various categories of goods, but they had not been able to introduce the element of quantity effectively into their system.

This quantitative, psychologically subjective solution fitted ideally into the spirit of the time, which, in that period, was obsessed by an expanding standard of living that went far beyond moderate requirements.

The mechanism of human needs provided an ideal trial ground for a number of highly complicated economic theories which operated with an acceptable basic principle but which got tangled up by trying to explain a reality in which their hypothesis was only partially active. Pressure on the consumer, for instance, which is so strong in our modern economy was a factor which could not be explained by subjectivistic economic thinking.

It must be restated at this point that economics, barring the socialistic and organic schools, remained the ideology of the rising middle class, which needed an individualistic and quantitative approach in order to reach their goal of greater spiritual, legal and economic freedom. This ideology grew quite independently from the actual development of the economic system, and it is amazing to see that there are at times even few contact points except in more specialized fields like money and banking.

The historical schools and economic history attempted to fill this gap, and yet today there are amazing loopholes in our history of the economic system and few to coordinate it with economic thinking or vice versa.

In general, economics was a part of the great movement toward a fuller conquest of the world. As a child of enlightenment and rationalism, it struggled firmly against existing bonds and was only in periods of reaction capable of viewing a stabilized world. As a science, economics is completely a phenomenon of a dynamic period — it was born when the hour was ripe and it lost a great deal of its general appeal when the civilized world began to strive frantically for the stabilization of its economic system through the creation of new forms of social and political control. The emphasis shifted to sociology, social psychology, social anthropology and related disciplines which take a much wider view of human nature and which may ultimately lead to a more correct analysis of human needs than economics provided.

In our needs our cultural and mental progress is reflected, and they create a changing pattern which can never be adequately analyzed by an economic approach, although it brings out certain fundamental aspects of quantitative relationships..

If we succeed in creating a stabilized and harmonious world, economics will be delegated to the place of a technical discipline but have no further significant role in creating the ideology of the world, at least not to the same extent as in the past. In a harmonious civilization there is a hierarchy of sciences which may become disturbed in times of upheaval and change but which, sooner of later, regains its position. In this structure, the science which deals with the production and distribution of goods should fulfill a function designated to it by philosophy or psychology. As long as it presents this final aim as a goal in itself, it tacitly admits a condition which no longer exists in itself, since the majority of the people feel that wealth for wealth's sake is no longer a permissible purpose of human endeavor, and has, in fact, led to the many dislocations from which our society has suffered.

Complete stabilization of our civilization is unthinkable, but it has become a generally accepted principle to attempt to keep economic change within reasonable bounds, although the means thereto are only tentative and incomplete.

The former violent upheavals belonged to a dynamic period when the development came to a temporary standstill, probably through a combination of economic and psychological factors. The growth of our modern economy has been spontaneous, by leaps, as any natural growth is. The idea of a planned economy is as such an indication that a period of economic expansion has come to an end, or is at least by many considered to be no longer of the same overwhelming importance, although this does not hold true for large areas of the world which, however, can bring about this development by a process of imitation rather than by spontaneous creation.

A planned economy in itself means an economy which would be stabilized or further developed on the basis of an existing system or by comparison to or in analogy with such a system. The original creation of our economy could never have been planned, as every creative process results from inner forces of which the individual only becomes aware through the process of creation itself. A completely conscious development can never be a creative one, and we can once more make the same observation that increasing consciousness or awareness which runs parallel to cultural progress may not be such a positive thing as we are generally inclined to believe.

The desire to stabilize our economy is indicative of a lessening of creative power at least in this field. It is not argued here that there is no great need of applying our energy in the first place to political, social and moral problems but often a lessening of energy in one field does not lead to expansion in another.

We will need considerable concentration to overcome this dead point which we have reached, although this concentration can only be achieved by desisting from the overwhelming materialistic emphasis which our civilization still possesses and which constitutes its greatest danger.

## CHAPTER XI

## RATIONALISM AND ENLIGHTENMENT 52

The relative simplicity of the process of thinking, if we consider only its fundamental principles, becomes a hopeless array of systems, ideas and theories as soon as we attempt to go into details. Even the most generally used terms defy an exact definition, and long studies can be made to determine the approximate meaning of a given term.

To a certain extent every human mind is a world in itself of which certain regions have contact with other minds while other parts remain hidden even to the individual himself. Knowledge of one's own mind has often been proclaimed as the highest ideal, and especially the minds of those who possess a great deal of awareness realize how limited, biased and prejudiced their knowledge fundamentally is.

The mind, as an infinitely subtle instrument, is, in itself, subject to growth and change, and therefore it is a complex undertaking to look for consistency in the systems of thought which were produced in one age or another. There is undoubtedly similarity, on different levels, but we could never find identity.

Tremendous efforts have been made to regard the mind as a definite unchangeable entity, a center of energy which was considered to have at least permanency in mass — if it is permissible to use this expression — but the attempts have never been successful, and their ultimate possibility can well be questioned.

Modern thought becomes more and more convinced that in almost all fields we deal with a process of growth, and we may as well apply this also to the concept of psychic energy. If we regard psychic energy not as a constant but as a variable, we would have to reorientate ourselves in the processes of philosophy. Philosophy may once more become the love of wisdom instead of the science which strives for general knowledge, a concept which in itself becomes untenable if we regard the subject of this knowledge as itself subject to change.

In that case, the problem becomes more of what type of change such and such a philosophy is indicative than whether the concepts themselves approach — and to what degree — an absolute knowledge whose existence we no longer admit. Why the medieval mind was so preoccupied with metaphysics, why it filled the world with angels, saints, demons, witches and sorcerers is a matter which should make us search for psychological change. We would almost say: for the laws of psychological change but even the concept of "law" belongs to one period and does not to another. On the other hand, the admission of change and growth does not have to lead us into the solutions of pragmatism, to the belief that a certain pattern of thought has value because it operates under certain conditions. Such an attitude would make philosophy the cataloguer of patterns of thought, but the concept of change re-affirms the task of philosophy or science even though its purpose is restated. It demands the consideration of new factors, of a new dimension which the desire for permanent and absolute knowledge overlooked.

It is of importance that we restate the leading concepts before we deal with patterns of tought of such alluring names as Rationalism and Enlightenment. The names themselves betray the purpose of these systems, which dominated the human mind in the New Era, in the period of terrific psychological struggle between the forces which regarded life as an eternal struggle between light and darkness and those who wanted to overcome the extremes of elation and despair in order to make the world a better place for human endeavor. It was a tremendous effort to bring the human mind within narrower limits and to channel its energy in order to direct it to law, morality, the exact sciences and less to the problems of the supernatural, which were not denied, but which were deemed to be inaccessible or open only to a rational approach. It is almost impossible to understand the grip which fear and imagination held over the human mind until late in the 18th century. It was fear of the supernatural which religion tried to overcome or to play upon, according to the sincerity of its representatives, and which colored life in all its aspects. Enlightenment and Rationalism were the forces which fought a slow and tenacious battle to overcome the interplay of fear and imagination, the two qualities which made life under simpler conditions bearable and unbearable at the same time.

If the human being lives under constant hope and fear of what will happen in the hereafter, this conflict will tend to make harsh conditions more bearable because a longterm psychological attitude will put an acceptable interpretation on them, yet the amelioration of material conditions is retarded through the same process of psychological distance.

To maintain this attitude, which was the aim of important social groups, the imagination was constantly nourished with tales of the supernatural, in its good as well as in its evil manifestations, and concrete as well as objective thinking was discouraged as much as possible. Death and devil walked at the side of the human being in every second of his life, and every attempt to free oneself from this paralyzing grip, whether in the form of boisterous frolicking or of serious intellectual efforts, was followed by a renewed attack of the forces which were insistent upon keeping their hold on the human mind. The elements of fear and imagination are always present in the human mind, but there has been a clearly marked change in their relative importance.

In the Middle Ages as well as in the beginning of the New Era, the average human being was quite ready to admit that a witch was capable of riding through the air on a broomstick, and thousands of unfortunates were tortured and burned for this reputed achievement, which today would probably yield the performer a comfortable income.

The margin between reality and imagination, between knowledge and superstition, was so close that the main question which was asked constantly was that of the possibility of knowledge itself. There was a desire to place more confidence in the world of the senses, while serious thinking inevitably led to the conclusion that the world as it appears to the human being cannot possibly be the world as it is in reality.

The entire period of the 17th and 18th century in France, England and Germany is dominated by the desire to comprehend the world by the powers of intellect and reason without recourse to revelation and supernatural power, a process which was and never could be entirely successful but which contributed a great deal toward the development of intellect and reason as factors of the human mind. The attempt to establish a system of cause and effect in Nature, to an "interpretatio naturae", apart from immediate sense perception, led always again to the question as to how far any law observed in Nature was in reality a law of the human mind. The efforts to establish a connection between the two ranged from the impossibility of such a connection, as in skepticism, to the pre-established harmony of Leibnitz and Spinoza. Yet, the New Era was definite in its opposition to the Middle Ages, to the belief that what exists in the mind as a result of revelation is an exact replica of reality. For this belief there was no longer room, and thus we can witness a continued struggle to establish order in Nature as well as in the human mind and the effort to ascertain how far this order also exists in the "real world", toward which no knowledge seems to lead unless we assume a certain pre-existing harmony between mind and world. The object as it comes to us through the perception of our senses is not the real one, as the development of the exact sciences made clear enough, and yet there is no reason to admit that the powers of scientific reasoning grasp a world which has a better claim to real existence. An experiment ultimately proves only what we read into Nature and confirms, if successful, the consistency of our reasoning but not the essence of matters. Reason may disclose other and new aspects of Nature, but now, as in the period of Rationalism and Enlightenment, there is no reason to assume that our knowledge is complete or intended to be complete.

We are still an unknown factor in an unknown universe, even though we have filled it with notions of forces instead of populating it with angels, spirits and apparitions. The change which has occurred has been exclusively within our mind, and we could even claim that many of mankind's former imaginations have been confirmed within the realm of reason and have been realized in a factual way, showing perhaps once more a parallelism between the mind and reality toward which our beliefs easily tend although apparent parallelism is not proved parallelism. In the same way as the Middle Ages had no better proof for the existence of God than that His image or a concept of His image existed in our mind, our modern thinking has no stronger argument for the real existence of the natural forces they operate with than their existence in our mind. If highly complicated calculations are finally tested by experiments, we are merely testing our own consistency, but we do not prove more than that an originally made set of abstractions has been logically developed. We do not prove the existence of a force or a reality or a substance which did not exist before. While it is conceivable that the human mind as well as the universe changes, the ratio of change in many cases is so infinitesimally small that, for all practical purposes, we can operate with the concept of permanent natural laws.

When Rationalism and Enlightenment were so concerned about the establishment of a rational order, it was the human mind which was demanding such an order for itself. [53] That this order led to a greater domination over natural forces was a by-product which may be accepted as a proof that, in whatever condition the mind is, it finds a counterpart in reality; but the changes of the human mind do not necessarily mean that our mental picture of reality becomes more accurate.

It might be accurate in all stages, but it might mirror different aspects of the same reality or its change might imply a change in reality; however this could not be easily argued, since the changes of the mind are too numerous to be acceptable as changes of a reality which, otherwise at least, appears to be of considerable permanence.

We can also observe the strange phenomenon that the objects on which the human mind focusses are always supposed to have at the same time the greatest reality. When, in the Middle Ages, God and the spiritual world were the matters with which the mind occupied itself, any doubt about the real existence of these concepts was a matter of life and death. In a later period when the human mind centered on "Nature", there was no doubt about the reality of these processes which could be "proved" by experiment, but it was quite permissible to regard God as a function of our moral consciousness while His real existence was deemed of considerably lesser importance. Thus, we can make the interesting observation that a function of the human mind which is strongly developed projects itself readily into reality, while a decrease in the importance of this function immediately raises the question as to the reality of the objects with which the function occupies itself. The clearest example of this is the primitive mind, which is aware only of its immediate surroundings while we can daily observe in ourselves that the importance of a place or person depends entirely upon its role in our consciousness. From this we could conclude that a complete cognition of reality depends entirely upon the condition of the human mind, and that the acceptance of growth or change in the human mind would preclude a complete cognition per se. We can only conceive the construction of an abstract human mind which by combining, coordinating and subordinating all possible attitudes would reach as close an approximation of reality as can be achieved. This is the task of the philosopher which was so masterfully achieved by the thinkers of the 17th and 18th centuries, who investigated all fields of learning of their period and attempted to draw a complete picture of the world which was accessible to them.

The factor which their thinking perhaps overlooked was the reason which compelled them so strongly to look for reason and order and the reason for their constant struggle to avoid metaphysical principles. These principles were frequently readmitted in the end, since they constituted the only realm on which mind and reality could meet one another. Another factor of great importance in that period was the first attempts to view the mind as a dynamic structure which does not reflect the world passively but which, in the act of perception as well as of conception, positively gives a form and structure which may or may not be those of reality. This admission of the dynamic structure of the mind was a great improvement over the Middle Ages, which understood thinking as a passive awareness of the universe. The tremendous struggle of the New Era for the clarification of the concepts of force, time and space meant that the utter importance of these structural qualities was fully realized, although, also in this case, it means a renewal of the question whether these qualities were inherent categories of the human mind or attributes of reality or both. The more reason was promoted to the main guiding force of the mind, the more reason and intellect themselves became the subject of investigation. This thread we can follow throughout the entire New Era: on the one hand, the desire to rely on reason and intellect, and on the other hand, the doubt, springing perhaps from metaphysical sources, as to the reliability of these instruments.

This doubt found its expression in skepticism as well as in the demand of the romanticists for a return to cosmic thinking, a demand which was made on a subjectivistic as well as a collectivistic basis. However, these reactions meant only modifications of the trend toward rationalism, which continued until the 19th and 20th century, and is only now somewhat challenged by demands for structural thinking or for the pragmatistic interpretation of thought as a predominantly social function.

The forms in which rationalism has appeared are too numerous to be dealt with here, and we can do no more than give a sketchy impression of its main trends, especially since most systems of rationalism were by no means consistent in themselves.

The entire development has been dominated by the growth of the natural sciences, as philosophy itself succeeded only gradually in freeing itself from the hold of metaphysics and found its strongest support for elevating reason to the role of the main intellectual agent in the scientific discoveries of the period. It destroyed the medieval philosophy that whatever is present in the human mind reflects reality in a simple parallelism, although this thinking insisted upon an hierarchical structure of reality which was based upon imagination and not upon observation and analysis.

The distrust of the world of the senses was of a moral rather than of an epistemological character, while the path of higher truth was not an intellectual or rational one but a result of revelation. Only the New Era discovered gradually that the function of cognition was more important than its objects and that the world of experience was not a given factor but a highly uncertain one of which real knowledge was at least doubtful.

The uncertainty in regard to the outer world became the source of a new approach, of an admission first of the uncertainty of the contents of our observations which hitherto had seemed more stable.

The categories of thinking which had been considered in the Middle Ages as possessing separate existence were seen in the first place as instruments to deal with experience, yet, at the same time, influenced by that very same experience.

A clear example of this trend is furnished by Cusanas, who, in his earlier period, believed that the absolute can only be reached by the negation of finite knowledge; in his later writings, cognition becomes the image of the absolute. Subjectivity is no longer the counterpart of absolute being but the force which enables us to take part in it. Mind and being are not identical, but there exists a harmony of contents between them which causes the human mind to project all relations of being.

The attempted separation of cognition from metaphysics, which did not succeed in Cusanas' case, became one of the crucial problems of the Renaissance.

In the Middle Ages science and art, metaphysics as well as history, were dominated completely by religion. Only with the Renaissance did they gain a separate existence, but the problem of their unity remains in force but as a unity of life rather than of thought. It was the most remarkable effort to regain an individualistic attitude toward life even though tempered by humanistic influences. To grasp reality in all possible aspects was the "leitmotiv" of the Renaissance, which, however, was only reflected much later by philosophy.

The excessive occupation with experience, the world of new inventions and discoveries set the speculative capacity of the human mind once more free in the metaphysical realm, as there was no connection between the realms of thought. This accounts for the tremendous amount of superstition which penetrated not only popular belief but also the world of science. The desire to capture the fullness of life did not make the Renaissance a critical period in regard to the processes of thinking, and it has been customary to regard the Renaissance more as a literary than as a philosophical movement. Yet, there is no great significance in the dynamic approach of the Renaissance which caused physics to operate with the concept of function instead of with the idea of substance.

Although the discovery of the "I", as an independent entity, was already of great importance, this concept could gain structural qualities only by its relation to the observations of the exact sciences — as well as by its artistic and romantic approach. Leonardo da Vinci was the great master of this penetration of reality by the mind in an all-embracing manner. However, the testing of the function of the intellect in this process came only at a later stage.

The first steps in this direction were taken by a deeper analysis of Platonic thought than the Middle Ages had been capable of. In Ficino's writings on Plato the problems of the theory of knowledge were brought out more sharply; previously the metaphysical aspects of Plato's idealism had occupied most of the attention. The role of recollection in the Platonic sense in the processes of our mind led to a certain awareness of the concept of consciousness, but only vaguely and hesitatingly. Ficino realized that all cognition means a gradual approach of the objective world by the cognizing subject, which means that both must have a common basis. The forms which the objective world assumes are creations of the mind and cannot be explained as the result of a purely receptive process. The information of general concepts is not the outcome of abstraction from a number of separate cases but a spontaneous creation of the mind. The science which was most instrumental in creating this deeper understanding of the processes of cognition was mathematics, which furnished the best example of independent creation by the human mind on the basis of reality and yet apart from it. It was typical of the Renaissance that art was the realm which was used to demonstrate the creation of ideas; Plato had found his original starting point in our moral concepts.

The thoughts of the Renaissance culminate in the idea of Lorenzo Magnifico that, while the Middle Ages regarded the world as a vale of fears to be guarded by pope and emperor until the Anti-Christ, the enlightened spirits of the Renaissance gained the belief that the visible world had been created by God's love as an image of a pre-existing world. The temporal world is seen no longer as a hostile world but as an extension of God's work.

The astronomic ideas of the period which regarded the world as the center of the universe gave further support to this positive attitude. The great innovation, however, was contained in the idea of development which came to the fore in the sixteenth and seventeenth centuries. It was the concept of force, which built a bridge from the supernatural to the temporal world: the latter was no longer considered as a result of non-being but as an expression of the absolute world which could be regained through the various stages of being. This more dynamic concept alleviated the understanding of Nature as the totality of this interplay of forces.

The continuation of the belief in natural forces, as expressed in magic, aided this trend of finding natural laws on the basis of a general world-image.

It is a new reality which the philosophers and scientists were struggling for: an understanding of the temporal world different from an uncritical acceptance as well as from a metaphysical acceptance. Anthropomorphical explanations tried to point the way towards an understanding of Nature, and the famous discoveries of Leonardo da Vinci, Keppler and Galilei created a desire to analyze in what way these innovations became possible. Mathematics furnished the key which opened the door to Nature, since its calculations which could be tested in reality were considered to represent the laws of Nature. Experience in the framework of mathematics was considered to be the true picture of reality compared with the world of superstitions of previous periods. The efforts to determine the exact role of the human mind in the creation of this picture were uncertain, and the problem of inherent categories was not clearly stated. There was a constant struggle between the belief in the animation of objects and the efforts to explain them in a mechanistic way. Only by stressing the requirements of mathematical and geometrical methods did it become possible to arrive at objective observations.

Thus, the earlier dualism in the interpretation of the world was overcome: the unmovable celestial world and the constant change in our world became both aspects of the same Nature and subject to the same laws. It is truly amazing to reflect about the fear which these innovations had to cope with: most contemporaries were so intent on preserving their mental patterns of the world that they refused to take note of the new discoveries. The certainty of their metaphysical beliefs meant so much to them that occupation with reality had a frightening influence on them, strengthened by the still existing fact that reality has a highly dubious character.

The new concepts were formed on the basis of observation instead of imagination, but the real existence of the contents of these concepts remained as much a closed book as of those which were purely imaginative. On the whole, however, the scientists of the New Era were convinced of the harmony of mind and reality. It was a problem which they generally did not make the subject of philosophical investigation, although "reality" meant to them the world as determined by number, time, and space and not by its immediate appearance.

The appearance of things is entirely subjective and has no connection with the objective world. It is a new concept of matter with which the New Era operates and which it derives from its mathematical and geometrical theories. This explains why weight was not considered until later to be an inherent quality of matter. The concept of necessity takes precedence over the concept of form which dominated Aristotelian physics.

It becomes the aim to understand movement and function, cause and effect, and to consider a complete knowledge of reality as unattainable and therefore irrelevant, although the attitude on this point remains uncertain in the works of most writers of this period. Knowledge of the absolute became less important than absolute knowledge of causal relationships. Galilei was the first to state clearly that an hypothesis which can be proved empirically deserves to be considered "true" although it means a limited truth which may not stand in the light of further reasoning or further experimentation.

The thinking of the Middle Ages had created an ideal world of which the existing world was considered an image but, often enough, the ideal world had been fashioned along the lines of the existing one. At no time, however, had there been any effort to test these two forms of knowledge experimentally: they were both based upon imagination with a haphazard adjustment to observation when the contradiction became too obvious.

The shift toward experience as the source of knowledge caused a great difference in the evaluation of logic: dialectic and syllogistic reasoning was no longer the road which led to truth. The hierarchical world it could build was not the reality which the exact sciences were exploring, although they discovered that reality escaped them the nearer they approached it: very much the same result which modern physics is showing today. This difficulty made the problem of method of paramount importance. The different ways in which the mind presented reality were a product of the attitude of mind, of the method whereby it approached reality.

Ever since Bacon's "Organum", the quest for the methodology of knowledge has come to the fore. It was in Descartes' thinking that this problem of analysis of the mind was stated most clearly.

The unity of the human mind is created by the unity of its approach, and cognition finds its ultimate justification in metaphysics which was introduced by Descartes once more to complete the structure of thinking. It is again the problem of the categories of thought which takes precedence over the categories of being, although a compromise was attempted in the metaphysical realm. The principle "cogito ergo sum" places the center of the universe in the individual but also reconfirms reality, as every process of consciousness is stimulated by a process of reality, though cognition is not a pure reflection of reality. Every process of thought requires a subject as well as an object. At one point the contradiction of substance and reality, of essence and existence, merges in the idea of God as the concept of complete and perfect knowledge. The affinity of the mind and reality is explained by Descartes with the argument that "God, as a perfect being, could not fool mankind".

Therefore, the cognition of reality although not complete must be correct as long as it is consistent within itself. This is why Descartes puts the individual at the beginning of his thinking: once the processes of the mind can be made consistent within themselves, they will also be true. It is an amazing structure which Descartes built and to which relatively little has been added by modern thought. The idea of God as a logical necessity did not mean a return to the autology of the classics and the Middle Ages; it merely reconfirmed Descartes' demand for unity of method.

It remained the difficulty of Descartes' philosophy that he used also inherent categories which exist apart from all contact with reality and which thereby introduce a mystic element into thinking. Fundamentally, the dualism in the thinking of the New Era was unescapable: the analysis of reality always led to the realization of the uncertainty of our knowledge of reality. The establishment of this knowledge of certain forces and relations then tended to re-establish the belief in the permanent value of ideas, viz. of those forces and relations, and this again led to the rebuilding of a world of ideas as a firmer haven of mental stability. Thus, metaphysics chased out by the frontdoor continuously returned via the backdoor.

Scientific investigation discloses that the world is not as it appears, while increasing knowledge of natural processes only furnishes a partial knowledge of reality. It will also demand the recourse to a higher principle to explain what is beyond our knowledge.

History has merely shown a shift in accent: our knowledge of natural processes has increased and, temporarily, a new discovery may blot out our fundamental uncertainty, but it returns as soon as we realize that our increase in practical knowledge does not bring us an inch closer to the universe as such. Whether we explain the universe in terms of good and evil, or of matter and energy, we must always face the question of the cause of the conflict, or of the process, and today as well as forty centuries ago we can do no more than to create an abstract principle as the cause of being. Whether this ultimate principle is interpreted in an anthropomorphic or any other way is immaterial, although it must be admitted that the anthropomorphic explanation is most readily acceptable to our mind.

The greatest step forward in the eternal conflict between mind, reality and the absolute was taken by Kant, who concentrated on the laws and structure of experience. Neither psychological forms nor material objects exist in an absolute way but only in the way experience presents them to us.

This eliminates the previous attitudes which had to project individuality and reality against a common metaphysical background in order to establish a relationship between them. Kant overcame this dualism by seeking the general forms of experience itself, whether it was experience of inner processes or of those of the outer world. It was a theory not of objects but a theory of judgments which combined the two facets of cognition.

The concept of judgment dominated the structure of Kant's philosophy, which started with purely empirical judgments combining the various elements of perception into the image of a given object. It is the permanence of these judgments which gives them an objective validity that goes beyond the immediate existence of the objects themselves. The permanence of our observations gives the world of objects a continuity which may not rest in the objects themselves. This process of objectivation leads to the formation of concepts which follow their own structural laws.

Kant tries to clarify this statement by comparing our consciousness in a state of dreaming and in a state of awakeness. In both cases the contents of our consciousness are the same but what creates the image of reality in one case are the structural laws of our intellect.

The laws of cause and effect prove the certain unity which exists between the world of our intellect and the world of reality although it is not proof of correlation of one to the other. Nature is not the world of the objects of our observations but the totality of their structural interrelations. In other words, there remains a subjective element in our knowledge of Nature and at no time can it be proved that knowledge reflects objective reality.

"The intellect as the creator of Nature" is the form in which Kant expressed the fact that there is no other objectivity than the objectivity of our judgments. The distinction in analytical judgments, those which contain a unit of observation, and synthetic judgments, those which give structure to the world of observation, aided in developing his critical philosophy further. Kant assigned a structural quality to the intellect which the earlier theories on the formation of ideas by a process of abstraction had omitted.

There is an opinion in the formation of judgments which gives them their validity when they are applied to empirical observations. The object is never the result of direct empirical observation but is created by the functions of the mind. In other words, the mind furnishes an image of reality which is its own creation and has no right to the claim of presenting reality as such. This is the major difference between critical and ontological thinking. The latter believes in the direct absolute truth of its findings while the former regards them as an image of the objective world which is in itself beyond our cognition.

The concepts of space and time, for instance, are synthetic judgments which are *a priori* products of our reason but not qualities of reality. Berkeley had proved that the concept of space is not the outcome of observation but derived from the analysis of observation.

Time and space are *a priori* concepts because we put these qualities ourselves into the world of our observations but do not derive them from it. This can be expressed more clearly by stating that we can imagine nothing without the attributes of time and space.

Kant's critical philosophy represented a highly significant step in the development of the human mind. It was the victory of analytical reasoning, and an almost complete refutation of the largely imagined systems of philosophy which had dominated the world for such a long period. For the first time a clear answer had been given to the question of what our knowledge really consists.

Throughout the New Era we can trace this growth of the rational mind very clearly, and it is definitely Kant's thinking which will be the starting point for further investigations of this problem.

When, at the end of the Middle Ages, the imaginative, metaphysical mind began to lose its appeal, mankind turned eagerly toward reality, a reality which had been the object of fear and which had been seen in entirely distorted proportions. It was the great deception that the world of reality when it was approached did not seem to offer any certainty and presented itself daily in a new light under the influence of the discoveries of the exact sciences. Thus, it became essential to establish a certain permanence in the world as well as in the human mind, and it is this struggle for permanence which shapes the countless philosophical systems of this period. Tired of the metaphysical approach, it tried to find a hold in the world of appearances, then in the concepts which the exact sciences created, and, finally, in the general ideas which the mind develops if it is granted the capacity at all to obtain a certain amount of knowledge.

Altogether the efforts to stabilize the human mind were not successful until toward the end of the New Era. We deal with the stage of history when mankind was trying to overcome its fears, but every new step created new ones, and the process remained a slow and wavering one. Metaphysics, which had been banned, re-entered the mind at almost every moment, because reason proved an instrument capable of dealing only with a part of reality and at its best turned out to be a highly unreliable element.

The attempt to develop certain sections of the mind is always only partly successful, as every new emergency will set those sections into motion which may not belong to the pattern of the period.

Let us try to visualize clearly what the period meant. The Western mind was outgrowing the stage of its youth, of complete domination by imagination, an imagination which aided mankind through a period of misery and uncertainty by creating the image of a future world, of a supernatural world, since it was too remote to strive for happiness on an earth which was the object of fear. It is strange to observe, however, that many of the wildest phantasies of the Middle Ages were realized centuries later in the realm of reason and science. Perhaps this proves that fundamentally the contents of the human mind are the same but that the process of development transfers these contents from the realm of imagination to the realm of reason. It is not the world which changes, or at any rate only at an almost imperceptible rate, but the human mind. Only the changes of the human mind hold the answer to the questions which mankind poses itself.

We have made the mistake of overlooking the structural changes of the human mind and of dealing with problems as if the mind approaches them on the same level. The desire to give permanence and stability are at the root of these efforts, which are denied by the very fact of the continued search for truth and knowledge.

The primitive mind is as ready to accept a supernatural world as the world of appearances. It is as uncritical in the acceptance of the dictates of its imagination as in its faith in the senses. The development of reason leads to a distrust of the function of our imagination as well as of our observations, or at least it tries to rationalize the imagined world. At a stage of greater vitality, imagination tends to be highly developed, but if the sum total of human energy diminishes, the power of imagination seems to decline first.

The world of reason, on the other hand, is neither a true nor a false one. It takes, as it were, a picture of reality which is consistent within itself but which can never be interpreted as the exact counterpart of reality. We operate with a relation between two factors: reality and the human mind; and both are only partially known to us. It is well-known today that the conscious mind is only a section of our entire mind: the subconscious as well as the superconscious are outside the realm of knowledge, while even only a small part of our conscious mind is dominated by reason. Thus, with a highly imperfect instrument, we take a picture of an object which we cannot see: a truly complex situation.

On the other hand, it cannot be denied that our rational powers have developed, but at the cost of the other organs of the human mind. Or let us try to go one step further and say that all science, all abstract thought, is ultimately a pattern which is created by our own uncertainty: let us therefore accept the world as we find it today.

To do this, we must stabilize our store of knowledge, which is essential to our civilization, but this very knowledge tends to show us the uncertainty which was the reason for its development. The desire to go beyond the accepted world, combined with strong economic factors, led to our control over natural forces. The desire to stabilize the world can only mean a decrease in the creation of new knowledge. A real stabilization carries the seeds of decay in it, since once our intellectual curiosity is lost, we would hardly be able to maintain our present store of knowledge.

The biggest danger which threatens the world is the idea that knowledge is more complete than it actually is. It would be better — and closer to the truth — if we realize that we really know only imperfectly a relatively small segment of reality.

The eternal debate of the New Era on the possibility of knowledge was a phenomenon which is indicative of a period of intense mental development. Its refusal to accept the supernatural as an explanation of everything as well as its distrust of the world of appearance shows a strong tie between the social and the exact sciences and an intense desire for consistency in all fields of thought.

Its approach to the world widened our knowledge of reality and sharpened the critical powers of the mind. It clearly realized, in the philosophy of Kant, that our capacity for scientific abstractions remains a capacity of the mind, although it seems to present aspects of reality.

The New Era was the period of adolescence of the Western mind, and its brilliance as well as its vitality made it the source of practically everything our present civilization has to show. Further progress can only come from intensive relations with other culture-groups in our world, as otherwise there is good reason to fear that the Western world out of itself will not create the new philosophy which is needed.

## CHAPTER XII

## THE SOCIAL THINKING OF THE NEW ERA [54]

It is somewhat disconcerting to consider the limitless number of ideas which mankind has produced and the ratio in which these ideas have been transferred into actual change. At times one gets a vision of people struggling on forever on this globe in much the same way and forever producing much the same ideas, even though in different combinations, with different stress, and within different patterns. If we could omit everything in social thinking which is purely a result of contemporary conditions and ideas, we would find that the variety of different possible solutions is very limited.

Our society has always the form of a pyramid, as the word society itself indicates that a given social group reaches the status of a group by a certain division of functions. If there were no division of functions, there would be no group and consequently no society. Even the smallest imaginable group, viz. that consisting of two people, would show that functional structure or there would be no contact of any permanence.

The division of functions which is the basis of all society is always limited to the same basic pattern. At the top of the pyramid we find those who have a leading role in spiritual, political and economic matters — whether these functions are combined in one chief or in a highly integrated structure is immaterial —, while at the bottom of the pyramid we find those who do the basic labor in all three fields but with a vast preponderance of economic activity, which always is and has been the root of all human activity. In other words, people need food, shelter and clothes as a *conditio sine qua non* of survival.

Then we find at all times an intermediary group which carries out special services, does supervisory work on a simpler level and forms in general the connection between the masses of the people and those at the top. The social pyramid may change in shape and size and in innumerable other ways but its form is an essential attribute of human society. [55] The form in which the members of a given society consider themselves does not alter this fact.

If, in a given social group, all members regard themselves as equal, they can only mean one of two things. They can mean that, at the moment that the social group was formed, they regarded one another as equal and were eager to keep differentiation at the minimum necessary to carry out the task of the social group.

Or, if the social group is already in existence, a definite statement of the desirability of equality means that the members of the group are eager to lessen their integration in order to join other social groups or in order to carry out certain functions which the social group does not embody. In the latter case people who stress a desire for greater independence or freedom generally are anxious to follow a new pattern of life, a pattern for which they have certain organizational forms in mind or a pattern which gradually creates itself the patterns it needs for its existence. Thus we can observe an utterly confusing picture of the growth of human society as long as we are members of it ourselves. It presents itself as a continuous struggle between social groups — large and small —, a totally irregular pattern of growth in which the social sciences have looked in vain for a certain regularity. There is no regularity in the growth of human society any more than there is in other processes, and we always have to tell ourselves again that we create patterns in the exact as well as social sciences only as a means to cope with reality, which in its entirety is too vast, too unpredictable, too tremendous to be grasped by our mind. Our mind changes and reality changes, and the constant interrelation between these two variable factors creates the dazzling array of philosophies, sciences, political and economic systems, arts, etc.

It has become the trouble with our contemporary society that its complicated social groups tend to create their own patterns of all aspects of life, with the exception perhaps of the exact sciences, which are considered valid by a large percentage of mankind. But it should not be overlooked that there are vast groups which, for instance, for religious reasons, accept the findings of science only in a half-hearted way or not at all. Finally the claim of the exact sciences is only that they aid to produce something useful, and even the concept of usefulness is a highly variable one. In view of the overpowering multiformity of modern life — or really of life for quite a number of centuries —, we claim the merit of usefulness also for the effort of simplifying matters. Yet this interpretation of usefulness also will find its opponents and its scornful critics, who love the complexity of things, since complexity has become the warp and woof of their lives.

However, let us return to our simple view that human society of necessity takes the form of a pyramid caused by the division of functions which are the reason for its existence. No revolution ever changes the fundamental form of human society: it changes only the leading group and replaces it by another one which mostly feels the need of presenting a new pattern in order to please its followers. But how many of these patterns are really new is a subject on which a number of disconcerting remarks could be made.

Fundamentally, since the days of Adam and Eve, people eat, drink, and sleep and — in order to do so they have to cope with their surroundings as well as with one another. They also have to procreate, or at least they have been inclined to do so, and it must be assumed that the inclination will continue for a considerable time to come.

This perhaps unbearable oversimplification of life is not so uninteresting if we direct our mind to the amazing world which has built itself upon this simple fundamental pattern to which even the most complex society can be somehow reduced. There is nothing alarming in this but it can only make us revere more the utterly amazing processes of Nature.

The desire to exist and to continue to exist is the basis of our life. Whether the intensity of this desire is subject to change is a matter we have somewhat touched upon in preceding chapters, trying to present a pattern which would correspond to a certain extent to the processes of anthropological growth which we may attempt to distill from the forms, patterns, etc. of our social structures.

The shift in focus from the metaphysical to the temporal world, the greater mastery over Nature, have been considered as stadia in a process of growth, a process in which progress assumes a different meaning from what it generally has. Most of our thinking has been self-centered and full of self-love, and we are not too eager to view ourselves as a part of a tremendous natural process which might mean that the clock ticks away the history not only of the individual but of mankind as a whole.

The tension of the mind has been the subject of some of our reflections, and we have tried to indicate that the decrease of this tension may mean progress, since it enables us to cope better with reality, but it may also mean a decrease of the sum-total of our vital energy. Thus we have attempted to create a sequence of three stages of development of the human mind as stadia in a process of growth. This pattern, as imperfect as all other patterns or possibly even more so, covers only the period which has been visible to a certain extent to the author, leaving out the numerous aspects of which he did not become aware and the subconscious and superconscious processes which are beyond the realm of our cognition.

The three stages, the first one of fear and terrific tension, the second one of a full-fledged attack for the mastery of life, the third one — which is in its beginning — the effort to stabilize life for a long period to come, although the word "stabilize" should not convey more than the idea of a slower rate of growth. Within this pattern, the aspects of our social problems change in focus as well as in intensity.

The first period, the ascetic or metaphysical one, looked for community life more on a spiritual than on an economic level. Its economic structure stayed simple until the late Middle Ages, when convents as well as the thriving Italian and Flemish cities developed a quite highly integrated economy. The hedonistic period, on the other hand, needed a strongly developed community in the modern sense of the word. From the town of the late Middle Ages it strove toward the creation of large national states with centralized governments with no further authority above them, although the Roman Catholic Church as a potential world-state as well as the idea of a universal law recurred at all times.

In its social thinking the New Era was as wavering as it was in its philosophy or in its faith in the ultimate validity of the findings of the social sciences. In actual social conditions the entire period is characterized by the increase in influence of the middle classes, which were the true carriers of the hedonistic approach toward life. They were in an eternal struggle with the nobility as well as the third estate, who both viewed their ascendancy with spite and envy. The middle classes, however, found frequent support in the monarchs, who were badly in need of a group to keep in check the nobility, which was forever eager to swallow the king if it was in a position to do so.

Therefore, if we want to view the process in terms of a pyramid, we arrive in the first place at a tremendous increase in the volume of the pyramid, since the population increase from the end of the Middle Ages until about 1900 was staggering. Relatively the largest increase was in the middle classes, thus making the pyramid of a different structure, namely lower and wider. It will be interesting to observe later on whether this trend continued in our present day. On the other hand, the greater spiritual unity had been lost since the days of Renaissance and Reformation, and the gradual creation of a national outlook weakened the general ethical basis which the Middle Ages had striven to create.

Psychologically this means that the pattern of the New Era was narrower and more immediate in its aims, although it had at all times to seek new inspiration from universal ideas, since a narrowing of our patterns always leads to a quest for general ideas.

Thus we can observe a trend like that of Rousseau's philosophy, advocating a return to a simple, unspoiled life, as well as a great variety of religious groups, of which many propagated direct communication between the individual and God. Religion in the New Era was less institutionalized than in the Middle Ages and less dogmatic, but it was of considerable influence as a social force. The approval of economic pursuits by Puritanism as a way of serving God is one of the strangest paradoxes of history. It proves the overwhelming force of the desire toward economic activity which had to be approved on religious grounds by an artificial detour.

This same trend is evident in the great stress which the New Era placed upon charity: it was all right for religious reasons to assist those who lived in poverty, but poverty was regarded fundamentally as self-inflicted and not as the result of poor economic organization. The middle classes attempted to follow the standard of living of the nobility, but the misery of the laboring class was regarded as no concern of theirs and as a phenomenon which would correct itself by the working of natural economic laws.

It is not surprising that the middle classes were mostly interested in stability of government as well as in as little interference with their economic pursuits as possible. This made the monarchy the preferred form of government, since it had all the elements the middle classes needed for their development. However, there was considerable difference between the various Western European countries in the ways in which this development took place. In most countries the king did not supersede all existing authorities, in spite of the concept of "plenitudo potestatis", but rather absorbed those functions which were necessary. Royal commissioners formed the basis of a centralized administration which had to overcome local vested interests. In order to increase the revenue of the Crown, the monarchy, notably in France and Russia, led to considerable stimulation of industry and commerce. Gradually the unwieldy local statutes and privileges diminished in importance to give way to the centralized administration of the modern state.

The king as a centralizing force was strongly in the favor of the middle classes, while the function of the court as an intellectual center did much to stimulate inventions and discoveries as well as new economic and political ideas.

The France of Colbert and Richelieu, of Voltaire and the Encyclopaedists, offers one of the best examples of this constructive function of the monarchy, although its too strong absolutistic tendencies led ultimately to its downfall.

In England a strongly centralized rule was less necessary because of the relatively isolated position of the country. After the revolution of 1688, which did away with the rule of the Stuarts, the foundation was laid for an early development of constitutional monarchy.

In Sweden the great power of the peasantry led to an early establishment of a parliamentary government. An interesting development took place in the Netherlands, where the early growth of a larger administrative unit, viz. the province, created an astonishing rise to power of a relatively small territory. The commercial and seafaring talents of the Dutch were set free when the feudal system was broken, but when the larger national states began to develop, its more decentralized form of government was no longer able to overcome this more efficient competition, and the country lost its position quickly to the surrounding national states. The trend towards a more centralized rule in the Netherlands was evident in the continued change from a stadholder who exercised centralized rule to the stadholderless periods when the jealous cities resented the concentration of too much power in one hand.

In Prussia the creation of a class of devoted civil servants, recruited from the rising middle classes, did much for the formation of a fairly flexible government which paved the way for Prussia's rise to power. In those days the influence of the nobility should not be overrated, since the Prussian kings frequently kept them in the seclusion of their estates in order to carry through the reforms which the bourgeoisie demanded.

The growth of bourgeois civilization received its first serious threat from the clamor of the lower classes for improved economic conditions as well as for participation in government. In theory the way for this was paved by the natural law theories which postulated certain absolute laws, having validity beyond the existence of written laws and regulations.

The theory of natural law had developed in Antiquity, either as a God-given law which established an hierarchical society or as the natural law of the individual which granted him certain rights which could not be alienated. Both types recur in the New Era: the natural law of the Church and of a number of philosophers conceives a pre-established order which should be recognized in order to follow the commands of God, while Rationalism and Enlightenment proclaimed the natural law of the individual, who does not have to enter into more obligations and, consequently, acquire more rights, than he chooses to when he enters society.

The natural law theories, however, show a considerable amount of dualism, since they were used to defend a more collectivistic form of society as well as to propagate an increase in individual liberties. Natural law should be seen as a reaction against positive, existing law, and what form it takes depends largely upon the system it seeks to combat. If it advocates a collectivistic society, it does so either by appealing to divine commands as made known by revelation or by postulating general moral and legal principles which embody a certain type of society deemed desirable. These principles are generally called "natural" on the assumption that they form part of the general system of Nature which the New Era liked to think of as governed by laws.

The individualistic theory of law which claimed a number of un-alienable rights of the individual as "natural rights" was largely an outcome of the struggle of the middle classes for a secure political and legal position. Here again the word "natural" was merely used because it had a sort of magic appeal in the 17th and 18th century, and nobody was greatly perturbed by the fact that these "natural rights" assumed the form of legal rights only in the case of the upper and middle classes while they remained moral principles for the third estate.

It is equally impossible to look for consistency in the theories on the most desirable form of government: the absolute monarchy was defended as strongly as it was attacked, and it was not until the eight-teenth century that there was a certain consensus of opinion that the constitutional monarchy was the most desirable form of government. This can be explained easily: in the more turbulent days of the six-teenth and seventeenth centuries there was a strong need for a central ruler, while the more settled eighteenth century made the middle classes eager to define a number of their rights as essential and inviolable by the monarch. Locke and Rousseau were the most able defenders of the rights which constituted the basis of the social contract and could not be assailed by an absolute ruler. Although the belief in the divinity of kings decreased considerably as the New Era progressed, the hereditary constitutional monarchy continued to be the most favored form of government as its stability protected the middle classes against the third estate as well as against a return to the feudal system.

The "natural condition" which was postulated as the original source of the rights of the individual was alternately seen as a vicious war of all against all, as by Hobbes, or as an Arcadian state of bliss and delight. Both concepts were hardly based upon exhaustive research but were simply presupposed in order to make the tenets of the author in question more acceptable. If the original state was seen as one of death and destruction, the individual was by necessity obliged to form a society as a matter of self-preservation. In the opposite case, when the original conditions were viewed as fairly desirable, it was more a matter of choice for the individual and left him the possibility to retain a number of rights which did not become a part of his social contract. Thus the concept of the social contract became a convenient fiction which could be made as extensive or limited as conditions warranted.

In every respect the New Era shows the eagerness of a youthful mind which rushes with enthusiasm from idea to idea, without too much bother about consistency and also without much awareness of the real reasons which made one idea important at a given time and another at a later moment.

The writers and philosophers of that period were charming and witty gentlemen of great learning but also of so much vitality that they most ably defended the interests of the groups with which they identified themselves. Frequently their desire to be consistent made them construct buildings which had to be patched up in the end as they had to fit their particular ideas into a general worldscheme, since the New Era was not capable of being satisfied with the limited approach that satisfies us today. If they solved one problem they wanted to solve all problems, so that they generally had to reintroduce the metaphysical elements which they initially tried to avoid. If it is our aim to present a general philosophical scheme for the world, logic demands that the entire structure be based ultimately upon one principle, as even two principles always require a third and higher one which dominates their interaction. Even efforts like those of Spinoza or Leibnitz, which operate with the concept of parallelism, have to give precedence to one principle in order to make the parallelism possible.

If, therefore, we admit that every philosophical system ultimately needs one basic principle, our choice is limited to a materialistic or a spiritual principle, and this is really nothing more than a play upon words. The New Era was fundamentally dualistic: it was dominated by the struggle between materia and spirit which it tried unsuccessfully to overcome. If we admit two forces which are opposed to one another, we have to give the one force precedence over the other and abolish thereby the conflict, or we have to establish a third one which regulates the interaction of the two. It always remains the difficulty of the theological assumption of evil that it must have been created for a certain purpose or otherwise God would not be omnipotent.

The New Era tried to overcome these metaphysical arguments but was not able to do so; it was not as strongly opposed to the physical world as the Middle Ages, but it was equally unprepared to accept the world as such, especially since the world proved to be a highly uncertain matter.

If the desire for consistency leaves no other solution for philosophy than the choice between a material and a spiritual principle, we do not progress one step. If philosophy becomes monistic, it makes no difference whether we consider substance or spirit the ultimate principle. Substance is in that case a form of energy, indicated by such vague words as "Nature", etc., while spirit also ultimately signifies a principle of action.

Therefore, we must understand the New Era as a period of hesitation, a period which was incapable of stabilization because its mind still wavered violently between extremes, but extremes within the realm of the intellect more than that of the spirit. There have been few periods in history when the human intellect showed such magnificent development as in the New Era, a development which definitely far surpasses that of today, although our judgment and sense of balance may be more developed at present.

There is no period, however, which requires more of a sociological interpretation of its ideas. The entire struggle between materialistic and spiritual principles is to a considerable extent a struggle between classes: the Church was by nature destined to maintain a spiritual approach, less unified in its Protestant variations than in Roman Catholicism and less frozen in a caste system, but it nevertheless maintained an attitude which made a full and final acceptance of the world impossible. This probably gives religion its eternal value, because a full and final acceptance of the world is not possible, and it is not imaginable that the idea of a future world will ever disappear from the human mind, even if it is viewed only as a principle to make life possible and bearable. The struggle against religion of the New Era was a struggle against dogmatic religion which stifled a further development of the human mind as well as a struggle against an excessive hierarchy, but it can only be stressed again that society "qua talis" will always show an hierarchical structure.

The conflict between religion and rationalism, between an ordered bourgeois society and romanticism, between economic progress and feudalism, between the exact sciences and superstition, is indicative of a growth of the intellect and a decrease in the spiritual approach to life. The human mind, so to speak, was in the process of acquiring a certain bone structure, but it was a process full of growing pains that cannot be brought back consistently to a few principles. The conquest of the world by Western Europe meant that the European mind was more active, more alive than that of other parts, but it also placed upon it the grave responsibility of justifying its power. This justification lay in its material progress and in nothing else: it is the development of the intellect not of the spirit which gave people power. The spirit as the deeper and more fundamental source of human energy uses up this very energy by the process of rationalization so that we must see our social and historical processes as an interplay of forces for which no final explanation can be given, since the existence of more or less force here or there or now or then is a matter which is not subject to explanation. We can only learn to control the use of existing energy but not its existence or non-existence. Therefore, by analyzing historical processes we may learn to use our energy wisely but we cannot add or subtract from its total amount. However, as the human being exists in a tremendous network of relations with Nature and with his fellow men, there is an enormous interplay of forces of which we know but very little.

The controlled part of Nature is controlled by the use of human energy and thus is possible by division and development of human energy. The amount and extent of this control expresses a stage in our development which we can analyze but not change.

The great variety of the New Era, compared with our modern civilization, shows that it was not a period of set patterns. Many approaches were created, and there was not the preponderance of economic factors which we see today. The conflict between employers and labor saw its beginning in the New Era, but, since labor was as yet unorganized, an amelioration of conditions was possible only through the influence of the churches or through the humanitarian thinking of some employers.

The cleavage between wealth and poverty was an ethical problem rather than an economic one, although classical economic thinking tended to the belief that division of labor and increased production would ultimately benefit the entire population. The mechanistic interpretation of labor, however, as a factor of cost to be bought against the lowest possible price, left little room for actual improvement. In fact, the hedonistic mind which was fundamentally individualistic did not show any great interest in the economic well-being of the lower classes until it was forced to do so by the growth of an effective labor-movement and by socialism when it reached its "scientific" stage. Why Marxism was termed "scientific socialism" is in itself an interesting psychological phenomenon.

The earlier systems of socialism, reaching back to the ideas of Antiquity, had been vague schemes of world improvement inspired by general ideas of brotherhood and organized economic living. Marxism, in its aims, was not so fundamentally different from the earlier schools of socialism, but it presented its scheme in the form of a prognosis based upon the recognition of natural laws and therefore as an unavoidable step in human history.

Using Hegel's dialectic method, it operated with a growth in stages in which each following one resulted by logical necessity from the preceding ones. Marx reversed Hegel's idealistic philosophy into a materialistic one, since he considered the "idealism" of the bourgeoisie as a subterfuge to escape the necessity of improving the conditions of the lower classes.

Again the dualism of the New Era and of hedonistic thinking was the main cause of Marxian thinking. If we separate it entirely from its social implications, it does not add much to philosophical thinking.

We already had reason to observe that the idea of substance as the basis of a philosophic system is meaningless, if we omit the relation to the author and his aims in society. Even transferred to the social realm, we can make the same remark: the famous question whether people's religion determines their economic system or their economic system their religion is utterly meaningless. If we separate religion from its carriers, it is entirely a psychological problem of what weight religious ideas carry in the mind of a given individual at a given time.

The belief in a future life functions as a psychological mechanism which carries us through periods of stress. If an individual on an isolated island were to live under favorable conditions, the metaphysical part of his mind might never become activated.

If, on the other hand, we separate our economic activities from the structure of our society, there would not be the elements of oppression which in a society may give food to metaphysical beliefs. In other words: pressure on a human being creates the use of certain centers of the human mind which otherwise may remain dormant. Whether this pressure is in its origin spiritual or economic makes a difference only in regard to the susceptibility of the individual. Bad economic conditions whether inflicted by natural factors or by human mismanagement cause a mental reaction which can be metaphysical if guided that way or if mankind finds itself in a stage which is inclined toward this type of reaction. On the other hand, if mankind is in a stage which is dominated by fear of the supernatural, it will be less successful in its economic pursuits, or, if in another stage, it is dominated by social institutions which are metaphysical in slant, it may not give so much attention to purely economic solutions as it would if these institutions were not present. Marxism, although noble in its motives, presented an oversimplification, since it never separated the ideas from their carriers and was consequently neither successful as a sociological nor as a philosophical system. Its real meaning was that the hedonistic outlook on life had also reached the lower classes, although Marxism, while claiming the economic benefits of the other classes for labor, was at the same time a negation of the system which had created the higher standard of living. The freedom which had enabled the middle classes to develop our modern economic system, had not benefitted the lower classes, and they demanded control instead of freedom. The economic freedom of the New Era had created a system under which profit had become more important than the fulfillment of needs, although this same system managed its own salvation by resorting to mass production in order to obtain larger profits. Mass production demanded mass consumption, and this promoted the worker automatically to the rank of a consumer for which he had been striving so hard. Thus, once more, Nature itself created the pattern which the times demanded, though this was achieved in some instances by evolutionary and in others by revolutionary methods.

This change was brought about partly by the activities of the working classes themselves, partly by a retrenchment of capitalism which, after the second half of the nineteenth century, had to cope with unexpected difficulties which it proved utterly unable to overcome. It is again one of history's paradoxes that the hedonistic attitude, the philosophy of plenty, finally had to cope with unemployment and poverty as its gravest threat.

The economists of the period had no solution to offer, although the number of treatises written on the subject was staggering. In reality the cause which created unemployment was the hedonistic mentality itself, which was not capable of a more structural form of thinking. Its quantitative business approach, which was based entirely upon the concept of profit, did not realize that the unlimited encouragement of mass production disturbs the relationship between various categories of goods on the market. Mass production of product A will give this product a relatively lower price while the prices of goods which cannot so easily be produced on a vast scale will remain relatively high. This means, roughly speaking, that in an industrial economy prices of farm products will be high in relation to industrial products from the viewpoint of the consumer. As there is always a tendency to purchase lower priced products insofar as substitution is possible, this will give a certain twisted structure to the demand of the consumer. On the other hand, the prices will be low in terms of the producer who has to compete with the industrial market so far as labor cost, materials, equipment, etc., is concerned. Therefore, since his margin of profit is small compared with the industrial producer, he is forever clamoring for higher prices although the prices are already high for the marginal consumer, viz. the unemployed in periods of depression.

It is obvious that the problem of unemployment is more a consumption than a production problem. If the working class is considered in its entirety, its share in the national product would remain the same under stabilized conditions. If the national product increases, labor will, sooner or later, receive a larger share; if it decreases it will ultimately receive less.

Under a hedonistic society production becomes irregular and erratic because the individual is in a position at all times to produce new goods which upset the equilibrium and which aggravate the trend towards unbalanced production.

The temporary profits, derived from a successful new venture, stimulates other ventures until finally the realization sets in that the increased income of a part of the population hardly buys them more goods or at least not those goods which are most essential for human happiness.

This realization leads to a loss of confidence, which, in turn, leads to a so-called depression. It should not be overlooked that hedonistic society in regard to the individual consumer assumes that more and more needs will develop which will demand more and more goods in order to satisfy them. This idea would have found little support if the trouble had been taken to analyze the needs of people who are really at liberty to develop and satisfy needs as they please. If we omit those things which are purchased for social reasons, we would find that the needs of the upper classes in most countries are relatively simple. In order to maintain themselves they generally discover that a relatively simple life keeps them in better condition and more able to withstand the attacks of those on the lower rungs of the social ladder.

It is more the tortured middle class which exemplifies the ideal of hedonistic society. These people live in houses larger than they need, buy dozens of things they have no use for, stagger to vacations which give them no rest, and are, in short, the slaves of the needs which they were told to develop. And they did develop them because their instincts whispered to them that they themselves were a cog in the machine. Ultimately this process makes their lives a form of refined, prolonged and self-inflicted torture, driven by the fear of poverty, of disease, of ignorance while they lack the wisdom which the simple people as well as the upper classes possess of striving for balance and independence.

It was this distorted dream of wealth which finally meant the decay of hedonism. By the time the fuller life, that centuries had dreamt of, was reached, it proved to be far from the state of perfection which the Western World had hoped for, and this realization was accompanied by the sneers of the rest of the world, which had admired the achievements of the West but had also seen the unhealthy elements it contained.

The end of the nineteenth century does not offer a pretty picture to behold. Excessive greed and lust for power of a society which had eagerly taken up all the attributes of a caste-system in order to protect the owning classes against the lower ones, the class struggle which was fought with viciousness and bitterness, and all this sordid glory covered by nationalism and patriotism which repeated the same vices on an international level. It was a far cry from the days of the Puritans who conquered the world for the glory of God.

Late hedonistic society was the world of the luxury hotel and the slums, of the fashionable watering places where people cured their often self-inflicted diseases and of drab rows of depressing houses, of the psychological problems which the disregard for health and balance had created, and of an overwhelming sensation of fear which accompanied people from the cradle to the grave. These fears they overcame by a senseless artificial heroism and a rather ridiculous sense of honor which was a device to protect themselves against other people by a code which only a leisured class could follow with success.

It was the period which created the realistic novel, the labor movement, sports, the desire for social measures, internationalism and a thousand other trends which indicated that the time for a fundamental change had come.

It is an amazing thing that the human mind at all times reflects the ills of our society and indicates the way to cure them. The very form of hedonistic living created a mind which began to strive for a new approach. The morbidity, the domination by fear through excessive class consciousness, the inhuman greed of many people, made the human mind seek a way back to health and happiness.

Yet it would be entirely wrong to arrive at a negative judgment of the period which created most of the world as we know it today. There is no reason for any nostalgia for the Middle Ages, nor for any fear of the future which will still be based, to a large extent, upon the developments of the Western World of the New Era. Modern industry, the root of our present civilization, owes its origin to the discoveries of that period, while our modern economic system, with all its shortcomings, would never have been possible but for the expansion of Western Europe in the 16th and 17th and 18th centuries. It was in that period that the dream of a world state, although already known in Antiquity, caused the beginnings of the growth of international law which is approaching the realization of its most cherished ideas of world organization.

The two ideological systems which now dominate the world, viz. the American ideology and the ideology of the U.S.S.R. are both derived from the Europe of the New Era, and are both a denial and an affirmation of it. They both mean a denial of the European caste-system: the United States was born as an outcome of the worldwide revolution of the middle classes against the feudal system, while modern Russia is the result of a revolution against its own feudal classes as well as against the threat of domination by Western industry and capital. It owes its origin to a later reaction against the hedonistic world than the United States but in many respects it is more a difference in degree.

Socialism, in its numerous forms of social-democracy, scientific socialism, labor socialism, state socialism, even national socialism, are all an outcome of the opposition to the late hedonistic world which never developed in the United States, since there the expanding economy of a vast continent gave less room for the darker sides of the late-capitalistic period.

By a combination of factors the United States was capable of solving the most difficult problems by an evolutionary process, aided by the fact that its vast territory and increasing population gave rise to the phenomenon of mass production which had to raise great masses of the population to the rank of mass consumers. This process was not possible in Europe and it has not as yet developed in Russia, although the trend is in the same direction.

It is obvious that Russia could never have developed a modern economy unless under state control. Once a country is surrounded by economically fully developed countries, it cannot overcome the handicap of having started later unless under a strictly centralized rule which does all the planning and enforces the sacrifices which are unavoidable in such a process. Whether it is "good" or "bad" of a country to be eager to develop its economy is a question which is on the same level as asking whether it is good or bad of a child to grow up.

It may cause trouble to the parents but it just grows.

However, these arguments have led us somewhat ahead of the subject of this chapter, viz. the social thinking of the New Era. In the gigantic and infinitely subtle process of mental growth which we are attempting to sketch, the building up of patterns always indicates its own short-comings because they prove hard to maintain and because at all times the mind contains some of the aspects of other periods than the one to which it is assigned. Yet it is amazing how much the average mortal is dominated by the thinking of his period, and what long, hazardous and painful struggles are necessary before a new idea is accepted by the mind of the period.

There is no lack of new ideas at any given period of history, but many of them may never be uttered and many more may be expressed but die the same instant because they find no response. It was the charm and strength of the New Era that new ideas were numerous — and that the inclination to burn or torture people for expressing them gradually diminished until this was finally definitely frowned upon, although it was really only in the 19th century that this enlightened viewpoint became general. In the New Era Europe's caste-system had not yet become overly rigid: deserving commoners became nobles and even in one or two cases kings, and if an enterprising young man had no outlet for his ambitions at home, there were the vast territories in other countries where knowledge, shrewdness, hardiness and perseverance were likely to fetch a high price. Continuous wars and numerous diseases made the average life-span short compared with that of today, but life was full of color and adventure. The farmer lived through wars and pillaging, the artisan was far more migratory than our modern worker, the merchant held on to most of his profits, art and science were in great esteem, and the nobility lent charm, manners and military and administrative talent to a diversified world which was intellectually very much alive and able to marvel at inventions and discoveries by the hundreds. So long as wealth was not desired too much for wealth's sake but more for the power and splendor there was nothing much wrong with it.

People of wealth sponsored the arts, took delight in beautiful mansions and castles, and paid much attention to grace of manner and appearance. Too excessive lust for power was checked by Christian conscience, which remained quite alive through the 17th and 18th centuries and only became rather dormant in the 19th century when the social system began to show much more rigidity.

The excessive concept of honor may seem artificial to a modern world, but it was a natural consequence of the morals of the period, which placed a rather strong accent on birth and which had a watertight system of morals which might be violated a great deal in practice but little in theory. Women were trained to swoon at the proper moment and men to be at all times strong, masculine, protective and noble. It was the dream of the period, and how far reality conformed to it was a problem which was largely relegated to the subconscious and only began to bother the human mind in the stage of decay of the hedonistic approach to life. Then it became the favored topic of literature and psychology, which through their awareness of these problems paved the way to a new attitude.

Fundamentally the New Era had an optimistic spirit which believed in knowledge, political equality and economic progress, and which saw life as a process of continued improvement. It created the theory of evolution, which sees Nature as a process of growth but did not ask the question when and how this growth will come to an end. The world of the Middle Ages was stationary, the world of the New Era dynamic, while the following period should show a measured and controlled progress.

There were occasional reactions of pessimism in the New Era when the belief in progress faded. The pessimism expressed itself in the finding of natural laws like the iron wage law, which limited or denied the concept of progress and created the picture of a world which could not show any fundamental improvement. Generally, however, the finding of such laws already implied the possibility of a possible exception to their limited validity. The iron wage law, for instance, was not maintained long by economic theory although it was picked up again by Marxism for political reasons.

Thus, we get the picture of the hedonistic period as the one in which mankind tried to conquer the world, an undertaking in which it finally failed when it reached the limits of knowledge as well as of economic progress. The entire struggle of modern philosophy was the attempt to show that perfect knowledge is possible, a struggle which increased and widened our knowledge but which also made it clear that we ultimately deal with the relationships between two factors, both of which are only partly known and will probably remain partly known forever.

In the economic field greater wealth was finally achieved for more people than ever before, but it was wealth in which but little variety could be made by the individual, while still a large percentage of all nations struggled hard to keep body and soul together. The realization that the millenium had not been reached led to a period of skepticism and despair, and the desire to achieve wealth at the cost of others — a time-honored shortcut — finally led to two most disastrous world wars from which a wiser, wider and more balanced world is gradually emerging.

The two major lessons which the hedonistic period taught us are that neither complete knowledge nor unlimited wealth are possible, at least not with due regards for the rights of others. It also taught us that life is less elastic, less flexible than the world had assumed and that we have to learn to accept certain fundamental truths from which there is no escape. Character is a quality which the next period will need almost more than knowledge.

If it was enterprise and individual energy which made the hedonistic period great, it was lack of restraint and egotism which caused its downfall. It takes courage and daring to build empires, but it takes wisdom and tolerance to maintain them.

It is wisdom instead of knowledge which the modern age requires, and tolerance instead of egotism which has taken the place of justified progress. There was much of greatness in the hedonistic period, but all its greatness should not prevent us from realizing that it has definitely come to an end.

## CHAPTER XIII

## THE REACTIONS TO THE HEDONISTIC PERIOD [56]

Since for the sake of clarity, generalizations and simplifications are at times permissible, it seems justified to stress that Western civilization in the period 1500—1900 focussed its energy upon the development of the intellect rather than upon that of the other attributes of Man. Inherent in this tendency was the magnification of the intellect into an instrument of tremendous importance, seen as capable of gaining complete mastery over life. Knowledge was considered to be the function of the intellect, and it was tacitly or not so tacitly assumed that the extension of knowledge was synonymous with extension of happiness.

The drive for expansion of needs was at the root of this belief: expansion in terms of conquest and explorations, expansion in terms of inventions, expansion in terms of commercial and industrial innovation. The heroes of the period were the conqueror, the explorer, the inventor, the merchant, the entrepreneur, and also the artist, to whom the role fell to preserve the elasticity of mind and imagination while, at the same time, presenting an image of reality that brought it closer to the average person than the earlier symbolic presentations. The symbolic function had not been lost, but it had decreased in significance as well as changed in contents: it also had gained a relation to the natural instead of to the supernatural world. This change in function meant that art was becoming more independent as the creator of symbols and was able to attempt to formulate its own goals in terms of a more or less "direct" reflection of reality, freed from the weight of an already formulated symbolic system.

In this fashion it was able to exercise a much more dynamic function and to shift from extreme naturalism to extreme symbolism, whenever the dominant culture pattern threatened to freeze either one of these or any of the intermediary patterns into anything resembling permanence. On the other hand, art had to place itself in marked contrast to religion, which continued to give definite contents to the symbolic system as a rational interpretation of its own function.

In this way, the social significance of art gained while that of religion diminished, perhaps partly because art possessed this much greater freedom in relation to its contents and was able to react to the emotional frictions which resulted from rational patterns, superimposed upon a fundamentally irrational world.

The continuation of the symbolic function in a rational period was indicative of three basic factors. In the first place, the necessity of the symbolic function as the long-term attitude even in a period in which the present was gaining fast over the past and the future; in the second place, the emotional frustration caused by rational behavior-control set off a symbolic reaction; in the third place, the symbolic reaction remained the realm of last principles in regard to the direction in which science moved, again functioning as the mirror of the underlying drive-structure, but in this case having no direct bearing upon frustration but upon a normal emotional constellation.

The first factor remained largely within the field of formalized religion; the second in that of the individual and emotional religions as well as of art, especially in the form of the novel; the third as the realm of philosophy and frequently of poetry and music.

The three factors also contain the weakness of the rational reaction: underestimation of the insecurity of the long-term aspects of life; neglect of the necessity for a sufficiently direct outlet of emotions and drives, the attempt to rationalize the realm of last principles, which as such belongs to the symbolic function and cannot be subject to any satisfactory rational analysis. This latter attempt tends to undermine the symbolic reaction by doubting the validity of its principles, so that a reaction sets in whereby the findings of the intellect are considered insignificant compared to the firmness of beliefs. Beliefs are supposed to be like "rocks", while nobody has as yet claimed that this would be a desirable attribute of knowledge.

Consequently, the reaction against the dominance of the intellectual function takes place in three forms: a desire to reestablish beliefs, a desire to give more room to emotional life, and a stress on intellectual limitation to those topics that are approved of by the symbolic system.

Again we can observe how Nature brings about a certain readjustment: control-knowledge led to the expansion of needs, but this expansion ultimately causes decadence because the needs which were extended were physical and intellectual ones; thus the balance between the three basic reaction forms began to be threatened. This brought about a decrease of the interest in intellectual growth until a new equilibrium is reached.

A complicating factor is added if we take into account that the basic reactions differ in the various social classes.

The rational attitude was largely the creation of the middle class, which had the lead in inventions, technological innovations, development of the sciences, etc. It could expand only via the economic system so that there was constant interaction between invention and practical application. The development of rational philosophy, on the other hand, was more the achievement of the upper middle and lower upper classes, which were less prompted by economic necessity but which had to establish a connecting link with the metaphysical pattern of the preceding periods, as the expression of the drive for social continuity.

Since the middle class was hindered in its desire for expansion by the remnants of feudal controls, it had to strive for greater freedom; thus the idea of rationalism is invariably connected with that of greater liberty — largely seen as the extension of political rights as a means of combatting the influence of the aristocracy. There is no necessary or logical connection, however, between rationalism and political freedom, and this can be explained only in relation to the specific stage of Western civilization.

It should be pointed out, on the other hand, that, if the possession of "reason" as the capacity for logical thinking and the working out of cause-and-effect relationships is considered to be a general human attribute, then the conclusion results that all those, possessing this quality, should have also equal political rights. This interpretation of reality has been frequent but not quite so frequent that it has to be identified with the concept of rationalism.

Most rational philosophers and social thinkers, like, for instance, Condorcet and Turgot, were cautious enough to see the "rational stage" as a future one, since they certainly could not observe it in the society of their own days.

The idea of the rationality of life was the main tenet of the symbolic system of the New Era, and as such it colored actual observations completely which were made to fit into this preconceived notion.

The justification of this attitude was deemed to be furnished by the exact sciences, which dealt with processes that showed a much higher rate of regularity than those of social life, of which the observer himself was automatically a part. Thus the rational attitude found its confirmation and support in its apparent success in the exact sciences, and it was not until much later that it was realized that, also in regard to those fields, human intellect is not an impartial and objective instrument.

Since the rational attitude came to its strongest fruition in the middle classes, it is not astonishing that a more skeptical reaction as to its merits should develop in the other classes, and the more successful and complete hedonism became, the sharper were the reactions. These reactions had to deny the basic concepts of rationalism or to assert that the leaders of society were incapable of being sufficiently rational. Both these responses occurred, and it is not at all amazing that the latter was the first to come, since it implies that the belief in the ultimate victory of rationalism still persisted and that its partial failure was attributed to the "wickedness" of Man, who continued to ignore the dictates of "reason", sometimes written with a capital R.

This attitude could easily come to the conclusion that the trend toward rationalization had come to an illogical termination with the national societies, since — according to theory at least, although here the cleavage with actual conditions was extremely sharp — there was no reason to assert that "reason" could exist only within the borders of the national states of Western civilization. Those critics overlooked, however, that the concept of rationalism was a part of the symbolic system of the middle class of the Western world, which owed its rise to prosperity, to its growth within national states and their protection; it only belatedly realized this itself. But the middle class, having sired the entire process, was soon to become its oppressor when the third estate grew restive about the continued absence of the promised paradise.

Yet it did not abandon the dream of rationalism, nor its contents, namely the paradise of need-fulfillment of the individual, but it began to be extremely critical of the way in which the wheels of rationalism creaked and moaned under the hands of merchants and industrialists.

Another class which cast an eye of semi-disapproval upon this rationalist middle class paradise was the aristocracy, which had no appreciation for the extension of middle class needs and could have no sympathy for the liberal theories of the state which wanted to restrict government to the function of a policeman who was supposed to become superfluous when the millennium of need-fulfillment was at hand. Success makes human thinking shallow, and one can only marvel at the superficiality and disregard for reality that was expressed in many of the theories of progress, prosperity and patriotism, the hallowed triad of the New Era.

There is no reason to doubt the desirability of progress, but it is not a tree that grows into the sky, and such a vision is only an indication of a dynamic social stage with strong symbolic presentations.

The strongest reaction evidently had to come from those groups which witnessed and contributed to the rise of the middle class but were thwarted in their own desires for a share in the increasing total national incomes. It has been pointed out that this disillusion was not so much caused by the malice of the capitalist and managerial group but more by the mechanistic and quantitative thinking of the period, which overlooked the structure of needs and assumed that the increase in industrial production would automatically increase prosperity. The basic error was that prices rose more sharply than production, so that those products whose production had not been increased to any comparable extent rose in price, and to those categories belonged the basic necessities of life, namely food and housing.

The belief that profit stimulates production, and that increased production means increased prosperity for all, was a dangerous half-truth; and it is entirely natural that this idea was rejected by those groups whose very lives proved its inadequacy, namely the laboring classes. Of course, the element of a power struggle entered also into the picture, but the ultimate fallacy lay in a lack of structural thinking, since the faint protests of religious and agricultural groups were ignored, at least until the beginning of this century.

The thinking of the working classes shows an exact parallel to the emergence of the middle class attitude, only it came a century and a half later, so that it had to embody the events of the intervening period in its symbolic and rationalist reactions. It started out with a general symbolic reaction, with the image of a future world of freedom and prosperity, with the absence of all restraint and coercion. This utopian socialism occurred in many different forms and led to the establishment of a number of socialist and communist communities which all failed after shorter or longer periods, mostly because any social group in order to function has to develop the same basic functional structure; the expected classless societies did not emerge in reality or the groups fell back to primitive forms of living, which hardly succeeded in achieving satisfactory need-fulfillment.

The gleeful observations of critics that Man cannot work without the profit-motive were much less to the point, since many societies have operated without that mechanism; it was rather the persistence of structure and the resulting functional divisions which led to disillusionment. It should be observed, however, that economic progress and need-expansion have to go hand in hand; it is entirely logical to establish a reward for greater achievement in terms of the possibility of need-expansion. If achievement is sought for in artistic, intellectual or scientific endeavors, it has a much less direct connection with a visualization of reward in the form of an increase in the standard of living. But it would be hardly rational to expect someone to produce more economic goods without expecting a proper share. This might be done under strong symbolic pressure, but it can never last long, since materialistic goals lead to materialistic attitudes, and the two will be of necessity combined in the consciousness of the individual who is a producer as well as a consumer. The consumptive aspects can at best be postponed with the promise of later larger rewards, as is done, for instance, in communist societies which use the concept of outside pressure as a motive for keeping consumption low in relation to production. But also under those systems it is necessary to give in to some extent to the pressure of the producer for a reasonable share in the products of his work. It is one of the ironies of history that the concept of a surplus, taken away by an "unproductive" class, recurs also in a communist or socialist economy, proving that this friction results from the inter-relationship of functional classes which exist in all societies. There is no rational way of determining what the share of each group is in the total product, and a result can be reached only by bargaining and compromise in terms of a need-structure which is partially historically and socially determined. Apart from basic wants, people do not know why they have certain needs; they are part of the cultural heritage as well as of the social status system. The individual who determines his needs purely upon the basis of individual desires is a very rare one and needs considerable courage, as well as an antagonistic frame of mind.

The stress of socialistic groups upon the sole productivity of physical labor is a typical example of the fact that our thinking is largely class-determined unless this is counteracted by extensive educational and cultural programs. The thinking of the lower classes tends of necessity toward an interpretation of life in terms of the short-term, natural reaction, combined with rather strong symbolic presentations. This leads to an underestimation of the other social functions, so that an attitude results which places the main stress upon the more directly visible results of physical labor. This attitude will increase in intensity, the more it appears that the total goal of the society as a whole — for instance, increased prosperity — is reached by only a limited group and the resulting class-friction magnifies the attitude in question. On the other hand, increased technology lessens the distance between the classes, since all functions begin to require more rational control in terms of coping with complex technological equipment unless we finally reach the situation in which rational control-patterns are possessed to such an extent by skilled labor groups that they acquire a considerable hold over society and threaten to become the dominant group. This, in turn, forces the control group into the largest possible use of techno-logical means, largely in the field of communications and technological innovation, in order to ward off the danger of a possible loss of control.

The more petrified a society becomes, the larger this threat, and it is again an irony of history that this potential danger is larger in a less elastic socialist society than it is in a free one, where the rate of inno-vation tends to be higher because the tendency — which each society possesses to a varying degree — to freeze its patterns into permanency is less pronounced. For this reason, the "inefficient" organization of a free society leads ultimately to better production possibilities, since it preserves this higher rate of innovation. Once, the society as a whole becomes less dynamic, the rate of innovation falls off, and this will lead toward stabilization, even if the society continues to pay lipservice to symbolic institutions of a more active past. On the other hand, it should not be overlooked that in the early stage of the dynamic period of a society strong central control is needed in order to ward off a relapse into a static attitude. Consequently, it is essential in each specific case to determine as accurately as possible in what stage a society finds itself, and some possibility of measurement is given by the intensity of the symbolic reaction and the number of technical inventions and innovations.

Theoretically, a mature dynamic society, at present labeled by the term "Western free society", is stronger than an intensively controlled early dynamic society, but a reliable measure is not to be found in the symbolic presentations of the societies themselves but rather in the cold facts and figures in regard to the rate of change, which can be calculated most accurately in the field of technological inventions. If this rate confirms the symbolic picture, all is well; if not, it would be wiser to attempt to stimulate the elasticity of the society as much as possible.

Since the growth of each society is dependent upon an increase in technological control, it is evident that it will show a strenghtening of the status of those groups that are most essential to this process. Consequently, it is not an accident that the labor groups gained in power as a result of their organization, etc. but a phenomenon that must be attributed to the changes of the society as a whole.

Technology gained in significance, and with it rose the groups which are its carriers. They organized as a result of their gaining awareness of their significance, but their function was the "cause" of this process, insofar as one can talk about "causes" in regard to social processes.

The gaining of power of the lower classes of a society when it matures is a sociological law. The more mature a society becomes — up to the point of reversal of this process —, the more complex its technology, the greater social cohesion is required. The gains of these groups can be in political or in economic terms or in both, but the process itself seems practically an automatic one. If the control groups of a society try to suppress it, they merely retard the process of growth of the social group as a whole and endanger their own position to the degree of the dynamic potentialities of the group.

The reason why the process of technological innovation led to a greater class-friction in Europe than in the United States must be attributed partially to the higher degree of class-thinking of a society of greater "culture-age", although the ratio between Man—Natural Resources played also a very significant role. The upper and middle classes of Europe had been more saturated in their desire for expansion; thus they lacked the elasticity to expand the social pattern in such a way that it gave proper status to the carriers of technical functions. As a result, these groups had to make use of the power they already possessed in order to secure for themselves a social status which corresponded to their function.

It is quite logical that they regarded the industrial and mercantile classes as a retarding factor, although to deny their function as such was a purely symbolic manipulation, due to high emotional tensions. The tensions between those groups led the middle class to reconsider its position in regard to government and to advocate a strengthening of government in order to cope with revolutionary tendencies. The strengthening of government created greater cohesion within the societies but by granting the working classes a rational status. Since this increase in status involved an expansion of need-satisfaction of these groups, it gradually began to become clear that the greater the consumption, the greater the production, so that the once dreaded process of status gains of the working classes proved to be a positive instead of a negative factor.

However, the "mariage de raison" between business and government caused the working groups at first to extend their view of a constraining and retarding influence of business to government and to evolve an ideology that was international rather than national. The way in which governments succeeded in granting status in relation to function to the workers is an exact measure of the degree to which the latter remained international or national in their ideologies. The more successful the process, the more the international accent faded, or at least it was brought within an acceptable civilizational framework. In some cases, like the United States, the international ideology never even took hold, due to an open class-system, caused in turn by an extremely favorable ratio between Man and Resources and the high mental elasticity of a social group without patterns that had been frozen over a long period.

It is evident from the foregoing that, so long as a society is dynamic, it will automatically show a certain amount of class friction, since each innovation creates a "carrier-group" which has to gain its status within the already established pattern of the society. Whether a society can keep these conflicts always within rational bounds is entirely a moot question; it depends upon the rate of change, the natural basis of the social group, the rationality of its members, the rate of cohesion, etc. In general perhaps it could be said that the better the interclass communication system of a society, the more likely that all change can take place via rational channels, but, on the other hand, history shows that many of the most basic changes of society have occurred via the mechanism of violent conflict.

Perhaps one of the main reasons of the growing resistance to the hedonistic pattern was the application of concepts which belonged to the behavior-pattern of the merchant to a society which had already outgrown that stage. The mentality of the merchant of the New Era was conditioned to the concept that it was wiser to sell at high prices to a small group than at lower prices to a larger group, partially because the considerable widening of the consumptive powers of this latter group was hardly feasible. This attitude was maintained in the period of industrial expansion, so that a group emerged whose needs expanded beyond a degree of rational necessity while the "too much" on one side was matched by "too little" on the other.

Thus a truly hedonistic pattern arose which was characterized by the development of superfluous needs, and the resulting neuroses in turn contributed to the indecisiveness of the controlling groups, which did not make the changes of which they themselves felt the necessity. In addition to that, the large business and industrial enterprises created themselves a managerial type who was different from the original owners as he was more aware of the danger of loss of power, and, therefore more technical and efficient in his thinking.

The hedonistic type did not fit the largest types of modern economic organization, neither did he possess the capacity to understand the mechanization of society as a whole. His behavior, especially as a consumer, was largely symbolic status rather than functional behavior, and, in modern society, the interest in this type of behavior is definitely waning. We are not longer particularly impressed by "conspicuous consumption" and the leaders of modern society, are, on the whole, inconspicuous rather than noted for extreme behavior-forms.

The epicure, the art-connoisseur, the collector, the skillful and accomplished traveler, the man of graceful manners and brilliant conversation, the Don-Juan or Casanova-type are all becoming relics of the past, when there was a great deal more of conscious and studied behavior. Since we all have admitted to being human, there is no reason not to behave more or less naturally, and that is what most people do, so that the degree of awareness in personal behavior has undoubtedly diminished.

Our moral judgments are also in the realm of "more and less", and most people display a marked distaste for absolute moral judgments which run contrary to our generally historical and sociological explanations of human behavior.

All these changes were long and difficult, however, since they resulted from a change in Western society as a whole in which class distance diminished so that the more extreme forms of class behavior, on both sides of the scale, have disappeared. In addition, social mobility has so increased that more people have experienced the various layers of society personally. This has not resulted in their being more impressed than those who know the higher or lower layers purely by reputation. We have also abandoned the cruel attitude of applying equal moral judgment to people of different status, an obvious and malicious injustice that needs no explicit condemnation although it still partially prevails in our legal systems.

One might view a possibility of stabilization of our society in the fact that the dynamic period of Western civilization has created a social pattern which keeps Man in a certain tension. It would be of crucial importance to determine whether this tension corresponds to the normal activity of a mature human organism. If this should prove to be the case, there would have been good reason why the extreme stress on the development of the intellect of the New Era had to come to an end. This attitude led to a neglect of the physical and emotional attributes of Man as well as of the symbolic function. If this assumption is correct, the reaction would have to focus on physical development, emotional life and a renewal of belief and art, as parts of the symbolic pattern.

All those factors did show a renewed growth in the last decades of the 19th and the beginning of the 20th century, partly as a continuation of romanticism.

The interest in physical exercise and sports was partly military and patriotic in origin, especially in Germany, but it went far beyond this limited goal and became a part of Anglo-Saxon life first, and later on of all Western countries. It became a cultural factor of such importance that today it is one of the most significant segments of modern life, ranging from an almost religious devotion to physical strength to casual and haphazard participation. But there is no ideology left in modern life which preaches the neglect of the body for the benefit of the soul, and the idea that soul, mind and body are interrelated is a general one, although its scientific expression has not been adequate, because of our lack of knowledge of the interchange of energy within the organism.

Our entire high standard-of-living philosophy is based upon the same assumption that relative organic equilibrium can be reached only by keeping the "physical" organism in a certain condition of balance. We are quite well informed about the amounts and type of food, about required temperatures, useful amounts and types of work, rest-periods, health care, etc., but we are much less well oriented in regard to our intellectual needs, and there is an almost complete absense of reliable material about the fulfillment of the symbolic needs of Man and the degree to which this influences his mental and physical reactions. We do know that these three basic reaction-types influence one another, but in what way this occurs and how organic equilibrium can be reached via physical, mental and symbolic means has not been drawn purposively within the orbit of our studies. A certain amount of experimentation would be quite feasible and might show amazing results.

So far we can only observe that Nature herself seems to be striving for this balance, and social processes demonstrate us how the makrokosmos of society is attempting to bring about a certain equilibrium, so that it would be feasible to draw conclusions from this makrokosmos to the mikrokosmos of the individual.

It seems that Man in a stage of relative maturity would need a fairly strong symbolic system, but without too specific contents in order to avoid interference and conflict with intellectual processes, a highly developed system of technical and social control knowledge, seen as a pragmatistic process that does not and should not lead to "absolutes" or attempts at complete control, as well as a wide and untrammeled realm of physical and emotional activities, curbed however by a sense of measure and social responsibility, but also with no formulation of moral absolutes. The only constructive absolute would be a belief in Man and the Universe and an attitude of veneration toward the great symbolic leaders which mankind has produced. A balanced world would have to attribute equal value to the great world religions, and a judgment of "higher" and "lower" in regard to them would be an expression of civilizational imperialism.

A fusion of religions would enrich our symbolic life and might help to overcome the cleavage between religion and art, which has been purely to the detriment of the former, since many people seek symbolic satisfaction either in modern art or in religion but very few can reconcile the two. This may be due to the processes of rationalization of religions, which have made them into socio-political rather than symbolic organs. This function was extremely important so long as government was underdeveloped, but since government has taken over —and probably to a degree which even hampers individual development and initiative — the institutional care of the individual, there is no reason why religion should not return to its inspirational function. It makes very little use of modern art, because it is hampered by a pattern that, if taken literally, is really the dominant social pattern of preceding culture periods. If taken symbolically, the point of logical consistency and literal conformity loses its stringency, and much could be done to enrich religious life to such a degree that it would appeal more to the emotional needs of Man.

The religious person is not concerned about logic and rationality. He seeks emotional support in an attitude that is deeper and goes beyond rationality and which aids him to gain awareness of the comforting eternal flow of life, the rhythm that is lost in our civilizational patterns and that is fundamental to the gaining of equilibrium and the bringing about of a state of relaxation and acquiescence that cannot be achieved rationally. This desire is basic to all people, and at the present time it cannot find an adequate outlet, an escape from the present that is not the result of hostility or frustration but simply the need for a wider outlook that is not charged with value-judgments and related to fear. Modern life has reduced Man's cosmic fear, and the concentration which it requires does not permit him to bring himself back to a state of anxiety. The anxiety is still there, underneath, but it needs a soothing rhythm of beauty rather than a translation into philosophic patterns that stir up intellectual doubt and lead to the recrudescence of fear.

The question "why" has lost much of its emotional weight in favor of an acceptance of life as it is, if it can be channeled in such a way that it avoids the shameful and unspeakable horrors of the past decades, which did not take place in spite of but because of our so-called rationality. If too heavy a strain is placed upon us, the reaction brings out all the frustrations of Man, but if we can avoid extreme tensions, we can also avoid what all of us have to be ashamed of. Knowledge and control are but one aspect of life, and in that realm there is no solution, because there is no answer to our basic fear, which merely becomes veiled and distorted and hidden by a sense of false security.

We should admit that life is mysterious and unknowable and worship it for these very qualities, which, once admitted, lose their horror and give a perspective that is comforting and reassuring.

"We do not know" is a better answer than "we know", because it shows greater strength and deeper insight than the flight into the haughty certainty which merely betrays doubt and fear. We all ponder, we all imagine, we all create worlds that are more pleasing than the present one, but why should we still transfer those qualities which we have all in common into something definite that makes us feel superior to the next person. As soon as our beliefs become definite, they lose their most magic and mysterious element, since they become communicable. As they reflect our most inner emotions, we should not want to communicate them but keep them for ourselves, guided perhaps by the awareness that we have them in common with others and led by sounds and forms that take the all-too individual out of them. Our beliefs need content so long as they fill us with fear, but they need only form when we have become mature enough to accept the majestic and gigantic flow of life itself. Then the urgency is gone, the pressing of time less immediate, and the sense of an impending threat disappears. We are no more and no less than the world around us, subject to the same laws, which none of our frantic efforts can repel or invalidate.

We come and we go, knowing not whence we came and whither we are going, but we march with millions before and after and around us, and with all these other creatures which are so much like ourselves. They follow the same stream, obey the same commands, but they neither ask nor worry. Our own nature dictates our fate to us, and whatever these dictates might be, they are part of a vast and overwhelming pattern in which everything is related to everything else, to the moon, the stars, the winds and the sea. They all fulfill a task and a function, but they do not seek to escape their fate.

If Man calms down and glances around him, the answer to the questions with which he torments himself has already been given.

## CHAPTER XIV

## THE DECLINE OF HEDONISM [57]

The breakdown of a cultural pattern furnishes one of history's most fascinating spectacles, since it offers the possibility of a study in reverse of the process of culture-formation. Basically the phenomenon is perhaps a neural one, a decrease of energy which brings forth a search for new reaction channels, a wavering between patterns of the past and a hesitant probing for new possibilities, of bitter group-antagonism and of the latter-day attempts of some, formerly disfranchised, groups to make themselves the carriers of the pattern which is entering upon its decline. As such, it is a period of overly sharp consciousness, of a last coming back into focus of the pattern with its full implications, leading to — what could be called — a cultural guilt-feeling and the frequently weird attempts to overcome this sense of the complete inadequacy of the habitual patterns, which begin to appear as strange conglomerations of ideas and symbols, without any visible or logical relation to the starkness of reality, suddenly all the more shocking when it appears without its customary rationalizations and its covering symbolic screen.

It also leads to the sudden realization of the separateness of things and people, of their being apart without any necessary relationship, so that society seems a phantasmagory of soulless puppets, operating in a sphere of almost unbearable lonesomeness. This re-emergence of anxiety creates the high emotional tensions which appear as the result of frustrations, caused by the taboos of the society, no longer purposive rules of behavior of the group as a whole but oppressive measures, enacted by cruel minorities in order to rob the majority of their right to life and happiness.

Through the mists and confusion of decay appears the notion that people have not really lived, that their bodies and minds have become warped under a set of rules that needs but to be ignored in order to save the individual, whatever may be the fate of the group. And perhaps this renewal of the individual and his breaking down of the barriers around him is the first step toward the formation of a new attitude that is born almost automatically from this blind groping for individual happiness and the emerging realization that this happiness has to be achieved within the limits of that of others or to be paid for at so high a price that its very purpose is annulled.

On the other side, we find those who clamor "decay" and contribute to it by the cramped awareness of their limited virtues; those who "hold their heads high" when the world around them burns, believing that it is sufficient to ignore the conflagration in order to combat the flames. But they render the function of bringing the outworn pattern once more into focus and to demonstrate clearly that it has outlived its usefulness.

This whole process was in progress in Europe around the turn of the century, more clearly visible now in retrospect than it was at the time, when the facade of the hedonist attitude was still hiding the overcrowded stuffiness of the living room as well as the filth and misery of the basements, and there existed only a vague uneasiness about the rumored stirrings in Asia and Africa where native peoples began to grow restive under the promises whose realization was eternally postponed.

The cleavage between dream and reality had become too great; the dream continued to have value only for those whose lives mirrored it at least to some degree and who clung to it in frightened desperation in order to save the world which had realized their desires. The more the masses arose in anger and disappointment, the more they insisted on the reality of their world, forced into a workable compromise only in those countries where the underlying emotions were not too extreme. But even there the anxiety continued, leading to the fratricidal spectacle of the first world war in which Europe re-acted its nationalist period which it had already outgrown.

If it had seen itself as a unity, its position would have been impregnable, but the underlying tensions were such that the threatening internal collapse was turned into the frenzy of an inter-European war from which no European power could have any rational expectation of gain. Western culture, however, was already no longer rational but dominated by an emotional frustration that was more imagined than real. The European mind had lost its grip on reality, but behind it all was already the image of unification beyond the national state. But the image seen in terms of time-honored power politics, namely as dominance by means of force by one power.

There was also no awareness as yet of the diminishing influence of European civilization as such, since European dominance was seen as synonymous with world dominance. Yet the final decision was brought about by the unbroken strength of the United States, guided by the instinctive desire to protect itself against the chimera of a unified, centralized, agressive European nationalism that was carried by German imperialism and not by England or France, which had already outgrown a purely European orientation as well as a desire for power for its own sake.

The shocks and disturbances connected with the transition toward a more cohesive, although mechanistic, pattern were to be many and farreaching, of which World War I was but one instance, and, for a period, it even re-established the cohesion of the Western nations. In the case of Russia, even the outer pressures exerted by a war were insufficient to stave off the collapse of a system that no longer gave cohesion to the dynamic impulses of a nation that had grown aware of its potentialities and its actual lack of any corresponding power.

Perhaps this was indicative of the fact that, in the period of World War I, the underlying conflict was basically a class more than a national conflict. The new type of civilization that was emerging required a different class structure, and ultimately it would also lead to farreaching structural changes in the world society, but this second factor was much less immediately visible, and it needed a second war to bring into focus the differences in the world society which had already taken place informally.

The emerging pattern demanded a different relationship between function and status, or rather an adjustment of new functions to status positions of a different type. Every time this kind of change occurs, we can observe that the changes in class structure first lead to the demand for a classless society. In order to rid themselves of the old structure, people develop the idea of abolishing all classes, and this catalytic process aids to bring about the transition to a new pattern. As the change is ultimately caused by a change in function, brought about in turn by a different need-structure, the criticism of the existing pattern is based upon a real or assumed divergence between function and class-status. Certain classes which no longer seem to carry specific functions are accused of a parasitic existence, but frequently the stigmatized function may have been merely overstressed by the old pattern and returns under a different disguise under the new one.

The breakdown or innovation of the class system brings an increase in the significance of social groups which had a limited role. So long as the national state was the dominant social group, all other groups, like family, clan, professional groups, political groups, etc., had a more or less circumscribed role. The national state was seen by the Western mind as the carrier of the late-hedonistic pattern, and the resistance against this pattern was in terms of an antagonism toward the national state. Socialism, religious thinking, etc. were frequently supranational because they believed that a new, more collectivistic pattern would need a different type of state or, preferably, would lead to the emergence of a world state.

The society which seems to be developing at present has not shown a disappearance of the national state, but the typical national state of the late 19th century, with colonies and dependencies, has lost in significance in relation to contemporary superstates which show different expansionistic forms as well as in regard to regional groupings and tentative world organization.

In other words, we can observe that the period of breakdown projected the tendencies of the future into Man's consciousness but these tendencies were magnified beyond their normal proportions because they functioned as motives for action. Action probably always requires a strong bias in order to overcome the basic trend toward an equilibrium, and periods of great action-intensity are in reality transitional stages from one equilibrium condition to a subsequent one, due to the basic cohesion of the structure of Man himself which does not permit prolonged departure from a condition of relative balance.

The transition toward the new pattern involved the following factors: an increase in the significance of technology; a rise in status, either by evolutionary or revolutionary means, of the carriers of technological functions; a greater class-cohesion, since production and consumption had to be re-adjusted when mass production became possible; an extension of governmental controls to bring about the various transitions but mostly the last mentioned one; a reorientation of society in relation to its control-group, which could no longer maintain the form of the 19th century liberal state that was the expression of a largely mercantile attitude.

The thesis of Marxism that this change of pattern, or any basic change of social pattern, is brought about by class conflict is entirely part of "symbolic magnification", although it is true that a change in function has to assert itself by a show of strength in order to bring about a change in status. But once the functional change has occurred, adaptation of status is entirely possible by compromise as happened in reality in the great majority of the countries.

Revolution seems to occur when the functional change itself is still a goal, so that its lack is attributed to the leading group, because the group as a whole feels itself threatened by the greater progressiveness of other groups.

In other words, the functional backwardness causes a desire to change the formal structure without the necessary preceding change on the functional level. This forces the control-group which gains ascendancy by revolution to establish strong autocratic central control in order to enforce the underlying functional changes with which the control-group is identified.

The change of pattern can take place in a far more normal fashion by gradual functional changes, which then express themselves in the formal structure. The alternative of establishing first the formal structure is a process of imitation of more powerful social groups, and this really indicates that the social group which operates in this fashion is in a less advanced cultural stage.

The natural creative process is obviously from functional structure to formal structure, and the reverse procedure is purely an effort to reach the same stage by a shortcut that can never be fully successful because a society functions only when there is a certain relation between functional and formal structure, and the emergence of the functional attitudes is a process that requires time. Achievement by imitation is not the same as achievement by creation, although the second may grow from the first. On the other hand, the first requires strong discipline, and once the discipline has become habitual, it may later on stimulate creation, since discipline may merge into self-discipline as a necessary condition of creative achievement. Imitation and culture-borrowing belong themselves to the early stage of the dynamic period of a civilization, and it is interesting to observe that this culture-borrowing takes place mostly from the group that is next in achievement to the group which attempts to advance.

Since the breakdown of the late-hedonistic pattern brought with it a certain hostility toward the national state, "classes" were seen and became in reality, to some extent, the effective social groups, so that culture-borrowing took place in terms of class ideologies.

Within Western society, the change did not succeed without violent conflict but it is interesting to observe that those conflicts arose in those countries where inter-class communications were poor, namely Russia and Germany. There was little or no contact between the mentality of the Westernized, sophisticated Russian upper class and the masses of the people while the main cause of conflict was probably inferiority toward the West, aggravated by lack of internal communication. In Germany, the new industrial upper class had absorbed the attitudes and mannerisms of the Prussian military nobility, thus making them unable to understand the desire of the workers for increased political participation as a result of their functional status-gain. Again in this case, the outer pressure of a lost war had to be added to bring class friction to the stage of open conflict.

In other words, culture change seems to lead to violent conflict when the combination of outer pressure plus poor inter-class communication occurs, because the ruled can blame the rulers for the outer pressures which are not felt as a function of the group as a whole.

It is therefore not altogether surprising that a class which as yet lacked a functional foundation borrowed the ideology of the Western

European labor class, which had partially reached both function and status for which the first group was striving. It is also interesting that this "borrowing" of socialism from Western Europe was done by a group which magnified a class ideology into the function of national symbolism because a set of symbols was needed to express the transition to a technological society. The more cohesion the society gained and needed, the more it had to stress the importance of the symbolic system as such, and the symbols of a society have no direct logical relation to its system of experience-knowledge. In other countries, class ideology remained closer to the realm of knowledge so that a cleavage had to result to the extent that the same ideology was used either as a symbolic system or as a pragmatistic economic theory, which could be modified and adjusted in relation to actual conditions.

When the new, neo-stoic, mechanistic pattern began to take a more definite shape, it had to establish an effective social unit in order to gain structure, and when this process had taken place, the friction between classes was partially transferred into friction between regional superstates. This friction should be partly seen as the emergence of the new pattern in the world society, but neither the functional nor the status roles have been determined in the world society to the extent that they have become institutionalized. This process of role determination can take place via means of gradual adjustment and compromise or via violent conflict, and a cynic might argue that the ultimate outcome in both cases would not be too different, since the leading roles will be determined by functional superiority whether this superiority will be factually demonstrated or merely accepted by indication.

However, it is of the utmost significance to realize that the transitional process which first took place within the national states is taking place at present in world society in its entirety.

If we apply this to world society, we can first observe that the factor of outer pressure is automatically absent but that the factor of lack of communications remains. If within relatively isolated regional groups functional and status reorientation would lead to such results that the class structures of those civilizational regions would fairly well reflect the functional structure, there will be no reason for extreme conflict between regions, except that the integration of world society as a whole would still be begging for a solution. An important factor which might lead to conflict is inner friction within the regional groups. If this factor can be eliminated, there is high probability that the problem of the structure of world society can be solved. The higher the integration of the Western world, the lower the probability of war, since there would be clearly visible power relationship between the world regions.

Two integrated regions, with an inner equilibrium, would not show the underlying extreme emotional tension that is needed for violent conflict, and it would be rational to assume that a limited communication-system would result automatically from economic, political and cultural ties which exist to some extent at the present time.

This argument is based upon the assumption that we are entering upon a period which shows a much stronger trend toward regional integration than toward a world society and the transition from national state to regional group is a far more natural and possible one than the jump toward a world society, which shows a purely formal organization without an underlying functional structure of sufficient strength. In fact, it might be for the best, if world organizations were to be strictly legalistic ones with limited goals while actual integration would take place regionally. There has been too much acting as if there were a world government while there is in reality no such thing, since there is no proper functional foundation for it.

The recent increase in the significance of regional organizations and the relative weakness of the United Nations seem to prove this quite convincingly.

However, it is time to return to the aspects of the breakdown and decline of the hedonistic pattern and the gradual change toward a more highly integrated society, caused in turn by the reaching of a higher degree of maturity of Man himself, which shows itself in a better co-ordination of his physical, mental and symbolic needs and a clearer view of the interrelationship and the function of these three basic attributes. It needs no special mention that this transition is one toward a long-term pattern which obviously will show a lower rate of innovation and change and which will entail new social forms, although the basic functional structure of society should be regarded as a relative constant.

If we consider that this society should be one, according to the law of probability, of considerable permanence, it is quite startling to reflect that it is of a mechanistic nature. The conclusion could be drawn from this that Man, in a stage of maturity, possesses only incomplete co-ordination of his basic attributes, although this might be the very reason for his societalization and for his living in a society which is organized in terms of strong basic class allegiance. In other words, the higher degree of societalization implies imperfect coordination as the basis of its existence.

Psychologically, this might mean that the high amount of direct or transmitted experience needed to be a successful member of modern society continues to place great value on control-knowledge, so that adaptation to the society prevents complete organic coordination. For this reason, we might expect that modern society will continue to show large groups — the young, the old, and the partially or non-adjusted — that will continue to show an only relatively low degree of adaptation to the requirements of modern society. We live in a society which is the condition of our existence through its mechanized processes, but at the same time these very same processes prevent us from reaching a rhythmic form of life, so that a strong need remains for the development of an adequate symbolic system in order to cope with this danger of overintensity.

From the datum of imperfect coordination it could be concluded that it would also be inconsistent to expect a logical relationship — or at least a relationship that could become subject of human knowledge — between emotions, knowledge and symbols, or perhaps it is quite reassuring to realize that we deal with relatively autonomous realms of which only one is open to logical reasoning.

The full impact of the mystery of life may aid us toward a more balanced view and toward an attitude of veneration and respect which can only benefit interhuman relations and revitalize the symbolic realm, which is undoubtedly underdeveloped in modern society. It is not surprising that the late 19th and the 20th century have shown anti-intellectualistic movements as a reaction against the overestimation of the intellect by rationalism, but those reactions were onesided and emotional and consisted of attempted returns to outdated symbolic systems or to the earlier social forms of personal leader-follower relationships.

Perhaps a visual presentation in diagrams of the transition from hedonism toward modernism may be helpful:

Diagram I

*Late-hedonistic society*

Psychological
dominant:

Acquisition of money,
largely seen as a
means of consumption
rather than of
production.

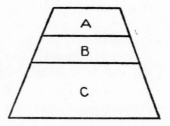

A:   Governmental function underdeveloped

B:   Business and industrial leaders: ideology of quantitative materialistic prosperity

C:   Workers: ideology of same type of prosperity but aimed at distribution
     of consumption in an international society

In the society of diagram I, we find an absence of a strong symbolic system although this function was carried almost surreptiously by modern art; an absence of long-term planning and control, partly resulting from the first deficiency; oversimplification in attitude B in terms of quantitative economic thinking (the more goods, the higher the prosperity, with lack of understanding for the structure of demand), continued insistence upon "freedom" although the emerging society required greater integration, equalized political thinking (equal political power to everybody) as a sign of breakdown of the structure of the old society and the transition toward a new one; in attitude C we find a strong element of symbolic thinking (the perfect society visible on earth), as a result of frustration, a clinging to the ideals of hedonist society although the extension of its benefits to all people required rationalized production, and rationalized production causes in turn a structured society, not a society of equals.

THE COMMUNIST REACTION

| Diagram II | Diagram III |
|---|---|
| *Western society* | *Lower standard of living society* |

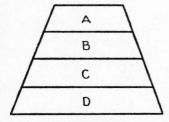

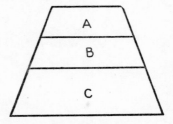

A: Government
B: Business and industrial leaders
C: Professions
D: Workers and farmers

A: Aristocracy
B: Small middle class (7 % compared to 15-20 % as "normal")
C: Peasants and workers ("Borrowed" ideology D as belonging to desired functional and class status)

Diagram IV

*The reaction*

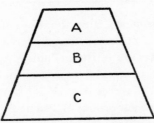

A: Strongly centralized government with ideology D reenforced into strong symbolic system
B: Beginnings of professional scientific middle class
C: Workers and farmers, organized according to pattern A

The group which brought about the transition from the situation of Diagram III to that of Diagram IV forms a strong self-perpetuating control group which seeks to reach or surpass the standard of living of the society of Diagram III. Thus, strong central control + strong symbolic system results from the need for cohesion in order to "catch up" with the more highly developed societies. Outside pressure given as reason for the need of central control and cohesion, in reality partly resulting from the beginning of a more dynamic stage of the society in question.

THE FASCIST REACTION

Diagram V

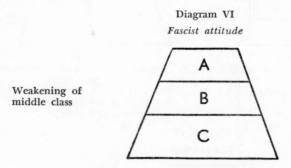

Entire society suffering from frustration of poor results of World War I

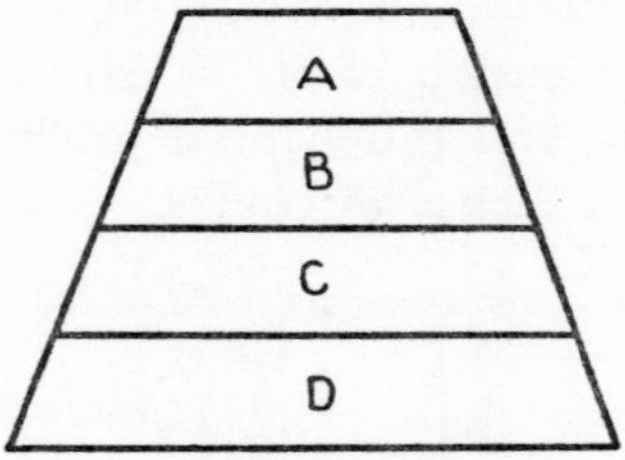

A: Weak government
B: Landed proprietors, industrialists, etc.
C: White collar, middle and lower middle class
D: Peasants and workers

Diagram VI

*Fascist attitude*

Weakening of middle class

Strong central government, with the resuscitated symbolism of the national state in terms of military strength, carried by group C, suffering most heavily from the failure of the hedonistic system and profiting less from gains of group D, achieved by militant socialism. Sees itself as the group which "heroically" serves the whole community because it tries to solve the conflict between groups B and D by force. First makes concessions to group D (socialist parts of program) but moves over to interests of group B, needed for national renaissance, after acquisition of power. Anti-intellectualistic because aggressive attitude toward the more succesful nations makes the taking of rather desperate decisions essential while the development of intellect and reason increases selectivity and broadens judgment, so that the decision of the "gambler against heavy odds" is no longer attractive. Conscious of physical "regeneration", since energy is no longer used to build up the more complex patterns of moral and social control, and introduction of the less selective "military patterns", resulting in the worship of pseudo-heroism (physical heroism in lieu of moral, intellectual or spiritual heroism). Shows the familiar pattern of considering the simpler attitudes of the past as more "virtuous".

Since these efforts run contrary to the more basic need of gradual technological, social and political organization, this type of society needs insincere and corrupt leadership. Odd mixture of dynamic elements ("heroic" expansion toward the outside world; hostility toward outgroup) and static ones (freezing of society into "estates"). Stresses in-group loyalty because integration into Western and world society has proved unsuccessful, due partly to lack of understanding of these groups.

### THE NATIONAL-SOCIALIST REACTION

#### Diagram VII

Entire society in condition of extreme frustration, due to defeat in World War I and to failure of effort to reach the condition of Western empire-owning nations. Lack of natural protection toward the East. Essentially highly dynamic society but with retarded social forms of industrial and agricultural feudalism, due to social worship of military organizational forms.

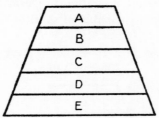

A:  Weak semi-democratic government
B:  Industrial, economic, agricultural leaders
C:  Professional middle class, partly with autocratic thought-patterns
D:  Frustrated lower middle class
E:  Workers and farmers

From diagram VII it is visible that the conditions for a severe explosion were given. The frustration in regard to the more successful Western nations was of long standing and deep because it was felt that the position of the Allied nations was perpetuated only by their combining against Germany, while Germany considered itself as individually more "tüchtig" than any of the other ones. It was overlooked that this "Tüchtigkeit" was largely economic and military, but neither political nor psychological, since Germany was a country of poor international judgment. The resentment against the Allies made Germany more of an "in-group", resulting in an already outmoded strong nationalism. Again the same phenomenon of regarding outdated social forms like military and industrial feudalism as a sign of superiority and greater "virtue". ("Deutsch sein heißt treu sein", "Durch Deutsches Wesen wird die Welt genesen" and equally sentimental slogans). Extreme sentimentalism as a reaction against extreme discipline (German "Gefühl": das Land von Dichter und Denker), combination of the two into the German beer-rituals, reaching from the students to the village "Stammtisch". Dynamic pressure resulting in extreme emotional dualism (high ideals, sexual licentiousness, numerous street brawls and latent cruelty). Same effort at physical regeneration, because of a lack of more complex control patterns (Nature-cults, youth movement, Free corps, political military formations, etc.). Racial superiority doctrine caused largely by jealousy of pedantic, officious lower middle class of the economically successful liberals and the more advanced free professions (magnification of their virtue of being "Teutonic", loyal to the state, etc. into pathological proportions; economic failure explained from "high ideals"). Same lack of integration into Western international society, due to the etatism of these two societies which was partly a "cause" of Germany's predicament.

Impending failure of internal functional status integration as most powerful motive of external aggression as Germany's internal economic problems were undoubtedly capable of solution.

THE NATIONAL-SOCIALIST ATTITUDE

Diagram VIII

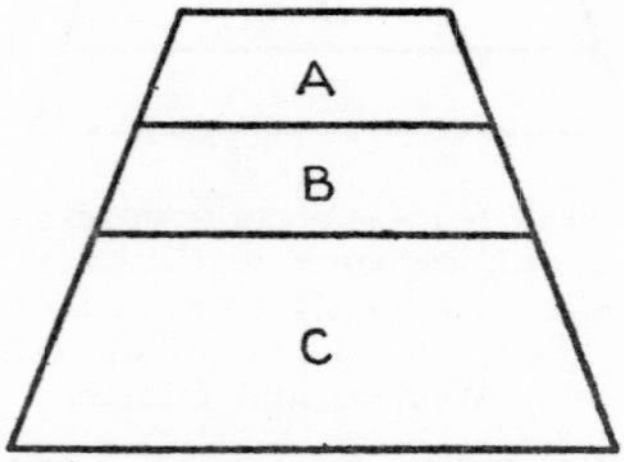

A: Military, self-perpetuating control-group with confused lower middle-class ideology. Odd mixture of power-, racial- and idealistic philosophy with strong eschatological undercurrents

B: Reduction of middle class to the needed professions through anti-intellectual bias, caused by the need for decisions against heavy odds; lower middle class irritation at half digested culture patterns

C: Organization of workers and peasants into "estates". Same attempts as in fascism to freeze the in-group into static patterns in order to generate enough energy for outer aggression. In this case, this was all the more successful since Germany was a much more dynamic society than Italy

REACTION OF MORE STABLE WESTERN NATIONS AGAINST
COMMUNIST AND FASCIST THREATS

Diagram IX

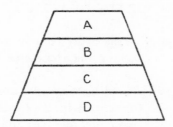

A:   Extension of governmental function in order to curb class conflict by
better distributive power

B:   Class of economic, industrial and agricultural leaders who strive for inter-class
integration within a free-enterprise system

C:   Upper-middle class and middle class, consisting of the professions, independents,
union leaders, etc. Group from which modern governments draw their "experts", who
attempt to regulate society on a "scientific" basis (remnant of the rationalism of the
upper class of preceding periods, belief in the "law of averages and the greatest
number" as an expression of the trend toward a more static society. The "normal"
person is postulated as the desirable one, namely the one capable of a certain equilibrium, from which, if general enough, a social equilibrium will result. The "scientific" approach to society also involves an attempt to take social problems out of the
atmosphere of class ideologies in order to reduce social tensions.

D:   Workers and peasants organized in political groups which assume semi-etatistic
functions in order to bring about the needed integration. The existence of these
highly organized groups gives a pluralistic aspect to modern society, increasing the
need for integration upon the public-law level. The fact that these groups all have
their own symbolic systems is largely due to their historical origins and may be considered as a cause of cultural diversity, although the lack of a unified symbolic
system also leads to a spreading of cultural achievement, and, possibly, some lowering
of standards. A novel which aims to be socialist or religious rather than a work of
art tends to suffer in quality.

On the other hand, a unified symbolic system can easily lead to rigidity, dogmatism
and intolerance, as is quite obvious in the case of societies whose inner functional
cohesion is still weak in spite of all symbolic presentations to the contrary.

Compared to European society, American society has been more
pragmatistic up to the present time, but it is striving hard for symbolic
content. The basic tenet of "The American way of life" is already a
limitation in terms of dynamic pragmatism but it is still far from
rigidity and stabilized contents.

If we consider that most contemporary national patterns arose out
of class ideologies, it would seem that contemporary Western Europe
is largely middle-middle and lower middle class in its attitude. The
United States would be more upper middle class if we refer the class
ideologies to the successful period of hedonist society. In all cases, however, modern technology has caused greater rigidity, so that the only
valid conclusion seems to be that effective changes in the formal structure of a society occur only after the functional informal changes have
preceded them.

## CHAPTER XV

## THE VIRTUE OF WEAKNESS

A CASE-STUDY, BASED UPON THE DIARY OF A BUSINESSMAN, WRITTEN
IN THE 2ND DECADE OF THE TWENTIETH CENTURY

Tomorrow will be my fiftieth birthday. In the morning there will be the usual celebration in the office, with the speeches and the presents; the afternoon will be in general for relatives and friends, and, in the evening, an elaborate dinner is scheduled for the inner circle. Theoretically I am looking at a very successful life, and yet I do not feel any joy or anticipation as I write these lines.

Perhaps I should ask myself the question why this is so. Do I feel as tired and empty as most of my friends look? Sometimes I think that I have wasted something more valuable and irreplaceable by being successful, and when I look at my two children, I can almost see how my own shortcomings seem to be magnified in them, and I fear they may not even have the courage to start on the road along which I so perilously traveled. My own parental admonitions to them are nothing but empty and shallow words which do not help me to overcome the feeling that their existence has been predetermined and that I am calling into a dimensionless desert into which sound cannot even penetrate.

When did I first get this feeling of struggling against forces much stronger than myself, when did I become aware of this terrible, hollow emptiness? The words I read in the papers and magazines beat at my brain as if they carried absolutely no contents. And yet there was a time that I was so convinced of progress and prosperity that I seemed to be marching along with an army of brave and determined soldiers. But soon after, the march became more like a compulsion, something from which I could not free myself, continuing merely because there was no way to break out of these ranks in which the others became increasingly as I was myself, being pushed on by those who seemed to be coming after us.

And then, perhaps it was five or even ten years ago, these pains started, as if my brain was being rent into two different parts. The one part was still reaching out for the life of my childhood; this was the desire to be part of a general human life that seemed to flow far, far below me but of which I could still hear voices and sounds and have these sudden vision-like memories. It was somehow a brighter life, not hemmed in by a rhythm that was carrying me away from the reality I still groped for so longingly.

The other part at times was very real, but it remained almost completely without happiness, except when the money I was earning enabled me to do something kind and unexpected, something really quite irrational. At those rare moments, the two realms blended into one another, and perhaps then I felt like the being that I had been as a child. Even in my childhood, however, this had been only in my imagination, because altogether too soon the world had been divided into a bright and a dark part. The bright part seemed so artificial and hostile that it was only out of fear of these merciless forces that I had walked on the side which lacked the mystery and surprise that were really so dear to me.

And gradually, — much later on, of course — it had all become habitual, and for a while this sharply lit world had become familiar, assuring me of my own strength as compared to those who stayed behind, afraid, as it were, to leave the darkness which — I then thought — was only hiding their weakness and incompetence. We were so bright and strong and so successful, setting up businesses and marrying nice girls with attractive dowries, and really calculating it all pretty nicely. We were not really calculating, of course, but we were just stronger than the others, and, since life consists of the survival of the fittest, they lived in squalor and misery and were always in debt while our tables were heavily laden. For this we praised the Lord although, if we had been honest, we should have admitted that we considered it all to be our own achievement.

But it would never have done to say this aloud, and, of course, we all had had a religious upbringing which proved to be very useful. It gave us the reassuring feeling that the good life was to continue into the hereafter, which was also divided into sections for the rich and the poor. Of course, it did not actually say so in the Bible, but the Bible was often controversial, and the visiting clergyman seemed to indicate that wealth had been approved of by the higher powers.

It was not so consistent perhaps, but fortunately we were much too busy to go into fine theological points, with directors' meetings and dividends on our minds. That was where one really showed one's mettle.

"What dividend are you paying this year, Kees or Jan or Piet? Can't tell me, of course, but you better make it good or I'll hide half of mine under reserves or buildings".

This was a good joke, and the boys all laughed loudly, their paunches growing a little each year with the dividends so that the heavy gold chains on their vests became more noticeable. Success also seemed to be connected with a lack of physical coordination, but that was perhaps because it all involved a lot of heavy brainwork. Other people were just not up to that, and sometimes we even had to drop somebody from the inner circle who would go bankrupt — losing some of our money — or commit another unpardonable sin, like voting for the wrong political party. One could vote only for the Liberals who stood for freedom, prosperity and sound money. The last was really the most important item. One does not want to slave away one's days and then find that all the money that has been piled up does not buy anything.

Those things happen only in bad countries to which warships and soldiers had to be sent to teach sound business morale. Not everybody was capable of being rational but, thank Heaven, there were enough people around who could run the world in an intelligent and progressive fashion.

It also seemed nice that Nature had arranged things in such a way that only a few people could reach this state of progressive enlightenment while the masses lived merely in the shade of it. This was the natural relation between leaders and followers, but it was disquieting that some people believed that the blessings of rationality could be extended to everybody, and, what was worse, they assumed that this process should be administered by an impartial government, while everybody knew that government officials were lazy people who could not make much of a living in the open market.

The rewards of the competitive system were the expression of a law of nature, not to be tinkered with by anybody, lest there be a lessening of efficiency and a falling off of profits.

All this was also reflected in the world of women. On the one side, the nice and respectable ones who were protected by the walls of morality, and there were those others who did not have much self-control and who were punished for it.

Just another example of the law of Nature which rewarded the strong and castigated the weak. Nothing could be done about it, and it was pure sentimentality to help the poor and the wicked, although a little charity here and there was all right, since even in this rational world there might be a flaw somewhere. Of course, only a temporary flaw that would be corrected automatically in the future.

The only trouble was that this rational world seemed to become emptier and emptier and that there was so much hatred against those who were doing their best for the benefit of all. Only if one kept going continuously, did these doubts not arise, but the triumphal parade then began to resemble a hurried flight. And out of it all emerged this feeling of being incapable to relax, of this maddening desire for the rest and sleep and peace which had disappeared into that other world. Was there more of it among the non-successful, the rejected and the hungry, or were they tormented by that same restlessness? Physically they did not have the advantages that we had, but their minds could not be like this eternal merry-go-round that threatened to revolve faster and faster until one, with a scream, tried to jump off it.

But there were no screams possible in this polite society, and the thought of the look upon the faces of the office staff or the children made me break out into perspiration.

It was about five years ago that I began to ask myself the question whether I could keep it up much longer. There were breakdowns here and there and people who suddenly retired or became very religious or even joined these movements to improve society radically. But what is there to improve about human nature when one really needs rest?

Then I also began to notice that I was afraid to retire. The rest and peace which I longed for were outside my reach, as if I was under a penalty that had made these goals for ever unattainable. The only realization which carried a certain measure of comfort was that perhaps this continued mechanical pace would wear me down automatically so that the moment of ultimate release would approach more rapidly if I only continued to operate under the same tensions.

Did I ever admit this thought to myself or only now while I am writing down these lines, awaiting the celebration that means another step on this road which has become increasingly burdensome?

Yet it could never have become a thought that formed itself into a goal, because the harness which hemmed me in did not permit deviations either to the left or to the right. It was as if I was riding in a car from which I could no longer descend, nor did I retain much control over its motion, except by certain operations which had become purely mechanical.

Perhaps I had become most aware of this since I had understood that my children were living in a totally different world. I knew that they despised me, as their mother did, but they could not have given any reason for it since I was an excellent provider and a thoughtful father. Their hatred was purely instinctive, because they lived in a world which had a high imaginative content while mine was cold and dismal and empty, containing only facts and figures and the credit in my bank balance. This was meaningless to them, although they wanted money as a means to escape the world in which I was living. They were striving for a rhythm that to them was practically within their grasp, but they never understood that I was desperately longing for this very same thing.

They did not want me as a comrade because by becoming that I would have lost the only quality that made me valuable to them, namely to provide them with the means to reach the world of their dreams.

I know that this sounds pathetic or even perhaps tragic. But I did not feel it that way. To me it was but another instance of the inescapability of the laws of Nature. I was carrying out the task that had been assigned to me, and that this task had cut me off from the possibility of communicating with my own family was really neither here nor there. Nature was cruel, and I saw this daily in the haggard and worn faces of the poor who tramped the streets with the same vacant stare that I felt in my own eyes. In them also there was no protest but even the dignity of those who carry a heavy burden, for which a rational explanation sounds like the words of a false friend.

In this same way I spoke with my children, carrying on polite and intellectual conversations or making nice plans for their vacations which they accepted with condescending tolerance.

Sometimes I took revenge on them and ridiculed their secluded world for its impractibility, but I really moved them only when I threatened to cut off their allowances. They had an aversion to society and its hierarchy of values, but I also knew that they were cowards who would never stand up for their convictions. Escape into an imagined world was the only thing that mattered to them, and they did not shrink from the idea that other people worked in factories or on farms so that they could spin their dreams upon a mountaintop.

Yet how could I reproach them when I myself had these same desires hidden somewhere deep within me? Nothing would have surprised them more than to learn this. I would merely have received a contemptuous look from their handsome but arrogant faces. I could never have become a member of their secret order which consisted of people who live only for their own emotions.

People who work can never hope to enter into these rare select cliques of the real connoisseurs of life. They are simply a later generation, destined to fade; but fading is what they really want to do.

How clever of Nature to let these people who live only for their individual benefit disappear, without causing so much as a surface ripple in the ocean that awaits a hurricane but is not concerned about the vapors that arise from it. Once they have gained additional weight they will return and run again through all these predetermined motions.

What puzzled me most was that this cycle, which was perhaps a natural one, seemed to move faster than it was supposed to. Was it to wear itself out in three or even two generations? Was it definite already that my children were to be failures or was there still a possibility that they might re-establish themselves upon a firmer footing? Perhaps some catastrophe was in the making which would bring this about naturally.

They considered themselves to belong to a higher social class than I did, but this belief was hardly founded upon a convincing reality, since their only function was going to be, as far as I could see it at the moment, to loan money against interest. That they would not even do themselves but they would entrust this task to a broker or a bank so that they would not be troubled with any of the unpleasant details of life. It would all be as I suspected their love lives to be: romantic on the surface but in reality quite irresponsible and even sordid and selfish.

Of course, I knew nothing about this, since they travelled a lot, but I could guess that the purpose of these travels was not an exclusively cultural one.

Had Nature in some secret fashion transmitted my hidden desires to them, or how was it all to be explained? I found no explanation, but I worried a great deal, and the thought was constantly on my mind.

Yet I did not hate them as they hated me. I loved them after my own fashion, but this fashion seemed to be quite inadequate, a reaching out in vain for something that must have escaped me many years before. Their hatred for me was caused by their feeling that I disapproved of them. And so I did; but it was not a voluntary action; it was something that came out of the whole constellation of my own life. I could not have been I and have approved of them at the same time. This they could not understand, but sometimes I thought that it would come to them many years later and make them feel badly.

The realization of this would inactivate them even more, since it would grow into a burden that would weigh on them as heavily later as mine was weighing on me now.

Did I really hope for some sort of a catastrophe? A hard lesson like a war that would make them wake up to what I deemed to be reality?

But this very reality had lost its convincing power even for me. It was merely an agglomeration of ideas and notions that existed by themselves like the signs on a shop that had stood empty for a long time. They creaked and moaned in the wind, with a certain weirdness that gave them a morbid attraction, and my mind continued to occupy itself with them.

Reality had become a philosophic problem that revolved for ever in my mind, although I began to notice that the emotional plus and minus signs seemed to follow a certain rhythm that alternated between being soothing and perturbing. In the soothing moments there was a certain acquiescence as if I were coming somehow closer to the world I was seeking and as if I could even regain the contact with those who were supposed to be dear to me.

In the last few years I could not fail to observe that my thoughts moved in circles and that no new ones were added to them. I absorbed the events of the day but they immediately fell into a pattern as if they had no longer the power to make me feel or think differently.

The thought of death, which perturbed me in my earlier years and caused sudden and violent fears, had almost disappeared or merely showed itself as the notion of a long and restful sleep that had even become desirable. It was very much like the autumn, full of sad beauty and more a transition to something else than anything that was final or a definite break in this rhythm of which I still retained a certain awareness.

But as I awoke to these wider dimensions, it began to occur to me that perhaps they could be re-introduced into our own lives. This quiet fire that gave a warming glow could be made to burn down all that which seemed so superfluous and ugly and perturbing. Underneath, it might even be carrying out this task, although I began to see more and more that it would have to break out into the open to be really effective. Once the flames would rise high, it would awaken these dormant, half-starved minds, insufficiently nourished by a sameness that was without power or force. A half-baked something that had not only been within me but that was really general and, because it was general, it would have to come to an end.

Was I to become a crusader then, a world-improver, a speechifyer? No, that could not be right because the hour was not ripe as the sounds would be like these nauseating speeches that I heard in political assemblies, repeating ad infinitum what had a grain of truth in it but the grain was so little that it all was like an advertising campaign. Use more soap and use more justice. All in one breath, as if there were no dimensions that had to stand out sharply in order to gain reality. But I began to see a structure that broke this equalitarian façade, of whose falseness I had become convinced although I could not have expressed what was wrong with it. It all sounded so nice and humane, so superior to my earlier arrogance and self-love that it had a ring of truth. Like not having any classes in a railroad car when we would be fleeing from a disaster. We would all of a sudden be brothers, and even my children would realize that I was their friend and they would smile at me and their faces would light up so that we would once more understand one another.

But what would happen, once the danger had passed? About this I fretted a great deal, and I did not succeed in getting a very clear picture. Maybe a little of the feeling that we are all human would remain, and perhaps we would build cars in which the first class was not so luxurious and there would not be the fourth class with signs 'Only for passengers carrying loads'.

But then afterwards? Was it not probable that people would forget again, or could we instill a dream in them that would preserve this warm feeling?

There was no answer when I looked at the drab and dismal streets of my native city, the rain pouring down upon the hurrying passers-by who looked harrassed and worried as always. True, a few houses were arising here and there that had an air of greater freedom and gave the feeling of a sense of space. Also true that perhaps there were fewer children in rags and with shoes into which the rain seeped through many holes.

Was it all a matter of percentages or did we really move forward, although at a pace imperceptible to the individual? Again I could not find the answer. There had been a lot of change during my lifetime, but it was as if it had not penetrated to the core of things, as if life moved underneath with a rhythm that was in reality eternal and repeated itself in majestic cycles of which we saw nothing but a short stretch of the hasty up-beat.

The up-beat was not the really important thing. It was a period of hurried growth that drove us along in a frenzy which caused the motion as well as that it made it possible. But beyond the cataracts, there was the quiet stream, invisible from below, and even the silence above was not audible through the din of the falls.

Of course, it was equally possible that this was all wishful thinking on my part and that the current was going to be faster and faster, finally breaking into a chasm in which we all would be smashed, prattling away about progress and prosperity.

Somehow this idea seemed unreal, as if it ran contrary to the steady downpour of the rain and the soft tatter against the window panes. In the puddles on the street there was this clear light that made them look as if they were bottomless, like the sea-eyes of the Carpathian mountains.

This all reassured me as if there could never be any question of any sudden or abrupt end. The ocean, the rain, the stars, the sky, the wind: they all spoke of eternity and rhythmic motion. I even gained this sense of permanence when I looked at the pathetic open-air market in the center of the street, the covers of the stalls, heavy with rain, flapping in the wind, and while I listened to the monotonous chant of the vendors to whom nobody seemed to listen. It had all been there before, I was almost certain of this, and many many lightyears away it would be there again. Once more I would be sitting in this little office with its simple wooden desk, in which the grain runs like trains going to distant lands, and there will be the little gas-stove with the bluish flames that have become so dear to me since they seem to be the only thing that is really alive and speaks of this world that I am trying to write about.

It is all very incongruous. These dreams that are not at all like the thoughts of a mildly successful businessman, but of course I can regard today as a sort of initial holiday. I am supposed to be reminiscensing on a day like this, but I should be different, more like a pillar of society. But a pillar supports, and I feel more as if I am being supported by those nameless masses who are not going to congratulate me on my birthday but who are more like a silent threat, giving me the feeling of being the prisoner of my own small success.

Perhaps it is this smallness that saves me. For the past five or fifteen years I have not gone beyond what I considered to be essential and necessary. I was no longer ambitious, and I did give away a great deal of money, more out of indifference than from a desire to be charitable. Even in my own eyes I have a few redeeming features, but they are few indeed. I no longer believe that I ever had any freedom of will, a freedom to think and ponder, to compare perhaps; but once things congealed into action, what was I but a particle that was being pulled to the left or the right, upward and downward? And after every deed my horizon widened so that I regretted many of my actions, but I could not really have possessed this wider horizon before.

Unless, and, of course, this "unless" remains the perturbing and puzzling factor. Unless I had not sold my soul in the beginning, but where was the source of a strength that I did not possess myself? Or was it this "getting and spending that lays waste our power" which has been my undoing?

Perhaps, at a much earlier date, I could have declared war on the whole of society, and today I would be one of those who tramp the streets. But I did not really have this possibility, because my whole background had predetermined me for the path that I actually took.

What is the use then of all these reflections? Is it that I merely want to reconsider things in order to obtain some sort of mental relaxation?

One writes and one talks but things remain pretty much as they were before. It is possible that I only torment myself with all these observations and that I would be much better off if I only looked forward to a happy celebration of my fiftieth birthday. Consciousness is but a punishment for those who lack faith and who too nervously glance at their lives, without seeing it in those dimensions that only devotion furnishes. On the other hand, it was plain common sense which informed me that I could not have led this kind of life, unless at the price of awareness.

And it was not only I who suffered from this. I could see it all around me. The desire to escape from tensions, the empty gestures and the vacant look. It was strange to reflect that it was as if we were all tired, an interrelationship that tied us all to the same chariot, at the price of the individuality which we had so highly valued.

The others, who had been less successful, and who had seemed so haggard and worn, appeared to be possessed of an unexpected vitality, a revival of spirit that made them sneer at us with a painful and convincing efficiency as if they tasted already the fruits of their future victory. How strange that we were to be defeated by this army of the worn and hopeless, whose eyes were looking in at our windows with this knowing glance. And yet they did not act as if these were our enemies but more as if they possessed a knowledge that was superior to ours because it was also capable of mercy.

Was this to be the future that we would have to talk to them and receive them as our equals? It would be like taking back, full of shame, a lover who had been rejected because her readiness to give had been too great.

And like the sudden fall of darkness, it came to me that perhaps this capacity for wordless giving was greater than the niggardly weighing of pro and con, the cautious postponement of today in order to be certain of tomorrow.

The same problem always repeated itself. Our marching orders were different, and there was no use to ponder about the fact that those who walked faster sometimes trampled upon the others. But if Nature wanted it this way, why was there this awareness, this weakening of fibre, and this slow torment which did not seem to lead to anything that was positive? Was there a hidden warning, or were we really supposed to convey these thoughts to others so that coming generations would not wear themselves to quite the same degree of morbid hopelessness?

Again I do not know the answer, and yet I hesitate to say that it is purely the cruelty of Nature. There is no cruelty in the rising of the sun, nor in the snow upon the mountains nor the sudden coming of a thunderstorm. Even the tempest across the frozen fields or the anguished cry of the trapped animal is full of a certain dignity, far from the frenzied actions of Man, unless also they are seen from a distance.

But this capacity to view life in this way must have a purpose. The animal is capable of joy or suffering, but it does not know that it is suffering. It merely feels it. We have this secondary reflection, this moving away from immediate reality as if it were without any importance.

Is this merely a mechanism to make us endure the present, even if it is without joy. But it is not without hope, because there are these images which have perhaps a twofold meaning: to lessen our conceit when all goes well and to make life bearable if it holds no rewards for the present.

Where does this put my pale reminiscences? They are perhaps merely vague memories, rising from the remnants of original emotions, to a gray-colored parade of distant thoughts which have lost their poignancy. Or they are perhaps the image of what I missed in life, an overbalancing of the negative because the positive — while it was there — was consumed at too great a speed, so that I was left with the emptiness of exhaustion.

The hours have gone by, and the streets are beginning to be deserted. There is no longer the soothing sound of the rain but merely a vague rustling of the wind. The dead things around me have gained a more intensive life, murmuring in their small voices to one another about events that took place so long ago and moved so slowly.

The blue flames of the gas-stove are beckoning me to leave so that there will be another day for them to look forward to.

I might as well set out for the journey which I have undertaken so many times. The short walk across the street, and then the streetcar which takes me home in fifteen minutes.

How dead these business streets look at night, more exhausted than a farm ever will. They speak of the same utter weariness, of the same failure of which I have become conscious today.

It is different with the buildings of centuries ago. In them there is still some dignity and vitality, as if they had preserved the spirit of the times of their origin. And it becomes better still when the streetcar reaches the canal that stretches to the outskirts of the city.

Here one can breathe a little better, although there is still this almost visible stillness, this lack of motion that is as disquieting as it is soothing.

The few passengers are all familiar to me. We have been riding this streetcar for years and know each other's names and businesses.

"Things are well?"

"Not too well but still what can one expect. The times are not so good any more".

And the voices trail off into the distance as if there is no need to repeat the thoughts that the others have too.

"But tomorrow ...", one of them remarks hesitantly.

I smile knowingly. And suddenly I feel some warmth that even among these strangers these signposts stand out so that we can all read them. The signpost to the past perhaps, to the things of which we know no longer how they really were. The things that fade into our dreams, and that suddenly may gain a different hue, brightened by a sudden emotion that spreads through the whole fabric of our thoughts.

"Yes, tomorrow", I say more brigthly. "It will be a great day. I have been blessed in my life beyond all expectation and far more than I deserved".

"It is good to be successful", the graying conductor remarks. "Good and soothing". This is where he is mistaken. All day I have felt the humiliation of success, its setting one apart from the others, and I know that they want to make me aware of my loneliness.

Suddenly I begin to long for the party, the noise, the shouting of voices. It will break through this circle of selfish thoughts and I will believe all the phrases of the speakers. I want to believe them: "successful businessman, humane employer, loyal husband, devoted father, the example of a progressive citizen ...".

Oh yes, I am all this, and I want to hear it again and again, to read it in the faces of my friends and of my children. Above all, in their faces. That is where my reward lies: the reward I have been waiting for all these years, with quiet desperation. If they would not fail me, then I shall gain this continuity that I so sadly need.

The streetcar has rounded the last corner, and for a moment I see already the quiet house. Here the silence seems less oppressive as if they are waiting for me, aware of my coming at just this moment.

This last block I want to stroll carefully and slowly, to feel the taste of my fate that has become neither bitter nor sweet.

I can see myself again now. A wanderer like millions and millions of others, even if they move only from factory to home, from home to factory.

In the sound of my own footsteps I can hear the footsteps of all those millions. They are catching up with me, perhaps ready to trample me down as I hear the sound come closer and closer and grow in volume until it reverberates like the blows of thousands of hammers.

But they pass me by. My virtues and my vices are too small for them, and they have not noticed me.

The quiet house lies before me. From the other side, the boy from the pastry shop approaches, carrying a large box.

"Good evening, sir", he remarks respectfully, and I nod in a friendly fashion as befits a successful citizen ...

## CHAPTER XVI

## BEGINNING OF A NEW CULTURE PERIOD [58]

The division of culture into periods has the one great advantage that it brings into focus clearly that our cultural patterns are determined in time as well as in space. Culture is not an absolute something that repeats itself for all peoples or native groups, although it possesses comparable structural qualities.

Some schools of contemporary anthropology tend toward the view that culture is ultimately based upon human needs and that these needs are a relative constant, so that cultural variety is to be explained in terms of a different relation between Man and his Environment. This so-called "functional school" seems to exaggerate in regard to the static elements of life, although this should probably be seen as a reaction against the strong dynamic bias of the evolutionary schools which developed over-simplified theories of stages which were supposed to occur in any social group in whatever environment it was living. A compromise between these two approaches would lie in the realization that changes in both factors, namely in Man as well is in his Environment, have to be taken into account in order to arrive at a satisfactory explanation of culture and its varying forms. It seems a rather simple point that, as Man can survive only under certain environmental conditions, the changes in the environment have to be less than the rate of his own organic growth. Consequently, Nature possesses a certain stability as compared to Man which has even led to the attempt to view Nature as subject to immutable laws, although the only observation we can really make is that the segment of Nature which is accessible to us is subject to less change than Man himself. If, for instance, the temperature on our earth would change radically, the survival of Man would become impossible; thus it is quite logical that, as long as Man is there to observe Nature, Nature cannot show any very radical changes. What happened before our presence and what may happen after our disappearance is purely a matter of probability calculations, based upon the regularities which Nature seems to possess, according to our limited capacities of observation.

To put it simply then: it seems justified to assume that the rate of change of the natural environment is lower than that of Man himself — Man viewed as an entity of organic life. Thus, in order to explain society, we shall have to give greater weight to the changes of Man and interhuman relations than we can attribute to his physical environment.

In this study, it has been attempted to view Man in his structural unity and to explain change from differing relationships between his basic attributes, while these attributes themselves are considered to be relative constants. These basic attributes are the energy forms of which the human organism is composed, while the processes of interchange of energy — and expenditure and receipt of energy from the outside — are partially reflected in and modified by the processes of the conscious mind. The mind itself seems to operate upon different levels and possibly in terms of different types of energy, although this point does not seem to be entirely clear at the present time. The structural law of the human organism would seem to consist of the cohesion which appears to control the interchange between the various energy forms and which constitutes the formal principle that makes Man different from other forms of life. But Man, of course, may also possess a form of energy which the other organic types lack. In the earlier parts of this study, some observations were made on this point, but they are purely of a speculative nature.

An attempt was made to show that we can distinguish definite cultural stages because the basic faculties of Man, in their interaction with the environment, develop differently, while a certain equilibrium is reached only in later periods when the organism has sufficiently matured. In the hedonistic period, the stress is upon the expansion of needs as the expression of a growing organism, and, as this expansion is only possible in terms of increased control over the natural and social environment, the development of the intellect becomes the crucial factor. This great importance of the intellect and of rational control leads to an overestimation of this faculty, which is considered to be capable of furnishing us with an accurate and reliable picture of the accessible part of the universe. On the other hand, the expansion of needs gradually leads to the formation of a group which is interested in consumption rather than production.

This attitude leads to a weakening of fibre, so that it becomes imperative to search for a new equilibrium in which the intellect plays a less dominant role, partly also because the late-hedonistic attitude and its need-expansion involves automatically a lessening of the control-function which, in turn, is dependent upon the intellect. In the new equilibrium, the symbolic function, activated by the suffering and neurotic disorders which result from the late-hedonistic pattern, becomes stronger. There is also an attempt to restore emotional life to more normal proportions through a revitalization of the "physical" part of the organism so that the emotional reactions are granted a realm of activity which is larger than under the early-hedonistic but smaller than under the late-hedonistic pattern. The intellect remains highly developed among experts as the continuity of culture, and its extension in size in regard to the number of its adherents makes a highly developed technology imperative, but it rates less as a social factor, although, since the two aspects are present in each individual, any general statement becomes hazardous.

There is less of "intellect purely for the sake of intellect" but, on the other hand, the increased socialization of the new equilibrium demands again an increase in social as well as technological control. In other words, the transition as seen over a long period is a minute one, a change in attitude that is in reality very subtle and that cannot be expressed in very definite terms unless at the cost of overstatement, although the focussing of our ideas needs a bringing out of certain aspects beyond their actual significance.

Consequently, the distinction of different cultural periods has a foundation in the reality of social life, but it also involves classification and as such the always partially arbitrary process of setting off one type more sharply against another than is actually possible. Yet there seem to be enough reasons to place the beginning of a new culture-pattern at about the time of the end of World War I, although cultural movements stretch over such long periods that one cannot hope to erect signposts with any great degree of accuracy.

Modern culture, however, differs sharply from that of the nineteenth century because it is more a culture of masses than of individuals. The leaders of the 19th century were bearers of definite cultural patterns whose full impact was limited to relatively small groups, but the modern leader has become a strategist who manipulates tremendous masses of people, with the advice of experts. Contemporary culture-patterns are definitely of a lower order than the preceding ones, as they seem much more concerned with the problems of direct survival than other periods were. On the other hand, the numerical basis of the leading world civilization has widened so that it could be argued that we are at the beginning of a new civilization which will only reach a higher cultural level at a much later date when the individual will begin to regain his liberty, which, to a varying degree, seems to be diminishing at the present time.

Early culture-periods are characterized by a small amount of individual liberty as the group is considered to be all important. We may be approaching a comparable state of affairs in which the individual has to be a conformist in order to secure his survival.

Again, however, we have the difficulty that a new civilizational type or pattern does not arise from a virgin soil, but that it is fastened to the past so that it presents only a certain analogy to earlier periods of comparable civilizational patterns. The ascetic pattern of India, for instance, has certain features in common with the ascetic attitudes of the Middle Ages so that they can be designated as belonging to comparable cultural stages, but much remains that has to be explained from specific conditions that belong exclusively to each individual case.

If we admit that the sequence of ascetic, hedonistic and neo-stoic stages is a permissible presupposition and acceptable classification, the problem arises that, while the neo-stoic pattern would be a late stage of European civilization, it would be an early one in the case of the United States and the U.S.S.R. If this assumption is correct, it would follow that the revival of the symbolic system would be more in terms of individual salvation in case of Europe, mixed individual and group symbolism in the case of the United States, and almost exclusively group symbolism in the case of the U.S.S.R. In the other hand, there would be pressure from America as well as the U.S.S.R. for increased group symbolism in Europe, since the extreme individualism of Western Europe, as a continuation of the late-hedonistic pattern, would be felt as a weakness by civilizations which themselves possess a much higher degree of cohesion. The degree of cohesion, obviously, determines the pressure as is quite evident from actual conditions.

It is of interest to note that these attempts to strengthen the group symbolic reaction in Western Europe has also led to a group symbolism that arises out of Western Europe's own strength, like the numerous regional economic unions, Council of Europe, Schuman Plan, European federationalists, etc.

Thus, we can observe a fascinating interplay of forces by which a new cultural pattern takes on a different function in the various dominant civilizations while there still is enough of a world society so that civilizational interaction produces a number of common features, although this is not immediately evident if matters are seen in terms of one of the contemporary civilizations. The common features are, however, not numerous.

In the first place, the complex technology of the modern superstates creates greater group-dependence of the individual than the more loosely organized hedonistic society produced. Secondly, modern means of mass communication also tend to increase this dependency by establishing a certain degree of mental uniformity. Thirdly, mass production requires mass consumption, so that it is no longer a feature of modern society to aim at low consumption and high prices. The interplay of production and consumption has lessened the possibility of gaining a relative freedom from society by choosing a simple form of life, because the intricate economic system hardly permits survival at a very low income level.

As a result of these factors, modern society is more highly integrated than that of the past.

How does this affect the individual?

In the late 19th century, the individual found himself in a society that was based upon the assumption of the independence of the individual. He thought of himself largely as a solitary unit whose major goal was to reach economic prosperity. The family was the only closely-knit social group in which the emotions of the individual were taken into consideration. For the rest, the individual of the 19th century was basically a lonesome creature, struggling for security in a supposedly rational world. And those who were capable of predominantly rational behavior did gain that security in a sufficiently large number of cases while the others fought a losing battle with increasing hopelessness. Obviously, the margin between high and low in this society was larger than in the present one, since the individual was driven to use his energy to the utmost, with no great social responsibility either asked or given. Control or lack of control was synonymous with good and bad, so that it appeared automatically as if virtue was rewarded and vice was punished.

This whole system was acceptable upon one basic assumption, namely that all individuals were equally capable of rational behavior, and that this depended upon their "free will". It is no revelation to remark that this assumption was entirely erroneous. In the first place, because it overlooked the structure of society, which limits the individual to developing only those mental and psychological reactions that are conform to his status and role in society. Consequently, if rationality is interpreted as a high degree of control, his class position will determine to a large extent how far he can reach this rationality as it differs from class to class.

In the hedonistic society, high control was required by the upper and upper middle class, involving a complex system of etiquette and manners, while the lowest groups in the social hierarchy lived in complete abandon under abominable conditions. Society felt little responsibility for this group because their suffering was considered to be self-inflicted.

It is obvious, however, that the pressures which the societal hierarchy exerted on them were such that — all other things being equal — they could not develop the responses that were considered rational by those who took a higher place in the social structure.

Secondly, the concept of the natural equality of Man is an ethical, philosophical, moral or political postulate, but it could never be determined by empirical science since we cannot observe individuals in an isolated position. Children, in order to survive, have to be placed within a social group, so that their reactions are always to some extent group-determined.

The idea of human equality is a concept which lessens tensions in dynamic periods when the position of the individual is fluid in the social structure. It is a symbolic concept that is the expression of a desire for high social mobility.

This again shows rather convincingly that symbolic concepts do not reflect "reality" and can never reflect it objectively because they are the expression of the frustrations and motive forces of Man.

The fact that modern culture seems to be much more devoid of symbols could be an indication that we are approaching a period, or have entered it already, of a much lower rate of change. Western civilization still retains much of the symbolism of the 19th century, but it has lost a great deal of its psychological impact. On the other hand, we have added symbols which show an increased sense of social responsibility, like New Deal, Fair Deal, Democracy, International Integration, etc.

They are indicative of the levelling off of social distance while they also represent an awareness of the structural aspect of society. We seek better distribution of income, not equality; we strive for full employment, but technical and professional qualifications become increasingly important; we still believe — although reluctantly and with reservations — in the principle of national sovereignty, but the United Nations makes a sharp division between major powers and the other nations; we think that education should be universal and democratic, but we create more and more institutions that strive for unusually high requirements.

Everywhere we see the same struggle: we retained much of the equalitarian symbolism of the 18th and 19th century as an indication that the dynamic element and the seeking of a new equilibrium still persist, but there is the new factor of a stronger awareness that any new form of society will have to conform to the structural laws that are basic to any society. It could be said that this would mean, politically, that the emerging culture forms tend toward conservatism or at least to higher integration in the form of numerous intermediary administrative links between, for instance, the citizen as employee and the citizen as employer.

The transition to a new culture form also reveals clearly that social growth does not consist of new institutions taking the place of old ones but of the grafting of the new upon the old, without a corresponding change in the symbolic system. In the modern Western states the executive branch of government has gained over the legislature, under the disguise of the "expertness" that is required for modern governmental functions, but we continue to assume that there has been no change in the basic attributes of our government and the fundamental separation of powers. The reason for this was perhaps that the lack of cohesion in the preceding society made an extension of government imperative, and this was considered to be feasible only via the executive branch of government, although other possibilities might have existed.

We can also observe a functionalization of modern society through the emergence of numerous powerful organizations like unions and professional groupings which break through the extreme individualism of the preceding period. Society is no longer seen as a conglomeration of independent individuals but as a structure of important power-groups which have a functional foundation. As long as these groups agree upon a compromise, modern society functions by finding a natural equilibrium, while it has become the function of government to maintain this rather precarious balance. This task is seen as a problem of planning, although some reflection shows that the foreseeable elements of social growth may have widened, due to our increased experience and better means of observation, but that the relation Man—Natural and Social Environment still rolls on as a sequence in time and space and is only revealed in each specific time-space unit. Consequently, planning can still take place only in terms of general principles for longer periods and large areas, while detailed planning could be effective in regard to short-term problems within smaller areas.

In this respect, modern society seems to be wasteful, and a great deal of the second form of planning is neglected, while it could be successful, in favor of the former. World-embracing general plans have become a part of our symbolic system and seem to fulfil more a ritual function than a practical one. Some of this can also be observed in the assemblies and committee meetings of contemporary international bodies in which one can detect a similarity to the chanted litanies of the priests of by-gone civilizations.

A counterforce is noticeable, however, in the trend toward regional integration where effective planning is far more feasible than upon a worldwide basis, where everything is measured against the not wholly applicable standards of contemporary American-Western European civilization, a continuation of the not too successful practices of the late 19th century.

The more pragmatistic American approach operates, however, with more flexible standards and has had a very favorable influence upon the more inelastic, although technically and socio-politically competent, European attitude.

It still remains probable that the most effective work can be done in areas which out of their own strength are entering upon a more dynamic stage and which need limited but purposeful aid, within the framework of their own capacities and whatever limited assistance might be available.

We can observe that the integration, which has taken place to a varying extent within the various nations, has not penetrated to a very perceptible degree in international society, which is seen more in terms of the symbolic concepts of the leading ideologies than in a practical fashion.

The problem of the structure of international society is carefully avoided, although it enters in disguise through the backdoor in the form of opportunistic distinctions of major powers, independent powers, semidependent and dependent powers, etc. None of these distinctions posesses a high degree of reality, but they are still used because international society remains the field of political forces which as yet await constructive channelling. If international society were also seen in terms of its actual functional structure, a workable world society would be quite feasible, since we have the necessary sociological, political, social and economic knowledge to give it the formal structure which corresponds to its functional foundation and to leave enough room for the dynamic forces of society. However, political tensions prevent this, and we still continue to create elaborate international organizations, involving considerable cost, as symbolic window-dressing.

This is all the more remarkable since it can be observed that the transitions which took place within the national societies are seeking to penetrate the regional and world societies, and those processes would undoubtedly run more smoothly if, by analogy, some degree of awareness would be reached of the direction which they are taking.

Until recently, integration within the national societies was feared because it involved a lessening of class distance. To those who were at the top of the social hierarchy this meant a catastrophe, because their own status was founded upon the building-up of special, complex and, frequently, highly artificial psychological reactions for which there would be less need in a more integrated world. As a result, they were convinced that the day of doom was at hand, but they overlooked the fact that it was merely their own private doom, which in no way coincided with that of the world.

In the same way, there are many who assume that greater integration of international society would lead to some indefinable disaster, and it is indeed not possible to see in what way such integration could occur in the present time. However, prior to World War II, regional integration of Western Europe would have been deemed an utter impossibility, but, a decade later, much has happend in that direction that was not foreseen and predicted by anybody.

It does seem, however, that it is generally a catastrophe of some kind which brings about social action. Without a challenge, desirable developments are reflected in the symbolic system, but actual movement toward these goals does not occur or only to a very small extent. Therefore, further integration of the Western world appears to depend upon the challenges which it has to undergo. If the communist world provides that challenge, integration would be a rational response. In absence of any pressure, however, there would be no sociological reason for any extensive developments. Since social life is more subconscious than conscious, it might even be possible to measure the challenge by the reaction, but such a procedure could also lead to dangerous pitfalls, since the conditions and culture stage of the social group in question constitute the other factors that determine the response to the challenge.

Social reality is just as evasive as reality in general, and we can only approach it to the extent that our thinking is rational, controlled and objective, and this is at best a question of "a little more and a little less". Since we are always ourselves actors in the play which we are trying to observe, near objectivity is possible only in relatively static periods or in the later cultural stages which show high intellectual development of small groups, with little or no mass participation.

Plato and Kant are an example of this. They both came at the end of a dynamic culture period which was by no means objective, but they had detached themselves from life because decline was already setting in. Consequently, they were capable of reaching a high degree of objectivity which took in all aspects of the preceding cultural pattern.

So far we have reached the conclusion that modern culture patterns are less individualistic, more integrated and more technological than the earlier ones. It should be asked what changes in mentality this involves and how this influences what is generally called "culture" in the narrower sense of the word.

The tensions of a society, as well as its social distance system, have a great influence upon the mental and cultural activities of its adherents. Tensions within a social group principally result under two conditions: in the first place, when there is pressure from the outside upon a social group, generally penetrating all layers of a society but transferred to the other groups by the upper class; secondly, when the society lacks coordination and integration so that automatically tensions arise in the form of pull and push forces.

The lack of coordination gives an aspect of irrationality to the society, while the absence of sufficient integration creates the psychological reaction of separateness and loneliness, leading to despair and morbidity. These elements were strongly present in the European society of the 19th century, which, in addition, showed strong signs of cultural fatigue, some of which have lasted into our present time.

There was a very sharp cleavage between the rationality of the accepted symbols and the way life was portrayed in the realistic and naturalistic novel as irrational, cruel, oppressive and wicked. The attempts at rationality of the leading groups were felt as an intricate system of studied wickedness by those who had no part in it and who saw it as a perverse persiflage of their own misery. The more the rationality and control were only a pretense, undermined increasingly by late-hedonistic styles of living, the more the conflict showed itself in its abysmal depth.

It was also the revolt of ugliness against the pretense of beauty, particularly in the magnificent French school of painting which succeeded in showing the deeper beauty of ugliness as compared with the conventional ideas of harmony or pulchritude. This lent a greater verisimilitude to their art than had been achieved before, and made it a part of the burning protest against the late-hedonistic pattern that ran from socialism to new forms of mysticism, reducing the defense to a growing awareness of their own shallowness and inadequacy. In art, the protest remained a pessimistic one, since it saw life in terms of its emotions and passions, and there was no reason to portray a shadowy world of weaker feelings to those who lived under the agony of their own intensity. The only way to escape the deadening pressure of this weight was to create a symbolic realm which was devoid of contents, a groping for a simplification of life that frequently carried itself to the extreme of purely abstract art. But there was, at least, the projection of a life of a lower emotional charge, a wishing for it as for the many things to come of whose real scope nobody was as yet aware, except those who portrayed it in terms of economic and political utopias.

To them, it never penetrated that their ideal world would lack the tensions which make the need to recreate reality an imperative one, in view of the distortions which are engineered by pressures of overwhelming magnitude. They did not foresee that art and science might be stripped of their strongest motive-force, of the urge to ward off the pall that a standardized and formal culture casts over the human spirit.

Art is an anguished search for reality, an expression of despair which only in creative periods can produce a certain harmony. Otherwise, its distortions are those of life itself, its striving for pure form a lack of emotions that engulf the individual because their very intensity prevents a solution.

Social distance is the other factor which increases the need for the symbolic function, either in the form of art or by means of a religious response. Since social distance is caused by lack of coordination and communication, it tends to reduce the psychic coordination of the individual, as he operates mostly in terms of one of the basic class- or caste reaction patterns. This, and even more the lack of communications, can cause an emotional vacuum which easily turns into anxiety, since the behavior of the leading groups appears to be incomprehensible and frequently whimsical.

This is quite noticeable in the periods when the lack of coordination is a salient feature, because the human mind itself cannot yet find proper coordination while its absence in society is a natural sequence of this.

In those periods, as, for instance, in Russia of the Czarist period, there is a deep emotional uncertainty in the masses of the people which expresses itself in the form of a devotional and mystic religion. On the other hand, the upsurge of these irrational feelings reaches into the higher classes, which respond to it by creating symbolic images of these tensions, perhaps as a means of warning the members of their caste who lack awareness and also as a way of establishing a minimum of communication via works of art. The social awareness of the great period of Russian literature — perhaps quite unequalled in the world — was certainly not accidental but arose from the conflict between a highly cultured but feudal upper class and the formless masses in which terrific emotional energy was hidden that could not be led into constructive rational channels. Russian literature vibrates with these tensions which gave it an emotional scale that could not be reached in cultures which had achieved a more rational form of life.

If one adds to this a vast and unexplored continent, the melancholy beauty of the landscape and the extreme changes between intro- and extravertness, there results a fabric of such variety and vividness of color that one can only marvel at it.

If we consider now that the emerging pattern of modern culture shows greater coordination and integration, as well as the modern means of mass communication, it is quite clear that we are heading for a culture of quite different dimensions, which is already visible although only through the growth of preceding culture forms. The fact that this culture could become a relatively more static one implies that the extreme emotional tensions are disappearing, unless it is assumed that this culture pattern would create again strong frustration. In that case, a more static period would be merely a stage to a new dynamic one so that we would not be really approaching any more permanent equilibrium.

This runs contrary, however, to the greater integration of modern civilization, which gives it a certain immobility that is tied closely to the desire for security of the average individual. There is also the factor that, while the national community has lost some of the freedom of motion of preceding decades, any free-floating energy can find an outlet by directing itself at the international community. If this were true, it would mean that high tensions would automatically result in the international sphere, but, apart from the friction between West and East, there is no proof of this, while one can point at increasing regional integration.

Consequently, it is permissible to conclude that modern Man may be on the road to a greater equilibrium than his predecessor; thus the lower rate of tensions would become an acceptable presupposition.

This would mean that while group-symbolism as a function of social cohesion might increase, the individualistic symbolic reaction in terms of salvation religion and artistic experience would tend to diminish. There are many indications that the art forms which presuppose strong emotional tensions are disappearing and are being replaced by art of lesser dimensions, in terms of achievements that are acceptable to the relatively rationalized masses.

Art as entertainment is gaining over art as a symbolic escape, and this deeper tendency is strengthened by the increasing organization of art, which makes it difficult to create outside the accepted channels of mass output. The movies, radio, mass concerts, book production — according to standardized types —, television, large housing projects, government buildings, etc. are all harnessed to the requirement of combining the artistic and the socially acceptable. The "revolutionary" art forms, resulting from the deepest frustrations of a social group, are left with a small field of operation, purely because the frustrations themselves are diminishing.

This would mean that art is becoming more and more a matter of technique and skill and less a matter of emotional expression, comparable perhaps to the cleavage between Roman and Greek art, where a somewhat related process took place if one regards Roman civilization as the later, extravert stage of a Hellenistic period of which Greek culture was the early period. Roman art, however, never reached the level of the Greeks, and one could argue that modern art cannot achieve the same as the great periods of Western Europe since the underlying emotional reservoir is being too rationally channeled.

In regard to science, we obtain a completely different picture.

If the coordination of modern society is increasing and social distance is diminishing, the pressure upon the individual is decreasing, but it is becoming all the more difficult for him to make his way through the various layers of society. The decrease of pressure would result in a reduction in very startling sudden inventions which probably require sustained long pressure on a still elastic mind, but the second factor would cause a continuation of technological innovation as a means of moving upward through the social hierarchy. The rate of inventions is directly correlated to the rate of change of a social group, in the same way as artistic production. Technological application of already existing abstract principles is fostered, however, by the integration of a society which enables more people to work on these problems and which holds out special rewards for success.

The integration of a society should tend to bring the social sciences into focus which are supposed to make contributions to these problems. Quite apart from their actual success, it should not be overlooked that science itself is a function of society. If interhuman relations become increasingly important — and this is a concomitant of integration and coordination, more jobs require qualifications in these fields, so that formal requirements are set up which tend to create college and university departments in those subjects.

The increasing importance of international relations to the United States has caused a tremendous augmentation in international relations departments, area studies, regional institutes, etc. in the various schools. This has made "international relations" into a "science", while the question is not brought to the fore whether it can meet the formal requirements that the older disciplines connect with the concept of a "science". To this it will attend later when it has become more firmly established so that it can reach the "theory-building stage".

One can show comparable developments for social anthropology, social psychology, sociology, economics and a number of the social sciences, especially those of a more recent vintage.

Sociology offers a convincing example. It started out, especially in the United States, because the opening up of a vast continent, the rapid growth of urban and rural communities, high social mobility, the mixture of many races and nationalities, created problems which were not met by any of the existing disciplines. The real impetus was given by society itself, but, since our society is competitive, a new science soon begins to look at its older brothers and makes the attempt to give itself the same formal structure of a body of theoretical knowledge. Whether this succeeds depends partially upon the position of science in general, and of the specific science in question, in the whole of the society. Our society is always willing to pay for the capacity to think logically — which is relatively rare —, but in a dynamic society the rewards for this capacity are much higher in the fields of action than in the field of contemplation. Next are these fields which are closely related to the active goals of the society, like the technical and medical sciences.

In cultures of an older type the contemplative life has a high social status but not in the dynamic stage of new civilizations.

As interhuman relations are increasing in importance, it is logical to assume that the social sciences will increase in importance and gain in status, even if one does not take into account that they still have a flavor of "culture", in the 19th century meaning of the word, although this flavor is rapidly diminishing. It is quite obvious, however, that their rewards are increasing rapidly as they entitle one to high government jobs, huge foundation grants, extensive travel, textbook writing, community analysis, and what not. As a consequence, there is a feverish search for a name which will appeal to the masses like: "Science of human relations", "Study of Man", etc., and the somewhat forbidding Greek and Latin names are being rapidly discarded, although, as soon as one opens one of these books, one finds oneself confronted with an intricate terminology as an indication of the professionalization of these fields. In fact, "word-invention" rates high, and, in that respect, the world does not seem to be changing very much: the Greeks started it and nobody has got over it since. But then, Man is a competitive animal.

## CHAPTER XVII

# REGIONAL CIVILIZATION IN RELATION TO NATIONAL CULTURES [59]

In the period of the emergence of national states, one finds also the gradual creation of the concept of nationalism and of national cultures. Especially in the second half of the 19th and the beginning of the 20th century, the individual was, above all, a Frenchman, an American, an Englishman or a German. He might also have been a Protestant or a Catholic, a rich man or a pauper, a socialist or a conservative, but, generally speaking, national allegiance came first, and, even if not all individuals felt that way, it was forced upon them in quite an effective manner by the will of the majority or, at least, a dominant minority.

The individual had no choice in the matter, since it was the general opinion that culture was a national product and a national concern. Even the class conflict was not strong enough to break the national culture patterns, with the exception of the U.S.S.R., where a class attitude became the creator of a national pattern, but even in that case it could be argued that the roles were rather rapidly reversed.

It has been stressed repeatedly and by many authors that nationalism and national culture were a rationalization-post-hoc: they occurred after the national state as a power-group had become solidified and had acquired the characteristics of permanency. After this process had taken place, it became inconceivable to think of culture except in national terms, although history points clearly to the fact that there is no necessary relation between national state and culture, as culture-formation is shown by all the social groups. But the average individual had been indoctrinated so effectively that this thought did not occur to him, although religion, socialism and numerous movements were worldwide rather than national, but they were always reshaped and recreated by the national cultures to such an extent that their supranational quality frequently became largely fictitious. Internationalism in art did not go beyond a polite interest in the achievements of other nations, although art, of course, had the real function of being part of the symbolic system of Western civilization as a whole and as such operated as a force against nationalism.

As national culture was the symbolic system of the national state, it does not have to be argued long that, as long as the national state was the most powerful social group, national culture was dominant.

When it approached a near breakdown in the late-hedonistic period, the non-national ideologies flourished and multiplied to an amazing extent, but the reconsolidation of the national state also saw their decline.

If culture is seen as belonging to the symbolic system of a social group, it is clear that all the concentric social circles have symbols and that they give the individual a choice and the possibility of a conflict in his loyalties. Consequently, a shift involves a shift in the efficacy of group symbols, and, conversely, the "weight" of a social group can be measured by the role that its symbols play in the society as a whole.

It has been argued that we are moving toward regional rather than national unity, even in the case of the two modern superstates, although to a lesser extent, than in that of the European countries. If this were true, we would have to expect a considerable increase in regional symbols, partially as the result of actual developments, partially in the form of wish projections. And what is even a more challenging question: we would also find a lessening of national symbols, except in the case of the two superstates, where international, regional and national symbols are superimposed upon each other and show a tendency to merge. In other words, in those cases we have national ideologies which operate with an assumption of universal validity. It is believed although rarely explained that the "American way of life" would be beneficial to all peoples, while the communists are never in doubt about the universality of the blessing which they can bestow.

It should be said, however, that in the U.S.A. the anthropologists are very vocal in their protest against the absurdity of such a claim and leave no stone unturned to show the "vita propria" of all cultures. But the story of ethnocentrism is an old one: the Jews regarded themselves as the chosen people; the Greeks, as well as the Romans, spoke of all others as "barbarians"; the Christians were certain of the inferiority of the unbelievers; the adherents of Western civilization only acknowledged their debt to the Mohammedan and Indian world at a late date, etc.

Ethnocentrism is a form of self-protection and only becomes slightly ridiculous when a larger social group begins to gain precedence. Today a Frenchman who believes only in the "grandeur de la France" is not much of a European; neither the English colonel Blimp nor the German who in his basement puts on his old military uniform and goosesteps around in order to impress his family. They are all tainted with the smell of mothballs, because a larger unit has already become sufficiently effective to make their purely national symbolism into a relic of the past, although it can become a part of tradition if it is really seen as belonging to the past and not as a projection into the future.

On the other hand, nothing seems harder than to create new symbols that really become effective. The U.N. flag does not make anybody's heart beat faster, because the idea it represents is remote and abstract and holds no appeal for the emotions of the average individual. It might be different to the soldier in Korea, but global allegiance is hardly within the nature of the present human being. Man is basically local unless he is nomadic, and the only way to create a more general allegiance is to force him into a less localized life via the pressure of a competitive system. If this force is absent, the crucial symbol of life is the home or the village or the town; only an artificial stimulus can give this feeling a national flavor but rarely or never a supranational one.

This factor is one of the great obstacles of European unity. The European is still a Frenchman or a Dutchman or a Norwegian, and one would have to hunt long for examples of "Europe-consciousness". Rationally people will give the expected answer, but emotionally they stay within a circumscribed orbit. Even the traveler of independent means who regards all of Europe as his home is not an example because he has lost old ties without acquiring new ones. He is not a part of any of the countries where he spends his time, and he knows that he is no more than a foreigner who might find some companions in comparable groups.

The social structure has its forbidding aspects: it really does not take in people who have no function and merely assigns them the role of "fringers". In this realm they dwell, having to create the illusion of "belonging" by a frantic emotional or social life that "fades, leaving not a rack behind".

Thus, it becomes the problem whether this would change if there were a regional functional structure. The answer should be in the affirmative because someone who spends a year for his company in Rome and the next one in Paris does not lose his sense of "belonging": the company is his "home".

But the difficulty is that there is not enough of an international or regional functional structure to create this type of generalized consciousness in enough people. The average worker, farmer, shopkeeper, artisan, professional, etc. does not move, and he even has an aversion which at times might be a form of jealousy for those who are more dynamic. One can observe this in any community: length of residence is a powerful factor in determining social position, and it ranks above wealth or functional status. In any community, the static forces out-weigh the dynamic ones, and there have to be many new communities, where this factor is absent, in order to overcompensate the trend toward conservatism. If there are groups of functional status but without per-manence, they form small groups like diplomats or U.N. people, but the local world intermingles with them only at the periphery. The fate of the returned colonial is a sad one: the social structure of the home-country has no definite place for him and he has to seek the company of those who are in similar circumstances.

If this thought is pursued consistently, we would arrive at the con-clusion that integration is not possible without economic unification, and this point is confirmed by the United States, which furnishes the only effective example of regional integration in recent history. In all other cases, like Europe of the present time, integration is fostered by external pressures, but as soon as the awareness of these diminishes, the unity seems to fade back to a much lower point and to stop at the level of possible economic integration, which is determined by local interest groups. There appears to be no possibility of overcoming this point, as every increase in prosperity, due to beginning integration, leads to higher prosperity in some sectors of the economy but tends to increase the resistance of other groups.

In other words, there is increasing resistance as the process progresses, so that the ultimate point that can be reached would be somewhere between complete independence and complete integration. But the latter is not possible under democratic political systems, since the resis-tance groups can use their political influence.

Consequently, there is no possibility of reaching a high degree of Euro-pean unification unless outer dangers can function as a motivating force, but even in that case unification would be only partial and sectional.

If these assumptions are correct, they must show their reflection in the symbolic system. Underlying strong integration trends would lead to spontaneous unification symbolism, but such symbols are most con-spicuously absent. There is no writing on walls of slogans like "Euro-peans, unite", there are no demonstrations, no leaflets that are passed from hand to hand. In fact, Europe does not give one the feeling that it wants to unite much beyond the mild degree that is represented in the formal international organizations like Atlantic Treaty, Schuman Plan, Council of Europe, and the numerous regional unions for re-duction of tariffs. Of those only the first two have achieved real inte-gration, but for the rest it is realized that economic unification should come first. This does not act as a motivating force, except where it is realized that it holds out specific awards for specific groups.

There are enough statements in political platforms, even "Yes"-answers in public opinion polls, if the question of unification comes up, but any real emotional enthusiasm is completely lacking.

The basic reason might be that Europe seeks security rather than adventure, and security and permanence take precedence even over a possible increase in the standard of living. If they can all be combined, so much the better, but, as soon as any doubt arises, the first two motives take precedence over the third one. It is also a strange but nevertheless observable fact that, as soon as a person becomes predominantly interested in security, he becomes relatively immune to an existing danger

The period preceding 1939 proved this very clearly: the forthcoming German bid for world power had been telegraphed a thousand times, but people in the democracies were blind to it. They were so bent on secure and normal living that these motives obscured their sense of reality, to such an extent that even clearly visible dangers were ignored or reacted to in a very limited extent.

In that case, for instance, reliable social science measurements could easily have given a convincing warning, but social science was too much a part of the total cultural pattern to fulfil its scientific role effectively. There should be an internationalized institute for the measurement of social tensions such as we have in meteorological institutes, but not within the framework of the present, largely political international agencies.

It is therefore not surprising that the U.S.A. has continuously pointed to the idea of aggression while the Europeans, unless prodded, shrug their shoulders. Their motivation is so different that the danger is not visible to them to the same extent, although, of course, we are basically dealing with a difference in degree and not an absolute one.

If the majority of the Europeans thought realistically and simply, it would be quite obvious to them that, apart from the actuality and intensity of possible aggression, the power-constellation has changed in such a way that common defense and an integrated economy are imperative.

In addition to the motive of economic security there is the factor of the inability to break through habitual thought-patterns which are no longer applicable to reality. In this respect, only an appeal to the large masses of the people, whose minds always remain somewhat elastic through the challenge of the problems of daily living, could be successful, since neither the middle, nor the upper classes seem to possess enough individuals who think concretely, or, if they do, they lack the capacity of creating a following. As a result, the unification of Europe progresses only slowly and in a piece-meal fashion.

An added complication lies in the situation of Germany, whose strongest motivation consists of the rise of Germany to a position of power to which the Germans feel that their functional achievements entitle them. This goal makes it desirable for them to integrate themselves with the West but they cannot forget the possibility of the much more important role that a united Germany could play, a development which could make them the leader of a relatively independent Europe that could follow an international policy of its own.

The slower the integration of Western Europe, the more hesistant the progress of its common defense, the more tempting it will become to Germany to direct its greater dynamic power at unification of East and West which could come about quite suddenly if the West loses belief in its own powers of integration. The relative unification of Western Europe makes it all the more desirable, however, for the Germans to wait, since the higher the degree of integration, the more important their future role, if one grants the assumption of their greater dynamic power.

This possibility explained to some extent the aloofness of England in relation to the continent as well as the wariness of France, which found greater attraction in the relative security of her own empire than in an uncertain function within a more unified Europe. As her own empire shows an unmistakable trend toward greater independence, the choice seems to lie between two negative possibilities or a clever combination of two negative aspects into one positive one. This the French have tried to do by attempting to draw her integrated parts into the European federation, but the rest of Europe turns a cold shoulder on these ideas which would raise many almost insurmountable problems.

The difficulty remains that, from the point of view of functional structure, the European countries reach beyond the confines of Europe, and a pooling of overseas ties is hardly feasible as the difference between the "have's" and the "have-not's" is much too great to make integration attractive to the first category.

Long-term thinking might make European integration the safest road, but it involves sacrifices, and the security-seeking spirit of Europe is hardly capable of giving future benefits of a political nature greater weight than the maintenance or increase of the present standard of living. Besides, the political system makes this quite impossible.

Recently, the difficulty of creating a united Europe has led to the idea of the Little Europe of the six Schuman countries, where common motivation might be within the realm of possibilities even though the present prospects are not too encouraging. It is clearly realized, especially in terms of the Netherlands proposals, that common motivation can only be brought about by economic unification. Thus, it is suggested that the six countries become a free trade area in which all tariff barriers would be abolished, although those toward the outside world would be maintained by the individual countries. This would involve some important changes in economic structure, and the problem again will be whether the European can face temporary losses and dislocations, even if they are cushioned by all sorts of governmental measures. A marked difference in standard of living might remain as this occurs within unified areas although to the detriment of some groups which would find the structural changes to their disadvantage.

Does this idea tempt the average Belgian, or Dutchman, German, Italian or Frenchman? Population movements of considerable size occur within Europe, as, for instance, the presence of several million Italians in France. But if a levelling-off of the standard of living occurs, the motivation for migration diminishes, the desire to remain in an accustomed place will again come to the fore. The young, the energetic, the adventurous would undoubtedly set out for the larger Europe so that an amount of cross-fertilization would be a natural sequence.

A European consciousness would gradually develop in a European Army so that we would ultimately get three strata: the Europeanized, the nationally-bound, the locals. If the Europeanized group would fulfil a number of vital and leading functions, they would ultimately amount to some 10—15 % of each population, roughly the percentage for the "leaders" in any social group.

The nationally-bound, as a sort of "European middle-class", would be about 25 % of the people while the rest, or 60 %, would remain local although "European consciousness" would be instilled from the top and via the processes of education.

The crucial point is whether the first group can be created out of a near vacuum and whether it can overcome the resistance of group II. The answer should be different for each country: the Netherlands has a strong international and commercial tradition and has automatically acquired an important role in all efforts toward economic unification; Germany has a strong dynamic element and would undoubtedly count on acquiring considerable weight; Italy, since World War II, has shown great impetus and is eager to acquire markets as well as an outlet for surplus labor; France is the "auctor intellectualis" of European unification but is hesitant about all its practical aspects; Belgium is not too certain that Germany and Holland might not gain too much weight in a unified area.

Big business, government, and internationalized artists and scientists are the forces working toward European unity, while the masses are in favor in theory, but doubtful in practice. The middle class thinks but without being vocal that, like by most modern trends, it will probably be squeezed a little more, while farming, if well organized, belongs to the big business category or to the middle class business type.

Since we live in a period in which the executive branch of government has gained in weight in relation to the legislature, it is clearly an issue in which power-groups will have to bring about the decision, and whether big business really welcomes unification is a big question-mark. Its structure is adjusted to the national pattern of Europe, and there is a great deal of friction between national subsidiaries, which would, in many cases, fear unification. The trend toward relative independence of partial social entities is also noticeable in big business, where the power of the main-office is certainly not increasing, in view of the growing realization that each "shop" is a social group with its own structure. As a consequence, unification of Europe would in reality lead to a sort of semi-governmental cartelization in which the weight of big organization would increase in relation to small independent businesses, although within themselves the big corporation would be partially decentralized.

This process is a natural sequence of the growing awareness of the laws of social structure, which give no longer the image of an equalitarian society in which the consumer is left to the mercy of those who can exploit him most adroitly. The idea of interrelatedness has diminished the realm of individual risk, also in terms of the consumer, but it has also limited the realm of free choice and the possibility of small, independent activity at the risk of the individual entrepreneur.

This change in constellation operates in the direction of the big corporation plus the governmental bureaucracy, so that it is quite likely that the trends toward unification will come to a certain amount of fruition. The opposing forces can wield political power only via the various parliaments, and the members of the latter cannot cope sufficiently with the "expert"-aspects of integration and their resistance generally weakens against the statistical presentations of the "planners". The latter are the witch-doctors of modern civilization, and their not so potent brews are nevertheless strong enough to unnerve the average individual, who has been indoctrinated to bow before "science". No one has the moral courage to stand up against the law of averages and to say "I couldn't care less", although the disappearance of individuality may be an indication of our search for a more static and permanent society where individuality would be as much out of place as in a well conducted orchestra. And why should we deplore it if the price of peace and stability is to be the unusual, the erratic, the brilliant and the unorthodox?

The simplification of life which seems to be in the making can perhaps be designed by the term "neo-stoicism", which implies that the human being concentrates on the business of living and does not worry too much about things which are outside his ken. It does not imply an absence of symbolism but a reduction of the dogmatic weight in symbolism, and, as a result, of its psychological impact. The energy-distribution within the organism does not leave too much room for the supply of energy to the symbolic reaction which most people want, in terms of general and rather vague ideas that make them feel a part of the whole life-process.

The building of greater social units is done with little participation of the symbolic mind, and, in fact, the unification of Little Europe lacks symbols almost completely. It is a predominantly rational and practical process, and the only symbolism involved is that it might prove a step on the road toward the integration of mankind as a whole.

This idea has a symbolic appeal and can be expressed via religious channels in which the brotherhood of Man has been indicated for a long time in a vague sort of manner. Mental hygiene and the psychiatric approach stress the importance of symbols as a means of gaining equilibrium, but the lack of concreteness of these symbols may prove to be one of the serious problems of modern culture.

The universality of the religious appeal of the Catholic as well as of the Protestant religions is an important factor but, since this appeal stops at the borders of Western civilization, regional trends develop which tend to correspond to religious divisions. If we talk about the Arab world, we think of Mohammedanism rather than of Arab racial unity, and it remains to be seen how far the world religions can adapt themselves to a changing technological structure.

Christianity has been rather successful in this process, but by a very gradual evolutionary process and upon the basis of the fortunate fact that the symbolic mind possesses a relative independence, so that inconsistency with empirical knowledge has not bothered the individual too much. This process will be far more difficult for the other world regions, where change is likely to occur at a more rapid pace, so that the conventional religions face a serious threat.

On the other hand, the social cohesion which religion furnishes is of the utmost importance, and a weakening of religious ties would threaten the needed integration whose technological foundation, on the other hand, cannot be easily adjusted to dogmatic religious beliefs.

Religion, as a cohesive force but with weakening dogmatic content, would be the solution toward which modern culture seems to be heading. Another possibility is the retention of dogma but a decrease in its psychological weight, an attitude which depends strongly upon the social and historical awareness of religious officials.

The modern mind, however, seems much less concerned about consistency than the rational patterns of the 19th century, which were sharply aware of the cleavage between faith and reason. The relative independence of the basic mental reactions appears to be higher in a period of more mature culture in which standardized stimuli cause standardized reactions, without this process being upset by excessively strong emotional impulses.

In other words, the basic trend towards a more harmonious culture pattern strengthens the independence of the basic social institutions, between which a working compromise seems to be sufficient to keep society in operation.

However, in regard to regional integration, the interrelation of the basic social institutions differs, because in the non-Western civilizations the function of the symbolic reaction is a far more important and intricate one. In this case, the importation of Western symbols is not always a wise process, because they appear as primitive and philosophically simplistic to the, in this respect, far more highly trained Eastern mind. The West appears as crude in its philosophy although skilled in its technology and technical knowledge, which are far sounder export commodities than Western middle-class symbols.

The inacceptability of these symbols for the Eastern mind may be a factor in causing an increase in cultural regionalism, since the blending of culture-forms with modern technology can be achieved only by the East itself, and Western propaganda suffers from its overly simplistic flavor.

For someone who is skilled in Hindu or Buddhist philosophy, talk about Western political democracy has hardly any significance. As a political system, it is as old as the world, and its blending with existing culture forms is a process that poses different problems in each case. By the drafting of Western political ideas on other cultures, much harm has been done, and it should be hoped that the idea of the fundamental structure of social groups will gradually cause a more adequate approach.

If we accept the viewpoint that regional unification can only be successful on the basis of functional integration, it would result that integration to a higher degree can only be expected, for the present time, in Europe. A certain grouping of nations around India and around China would be natural, but the process of unification inside these countries themselves is not as yet advanced enough to visualize them as a core around which other nations would range themselves automatically.

The crucial aspect of the new forms of culture which are emerging lies in Man himself. We can coordinate the technical and economic basis of our existence to a high degree, but can we coordinate the human being to any comparable extent? The answer seems to be a positive "No".

Everywhere we can observe that formal large-scale organization has not met with the expected success. In each large social entity, smaller informal groups have sprung up which ultimately become a factor that the larger social entity must recognize and give a certain amount of formal structure. In the large national communities, the idea of the separateness of the individual led to intense class struggles, so that social forms had to be devised which channeled this energy in a constructive fashion. The entire realm of formalized employee-employer relationships belongs to this category. But even within the factory itself, it became gradually clear that there was a marked social structure which is quite different from the formal hierarchy of super- and subordination. There are intermediary crystallization points of small groups, around ethnic or racial qualities which constitute a factor that cannot be ignored.

In the political realm, a comparable process took place. The relation of elector-electee proved entirely inadequate, and an intermediary structure emerged of political functionaries which operates in terms of the emotional expectations of small groups.

Everywhere the same phenomenon occurred. Also in the realm of education the relation of teacher-pupils had to be supported by intermediary forms which attempt to overcome the emotional separation of the pupil, who otherwise seeks compensation in small informal cliques which may undo the entire process of education.

Thus, the conclusion is warranted that emotionally Man cannot live in a general formalized structure but that his personal life demands small structured groups which then can be loosely coordinated into larger units, although on all intermediary levels the need re-occurs of having to bind the individual into a group which gives him a sense of "belonging". Sociological studies have brought out this problem very clearly, and they all point to the fact that modern technology needs a relatively well developed and coordinated individual who can no longer be manipulated with the techniques of a crude power-psychology.

If we try to run modern society by fear, we get individuals who are not of any great value in the complex machinery of modern society. A modern soldier is not someone who can be barked at by the drill-sergeant and learn discipline. He is an individual who needs a certain amount of judgment of his own in order to carry out a complex technical function. He is a collaborator more than someone who obeys blindly.

In this way, we seem to be heading toward a society which is based upon the awareness in each individual of the essentiality of a number of economic, technical and organizational functions so that he gains the relative independence which his own function gives him. This reduces the element of power, since the individual feels himself no longer isolated but as a member of a functional group which cannot be coerced but gives its cooperation upon the condition of receiving a reasonable share in the total products of the group. Products, in this connection, include also all the non-material things which have become a part of the life of a modern human being, like political rights, right to education, right to social participation, freedom of expression and freedom of thought. These "rights" are no longer seen as absolute but as "relative" rights, namely in relation to the life-task of the group as a whole.

Thus, the structure of our society is becoming increasingly complex, with the stress upon the relative independence of functional groups, which, in turn, depend upon satisfactory small group relationships.

While, in the nineteenth century, the total and general aspects of society seemed important (it was the period in which people dreamed of the perfect society) these ideas are now constantly losing in importance, compared to the imperative need of seeking a well-rounded existence within a relatively small group.

Even in social life, Society — with a capital S — is losing compared to the numerous groups and cliques in which the individual has to submerge in order to find professional and emotional security.

It is only as a part of this general trend that we see regional integration as more possible and more successful than the creation of a formalistic society which goes back to ideas of the 19th century.

The social structure is built from a foundation, and where this foundation of common interests is found lacking, — in turn the outcome of functional relationships — no sound or lasting edifice can arise. It is patient and painstaking labor, resulting out of the human emotions of nearness, likeness, and consideration that a working community arises. Blueprints may be necessary but, in a process of growth, reality never resembles the blueprint, because human life rests upon our ultimate drives and desires and our struggle for status and position and not upon anything that is entirely rational or that can be wholly planned. We may be able to understand whither we are going but we ourselves do not decide either the motion or the ultimate goal. We fulfil a task that Nature, within a gigantic scheme, has assigned to us.

## CHAPTER XVIII

## GLOBAL SOCIETY AND GLOBAL ORGANIZATION [60]

If one closes one's eyes and attempts to visualize our present world, one becomes aware of the extent to which modern Man is a group-animal. Wherever one thinks of roaming, there are people, governments, borders, passports, and even the mind can no longer rise to a vision of freedom. With a few possible exceptions, there is only relative freedom, and one can merely transfer oneself from one group to another; everywhere things are growing more similar, as in most places the world is becoming more populated, and integration results automatically.

This awareness, whether it is conscious or subconscious, limits the human mind and curbs its dreams, which no longer range into a universe of which we are beginning to lose our vision. Perhaps this process is a completely natural one: a change in the direction of our energy which leaves no room for the dreams that were no more than a reflection of the future. As this future has come near, the visions which heralded its coming are fading out, and nothing takes their place but the rhythm of ordered and regulated living.

Yet, there is justification for a certain nostalgia. As one may regret the passing of youth and the transition toward adult life, we might retain the feeling that our "progress" is not all gain.

The dimension "time" is losing in importance, and with it the sense of urgency and emotional tension is diminishing. These tensions brought a sharper awareness and a greater depth of thought than we are capable of now. Nature has become a stage-setting, instead of a part of our lives, to be enjoyed in a holiday mood but no longer offering us the escape which has become no more than a vague desire.

Yet the diminishing of social distance is as much a part of our time as the automobile or the radio, although it is an optical illusion that the decrease of social distance means the absense of structure. Our society is a structured one, but it is the awareness of this structure which is the changing factor.

When we strive for greater equality of cultures, we are merely seeking a new equilibrium which involves the integration of these cultures into a new pattern. The integration consists of a re-consideration of social distance in terms of functional differentiation, and the idea that these cultures or the individuals who adhere to them will become equal acts as the motivating force by magnifying the ultimate result beyond its actual proportions.

Once more, upon the stage of global society, we find a repetition of the processes which have occurred within the modern nations, with the one and basic distinction that ultimately there will be no territory left for the unchanneled forces of Man.

The class conflicts, the ideological controversies, the problem of integration versus freedom: they all occurred within the national states, and they now form the basic dichotomy of global society, with a number of intermediary shadings and stages that were less visible when the regions in which they occurred were regarded as a sort of outer territory of Western civilization that persisted against better judgment in the worshipping of outdated culture-forms.

In the formal organization of global society this structure is only partially expressed, because the United Nations is strongly under the influence of the symbolism of 19th century Western civilization, although it has moved toward the realization of structure compared to the League of Nations, which upheld the principle of political equalitarianism to a much higher degree.

Between the leading civilizations which express themselves in regionalism, we can observe the emergence of a structure that is not unlike the class-structure of the Western national states, because it has a comparable functional basis.

The free world of Western civilization sees this freedom largely as an economic one, since freedom of thought, religion and culture are the result of this economic freedom by which they are also limited. An artist who cannot find an economic basis for his work has only a fictitious freedom, which he cannot activate unless he finds support. The greater economic freedom of the West is largely due to its development as a modern industrial economy over a period of several centuries, whereby it has gained a position which the other world regions can only hope to approach by a far more concentrated effort. This need of concentration obviously means a limitation of individual freedom, and the eternal verbal ritual about freedom versus non-freedom has no more than a limited validity, although it mirrors a possibility of later integration when the functional distance will have diminished. In spite of all outer appearances to the contrary, there are indications that this process is taking place. The standard of living of the U.S.S.R. is far more comparable to that of the West than it was under the Czarist regime, and it is not clear how this process could have been achieved in so relatively short a time if Russia had not closed itself off from the Western world.

The situation is somewhat analogous to the relation between the capitalist entrepreneur and the managerial class, which led to a sort of "revolution" and ultimately to an adjustment within the framework of Western society. The change which took place was that the managerial class attempted to overcome the advantage of "condensed social effort" (capital) by more skilful and concentrated organization and by expert knowledge. The conflict ultimately resulted in a compromise which saw the reduction of power of the capital-owning group and an increase in influence of the managerial class.

Upon the surface, the conflict between the West and East seems to show a closer analogy to the class struggle that occurred within the Western nations, especially since the ideologies were borrowed from the upper middle class and the working class of these societies. But while the ideologies have, to some extent, been perpetuated, the functional relationship is a completely different one and resembles more that between a group which pitches capital and skill against a group which uses a more concentrated form of organization, comparable skill and less "frozen social effort" in the form of capital.

In other words, from the ideological or symbolic side, the cleavage in world society resembles the period of the class conflict in Western society more closely than from the functional side. This would mean that integration might be feasible if the symbolic system loses in weight, or — since the intensity of the symbolic system is the function of the cohesion of a society — if the West gains in cohesion while the East eases up. Such a development might be within the realm of possibilities if the level of consumer consumption would reach a comparable point in both societies so that a relaxation of inner controls would set in automatically in the Eastern world.

The functional relationships of world society are obscured by the interesting sociological fact — which can also be observed within the national societies — that the leading group attempts to impose its symbolic system upon the other groups, so that the symbolism of the society in its entirety is always weighted in the direction of the leading group. This group sets the patterns of thinking, creates the symbols and puts the organizational force of society behind them, while the symbols of other groups can never gain the same efficacy.

The same can be observed in international society. In the 19th century, nobody doubted that there was only one right way of thinking, namely that of the Western world, with its exact science foundation and its progressive political and economic ideas. It was only the "backwardness" of other culture groups which made them reluctant to accept the blessings which the West was ready to bestow upon them. Toynbee has pointed out very convincingly that the penetration of Western ideas into the other civilizations was relatively small and that culture borrowing took place mostly upon the technological level, while some lip service was being paid to Western political ideas which had, however, little bearing upon the actual power structure of those societies.

Many of these ideas still prevail, although we have become quite enlightened, compared to the nineteenth century, in regard to the value of the symbolic system of Western civilization. The European nations have learned this lesson in the hard school of experience when they saw their empires crumble, while the United States was frequently in doubt about the reality of its symbols in relation to its own society. *

Another factor which induces nations to view the problems of global society in the terms of their own symbolic system is a sort of inborn optimism, which might be a mechanism of self-defense or an ego-enlargement. If we speak about our own community, we generally talk in terms of a power structure, and the generalized symbols are used relatively little. But if we talk about a country thousands of miles away, we do not hesitate to say: "They are not ripe yet for a democratic system", although we take a skeptical attitude in regard to its function at home. As soon as we compare ourselves with other social groups, we magnify the merits of our own system, probably as a result of the competition among social groups.

This has even become an acknowledged social custom. If a man speaks poorly of his own country, he is deemed to lack taste, even if the factor of loyalty is not taken into consideration.

It remains the great difficulty that it is exceedingly difficult to obtain a clear picture of the functional structure of global society. A method which has been used is to multiply population by the available horsepower of the group, but it is an exceedingly crude method since it omits entirely the factor of group-cohesion. A nation with a high Man-horsepower ratio but an extreme class conflict occupies a much lower place in the functional structure than this ratio would indicate.

Another possibility is to take per capita income, but this method gives results of very doubtful value unless corrections are made for purchasing power. In the latter case, no clear picture is obtained either since the more complex the economy, the higher the price level, and an adjustment of income to purchasing power tends to obscure this factor.

It is clear, however, that global society gravitates towards the fields of high functional achievements and that global society changes only when the functional structure changes. As the global field has two focal points, the United States and the U.S.S.R., both these countries

---

* Especially in its literature.

are much concerned about keeping their functional strength at the highest possible level and at gaining support in areas of a high actual or potential functional capacity.

The trend has worked particularly in favor of Germany and Japan, whose capacity might change the balance of functional power.

On the other hand, all national groups tend toward self-determination, and an area like Western Europe, if it could gain unity, would have a strong motive to follow a policy of its own. The difficulty remains that while integration causes greater strength toward the outgroup, it weakens economic competition, so that the role of the lone wolf continues to hold a strong appeal. This role is only feasible, however, for relatively small nations, which are politically secure through integration in their area but attempt to keep aloof from far-reaching economic agreements as they see themselves as islands of a high standard of living. As integration tends to increase the standard of living, this policy could backfire in the end unless it is based upon very special economic attributes.

The aim of diminishing social distance in global society is a very interesting one, because it involves a great number of factors that are not too clearly realized. Western society has reached a culture-stage which assumes that organic equilibrium leads to mental equilibrium, but it overlooks that it is already an indication of beginning mental equilibrium that organic equilibrium is deemed to be a desirable goal.

The Middle Ages did not believe that physical health, regular work, etc. were of importance. On the contrary, they adhered to the idea that, if the body suffers, the spirit may triumph.

Again we see that Western civilization tacitly assumes that its ideas would be beneficial to all cultures. It overlooks the differing weight of the symbolic system in different cultural stages, and little success could be predicted for its efforts, were it not for the fact that social awareness in the world is increasing and that real changes are occurring upon the technological level. These are the really effective forms of change, and they furnish the measure for the possibility of cultural integration. Cultures tend to borrow the ideology that goes with their technological level, and, if, for instance, the West had attempted to bring China to a higher level of technical and economic development, it would not have been tempted to borrow the ideology and the methods of the originally "economically least-favored group". As the economic level remained low and no effective aid was given, it should be realized that the actual developments were normal and natural ones which have no bearing upon the idea of free choice, since Man's thinking is determined by his functional level in comparison to that of other social groups. At least, history seems to show a pretty high correlation between the thinking of a social group and its functional status.

A parallel to the conditions of global society is furnished by the relation of European nations to their present or former overseas territories and dependencies. In each case, the original arrival of the Europeans was followed by gradual economic changes which penetrated the native societies. In the 16th century, it was the East which had a higher standard of living than the West, but its social cohesion was so loose that it could not withstand the more aggressive policies of the Western nations. In that period, most of the culture-borrowing was done by the West, which had just entered upon the dynamic stage of its development.

Later on, the economic supremacy passed to the West, and it was only then that it began to attempt to impose its symbolic system upon the East. It is only now, after several centuries, that we begin to realize how futile most of these efforts were and how Eastern civilizations continued to follow their own patterns, which showed only very gradual changes under the impact of technological innovations. In the religious and artistic realm, the influence of the West is still weak, but Western political ideas spread if they begin to correspond to the economic stage that the countries in question have reached.

It was not Christianity which abolished the caste system in India but the development of modern industries and modern communications, rendering ancient social customs obsolete.

As the functional status of the native populations reached a higher level, they began to gain political awareness, just as the workers of the West had used their functional weight in order to gain political advantages. Society is a field of forces, and no social changes ever occur in a purely intellectual fashion.

People do not wake up to new ideas unless there have been already underlying changes of which these ideas can become the expression. Religious ideas, for instance, are accepted only under economic or political pressure and integrated into the symbolic system of the society in question, in which they gain a weight which differs completely from their original function in Western society. Many of these facts, of which social anthropologists and sociologists are fully aware, have been obscured by the reluctance of the average person to admit the only relative validity of his symbolic system. People tend to regard ideas in the symbolic realm as absolutes, because for many individuals conditional beliefs are a psychological impossibility. They have to possess absolute faith in their beliefs, and the idea that these beliefs are specific to the social group to which they belong is repellent to them.

Nevertheless, this realization is absolutely essential for the existence of a global society, since we can hardly expect the development of an extensive system of global symbols.

The growth of regional and global organizations is predominantly in the realm of rational behavior — in fact, they are based upon the rationalism of Western society — so that there is little room for the development of symbols, except some general ideas like the brotherhood of Man, the equality of nations, the four freedoms, etc., and all these concepts are aimed at a society in a highly dynamic stage, while one would be inclined to think that global society needs integration rather than a highly dynamic stage, which would undoubtedly lead to conflict.

But is world society dynamic compared to the national societies of the past?

We have seen revolutions and national uprisings in many parts of the world. In some cases, like that of Russia, they were the expression of strong functional changes; in others, they meant a loosening of political ties between East and West and even a, probably temporary, setback in the functional realm, since the newly gained political independence frequently lacks an adequate economic basis. The attempts at the creation of formal political democracies frequently leads to power societies which are oligarchies rather than democracies. To quote examples of this would be easy, but many instances will automatically come to the reader's mind.

In other words, the really effective increase of functional capacity has not been so widespread as one might assume, although Russia and India, and more recently China have made great strides, while Germany and Japan have regained a large part of their former power. On the other hand, certain areas in South East Asia, some South-Eastern and Middle European countries, parts of Africa, etc. may be falling behind, compared to their former capacity as a percentage of the total.

As a result, the West has lost in expansion, but it has gained again by integration, while the U.S.S.R. and its satellites show a high degree of forced integration. In the latter case, it is hardly possible to measure the actual degree of cohesion, although compulsory behavior may become habitual, as anyone who has been to school can easily recall.

Thus, from an overall viewpoint, the integration of global society has increased considerably since 1918, but it is no longer focussed exclusively on Western society. Western society regrets this bitterly and is quite vocal about it, though its own integration is due largely to the emergence of new centers of power, and no serious analyst of social affairs could maintain that this integration would have occurred without pressures.

One can only marvel at the infinite wisdom of Nature which, while people grumble, quietly goes about her task of creating larger and more effective social groups. Western society is still very much like the rich man who worries about the increasing prosperity of others despite the fact that his own position would be more endangered by an increase in poverty than by an increase in prosperity. If social distance grows beyond a certain point, it leads to a violent explosion, but there are still people who fail to see the interrelatedness of things and see their position as the outcome of individual achievement rather than as a status which is the function of a social system as a whole.

Nature alone is the creative force in human society, and Man follows the tune she calls, but his conceit frequently prevents him from recognizing this.

Western society then has lost some of its power, but this loss may easily prove to be the gain of global society. New regions can follow their own pattern of growth, and, as soon as a civilization reaches a certain point, THIS IS THE ONLY POSSIBLE WAY OF GROWING. Hence, the resistance to the symbols of the West. Not because these symbols are so bad; on the contrary, they are very good and not very different from those of other societies, but because new regional civilizations are emerging which have to insist on their right of self-determination.

Why lament that India is frequently lukewarm to the West? How could it grow to a strong civilization of its own if it had to operate with imported symbols, quite apart from the actual significance of these symbols, provided symbols have at all an actual significance.

It might be disconcerting to the West that China has chosen a road that is different from the one which Western paternalism envisaged. It cannot be overlooked that the right of self-determination is the characteristic of a civilization, as Toynbee so masterfully demonstrated, and that self-determination must include the right to choose the symbolic system that is or seems to be appropriate to a country's need. Upon the basis of international custom, the right of Yugoslavia to its own brand of communism is no longer disputed, but what is disputed is the right of countries to exert pressure on other nations.

This point has become a very complex one, since the sovereign national state cannot be regarded as the self-determining unit of global society with any great degree of conviction. The fiction is still maintained that countries enter supranational organizations of their own free will, measured by parliamentary consent, but, in the case of countries with a one-party system — be it a fascist or a communist one — this question becomes quite theoretical.

It could hardly be argued that a country with a one-party system cannot enter into international agreements because it cannot register consent. To do this is to attempt to force the acceptance of the political system of the West upon the entire world, while there are still Western nations where modern political democracy is functioning with significant limitations.

The idea that any group of citizens can form a political party has lost ground since — what could be termed — "the functional political parties" have gained such control that new political parties are practically impossible. If this is admitted to be the case, it becomes difficult to see why a multiple party-system is a better expression of the functional system than a one-party system with functional differentiation.

The political realm is no longer seen as the realm of "free choice" whereby the individual attempts to determine or improve his status via the political system. The "freedom" of the political system is limited by the interrelatedness of the functional system, and no political system of any society which wishes to survive can do without the basic functions of social life.

As the awareness of this relationship has penetrated the Western mind, it has become clear that political parties express the interests of functional groups, at least in contemporary society. As a consequence, their freedom has become a relative one, viz. to defend the interests of the members of their group insofar as these interests are consistent with the interests of other functional groups that are essential to the existence of the society as a whole.

A strictly controlled society does not even admit the relative freedom of these groups, although it has been argued in this study that the relative independence of the basic functional groups is an innate characteristic of our society, which cannot be changed by attempts at excessive centralized control. There are some indications that this centralized control is weakening somewhat in the communist countries, perhaps because it is not so effective as it is assumed to be.

The more it is realized that modern society has a functional basis, the more evident it becomes that "power", in terms of the excessive weight of one group or one nation, is giving way to compromise, the necessary result of the interrelatedness of the basic functional groups. Only those social groups can be regarded as independent which possess not the "cultural" but the "functional" right of self-determination, so that its decisions can be based upon sufficient strength to make them really effective. If this strength is absent, cultural independence does not give a social group enough status in global society to make it self-determining, although it may operate in a neutral sphere between the major powers. But the existence of such neutral spheres gives only a fictitious independence, and it would be hard to give any convincing examples of this.

If one regards sufficient functional strength as the prerequisite for self-determination, we have only two full-fledged civilizations: Western and Communist, with India, the Near East, China, and a unified Europe as regions which might grow to a relatively high degree of independence. Whether this development is likely to occur leads once more to an analogy with the former national societies and their civilizational groupings.

If it is admitted that global society is of necessity a structured one, the greatest strength can rest only in one group which embodies the leading functions of that society. If other groups had an equal amount of power, a global society could not emerge, because no social field develops among equal units. On the other hand, social development has very clearly shown the trend toward larger social groups, so that it would be an illogical assumption that global society could not develop to a higher degree of integration via the intermediary stage of stronger regional and civilizational unity in which we are living at present. If global society grows to this more complex form, it must show differentation rather than equality, although we could expect the same degree of relative functional interdependence that the leading national societies show.

Integration between West and East would probably be possible only via the road of extension of commerce, which, generally speaking, has been the initial stage of peaceful integration of relatively independent social groups. The other road would be via violent conflict, and the higher the degree of separation, the more likely this possibility, since purely formal contact through official international organizations may have modified war but it certainly has not prevented it in the past.

Communication on all levels is the first requirement for integration, but even that did not abolish, for instance, the European wars of the 19th and 20th century.

Again it is the element of compromise, based upon a functional division, which, as the novel factor of modern society, may prevent wars, by the realization that they are superfluous and would not affect a basic change in the functional structure of global society. Large-scale destruction would set human society back, but the relationship of raw materials — technologically effective population — functional strength could not be basically altered. Russian industries could not be effectively controlled from Washington, nor American industries from Moscow, if one wishes to put it very bluntly.

Whether the development toward global society takes place with or without violent conflict would not fundamentally change its course, as the wars of the past have been the expression of underlying changes but not the determining factor of history. In addition to this, the structure of our society has changed in such a way that violent conflict is no longer regarded as an effective way of settling disputes.

Within our national societies, violent conflict is definitely on the way out, since no party, for instance, in a labor conflict, can hope or even wish for a complete victory, which would upset our complex economic and social machinery to a much higher extent than the fruits of victory would warrant. It is important that the realization of this has spread among the people in general, so that it is on the way of becoming a part of our cultural pattern, even if it is to the detriment of those who pine for the days when people were more "real". The "red blood" of the past seems to be replaced by the gray of more complex neural reactions, and those who like the more vivid hue seem to be heading for bad days. But one cannot deplore the process of growing up, even if it leads to a certain paucity of emotions!

Of course, it means running considerably ahead of the present, to think now of a well-ordered world society and to express the fear that too much regularity and order may not fit human nature. But there are already millions of people who lead stable, normal lives, and they seem to be none the worse for it. Already Plato was concerned about the possibility of permanence, and he indicated that decay would some-day necessarily set in, even in the best regulated society. But this moment may be thousands and thousands of years away, since we may just be beginning to reach maturity; Man has lived only a short span of his total life.

In order to reach a permanent world society, it is essential that there should be a proper relationship between functional structure, formal organization and symbolic system. As the idea of equality works like a catalyst for social developments, it is worth asking whether formal world organizations should be more or less democratic. The United Nations has a democratic element in the General Assembly, but the Security Council is definitely oligarchic in nature. Even the designation "oligarchic" may be too strong, since it denotes a common ideological basis which is absent in the Security Council. Hence the requirement of unanimity, which has proved to be such a stumbling block to the United Nations as well as a condition of its continued existence.

Only if the functional structure of the world were more properly expressed in the Security Council, for instance, if the U.S.A., the U.S.S.R., the British Commonwealth, Western Europe, India and China were its members, would it be possible to have a vote by majority or by two-thirds of the members. At present, it is weighted so strongly in favor of Western civilization that it could not exist without the veto, which enables the non-Western members to assert the right to self-determination which — it should be said in all fairness and objectivity — they are entitled to possess.

Of course, a composition like the one mentioned above is more representative of the future than of the present, but formal organization should leave room for and be expressive of the principle of social growth, like the idea of equality in Western society.

The General Assembly is based upon this principle, but it functions mostly as a form of discussion without much actual power. There the principle of formal equality is at its proper place, because it enables smaller and medium nations to air their views, so that the Assembly works as a sounding board. The functional element is introduced by the Economic and Social Council and by the numerous letter agencies. It is noteworthy how strongly the functional outlook has penetrated the United Nations as compared with the League of Nations.

As the Security Council remains the main organ of the United Nations, a change in its composition as well as in its voting procedure would be the most important step toward making the United Nations a federation, with limited goals, of world regions, and this would be its most essential function, especially if it were placed upon a rigid legal basis.

The relation between informal functional structure and formal structure can never be a rigid one, in regard to the world of the present. It must leave room for development, and since future developments can be determined only in accordance with the laws of probability, the only justified observation seems to be that there is a trend toward regional integration which should find expression in the realm of formal organization. This leaves the question as to the function of the symbolic system but the more permanency a society develops the less the function of this reaction becomes, although it is one of the permanent attributes of Man.

Former China, as the example of a relatively static society, showed a highly intricate ethical system rather than preoccupation with metaphysics, and there is a comparable trend in modern Western society. Religion has become less other-wordly and ascetic, less individualistic, but more of a social force which deals with Man as a member of a group. Extreme psychological attitudes are no longer encouraged by the official churches, which strive for mental health and balance via the channels of the symbolic reaction.

The Church has also become a strong element in the trend toward the integration of small groups which do not find emotional satisfaction in the large, over-all social institutions of modern society. The small neighborhood church, dealing with the economic, social and personal problems of its adherents, is more a symbol of modern religion than the large cathedral, which operates upon the principle of mass appeal.

This may have given a class element to religion, but, on the other hand, it enables it to serve the more individual needs of its members. The civilizational bias of religion is still strong, but it is weakening through the influence of religious groups and sects which use Oriental elements and mental hygiene techniques.

A complete absence of strong civilizational elements would not be desirable, since the symbolic system needs content as well as form, and a formalized religion can appeal only to the mature members of the upper classes of a society. It is essential, however, that religious principles are regarded as civilizational rather than as absolute values, although there is enough uniformity in the world religions to leave a core of ideas and beliefs that the religiously inclined can regard as absolute, without becoming intolerant or bigoted.

A religious exchange program would be almost more valuable than the cultural exchange which is being so vigorously organized. Of course, the points that cultures or religion have in common are only the most general ones, while real art and real religion grow out of the life of a group and are perhaps more hindered by organization than they are aided by it.

Again it must be stressed that all which is "real" in life grows from the ground and belongs to those people who are most concerned with the vital problems of the group. All that is formal or conscious only touches the surface of the great forces that shape our lives.

Culture and religion cannot be made global by well-meaning programs. They will acquire a global aspect only when mankind as a whole has become aware of holding the basic values of life in common. Then, perhaps, will these values be translated into symbols that will stand out as guide posts. An art which in its simplicity appeals to everybody; a religion which speaks in a language that everybody can understand; a social science that is as aloof as pure mathematics from the bias and prejudice of daily life, and from the symbols of nations and civilizations.

# PART III

# REALITY AND SPECULATION

## CHAPTER XIX

## OUTLOOK FOR THE FUTURE

In all of us a little of the prophet is hidden, but also the desire to have certain ideas or beliefs about the future confirms to the spirit of the times. We no longer predict from the entrails of sacred animals but we try to derive comfort from what we can read out of statistical data. They tell us, in the first place, that mankind as a whole shows a high rate of increase, a lengthening span of life of the individual and a far greater economic power than the world has ever witnessed before. It is also true that the power to construct is matched by an equally strong power for destruction, but inventions in themselves have always been neutral. The use that is made of them can generally be destructive or constructive, depending upon a totally different set of factors.

The desire for a peaceful world seems to be quite general, but there is no unaninimity about the translation of this desire into organizational forms. It has been argued throughout this analysis that the underlying desires and drives of people are ultimately the motive forces of history, out of which — sooner or later — corresponding organizational forms emerge. Seen in this manner, this means that our desires are not yet strong enough to break through the national or civilizational patterns which dominate our thinking. It is in itself a tremendous advantage that we have progressed from national to civilizational thinking although not yet to a global outlook.

It has also been argued that it is more realistic to see social life in its structural forms than to interpret it in terms of general abstract ideas, which, if put into practice, immediately have to adjust themselves to totally different conditions so that semantic confusion is likely to result from overly simple ideas rather than clarification.

A realistic investigation of society shows us that the majority of the people are bound with their strongest interest to relatively small groups and that general ideas do not play much of a role in their lives. Those who deal with international matters within a given national society are a small group, and, if we are aiming for a peaceful world, the question arises whether there are people or groups of people who can feel and think in global terms, not as a matter of theory or as an oral behavior-form but as the expression of real concrete interests.

The answer to this question is that there are at present almost no such people, for the simple reason that there are no groups whose basic interests are or could be of a global nature. There are undoubtedly many individuals who have become civilizational rather than national in their outlook because a certain amount of common civilizational interests already exists in the economic, political, social and cultural realms. But there are but few comparable developments on a global scale, and the fact that many people probably believe privately that human beings are rather similar everywhere has no impact because it cannot be expressed in an effective manner, except perhaps by those small religious groups who want to be helpful to everybody for the sake of being helpful.

However, just as within the national states, small groups which had progressed beyond a national outlook could never prevent the upsurgings of nationalism, we cannot expect a peaceful global world, because there are a few groups and individuals who have freed themselves from their civilizational bias.

Social change mostly occurs when the underlying drives and desires of large groups of people become articulate in intellectual or spiritual leaders. These leaders, on the other hand, cannot formulate ideas unless they feel that a certain response is likely to occur. As long as the tensions between two *groups* or two individuals are high, there is no starting point for an effort at understanding unless the realization is present that understanding always involves a compromise, and a decrease in the power of complete self-determination. Thus, only if a lessening of power is acceptable to the parties concerned, a compromise becomes possible.

It is frequently assumed that the magic of "progress" makes it possible to compromise and yet to receive more. This is possible as long as increased integration is feasible, but there are limits to integration, and, from a certain point onward, compromise involves a sacrifice. We cannot build a united world by appealing to selfishness and on the basis of the shallow philosophy that the egotistic desires of the individual will be better served by cooperation than by direct satisfaction. This philosophy is a half-truth which has some validity under an expanding economy in regard to materialistic desires, but even in that case the individual has to sacrifice emotional and spiritual values. If we aim for stability, however, the half-truth becomes an untruth, and what is needed is the creation of a philosophy which shows life in its real proportions.

As a consequence, if the power-blocs of the world aim at preserving peace, they must be prepared to make sacrifices which might be of an economic or an ideological nature, but not by adhering to the misleading philosophy that cooperation will cause all sorts of additional advantages and lead to the millenium. Peace itself should be seen as the goal which is worth sacrifice and which needs no advertising in terms of uncertain additional benefits, like increase in the standard of living of all parties concerned. This would not be so in the initial stages, and there is little merit in trying to predict a more remote future.

If "competitive co-existence" is replaced by "peaceful co-existence", there might easily be an economic loss for certain groups and certain nations.

However, as historic forces gather momentum over a long period, it is more important to ask what seems probable in terms of long-term developments than to relate what seems almost within our grasp at the present moment.

The Western world has been highly dynamic for a period of three centuries but one of its off-shoots, the civilization of the U.S.S.R. has recently shown an even more rapid rate of social change, while China and India have undergone a "rebirth" by being able to direct their own development.

A compromise would involve a certain stabilization of the rate of change, which would mean that the social distance between the component parts would diminish, not only by an increase in the relative standard of living of the parts which have gained momentum but also by a relative decrease in the power of what is now commonly called the "Western world". Whether this is possible is basically a psychological problem in which the leaders of the Western world face an extremely intricate dilemma.

A reconsideration of Western philosophy seems almost imperative to this end as the dualism of Western thought seriously imperils the integrity of Western civilization. On the one hand, we have the continuation of metaphysical thinking in the religious groups without much direct bearing on the reality of Western life while, on the other hand, there exists the overly optimistic philosophy of progress which leads to vague and ill-founded concepts that are accepted at face-value.

Growth cannot be equated with progress because growth involves structural changes rather than equalization.

It has been the aim of this study to contrast these two basic concepts and to analyze how structural thinking could lead to a more realistic interpretation of Man's individual as well as of his social problems.

Structural thinking means a reconsideration of the attributes of the individual and a thorough examination of the question how an overall organic equilibrium can be reached as well as maintained in the successive stages of life.

Man is an equation between energy received and energy spent, but it is an equation which differs for each individual and, in regard to the individual, it should also express organic growth. Therefore, we must attempt to return to greater individualism without abandoning the advantages of an integrated economy, but, upon a sound economic basis, we should strive for as much cultural variety as possible.

Modern technology permits Man to plan for a reasonable standard of living, including a normal rate of increase, but if planning goes beyond this stage it tends to create false illusions. We cannot all be wealthy, and integration also means differentiation.

If a minimum standard of living can be achieved by organization, the rest of life could take care of itself under a relative great amount of freedom. If an individual wishes to go beyond the minimum, he can do so at the price of greater effort: if he wishes to satisfy emotional or spiritual desires rather than economic ones, he should be free to do so, as long as he makes his basic contribution, either in certain stages of his life or by average effort over a prolonged period.

What seems to be most urgently needed, in order to avoid the accumulation of tensions, is that as much free choice is given to the individual as is rationally possible. Cultural variety will grow by itself if the conditions for it are given.

Medicine, psychiatry and sociology can undoubtedly calculate what rate of tension could be considered "normal" for the individual, and, if the economists calculate the amount of goods needed, it is possible to determine the average effort and to adjust this effort to the rate of tension which would make continued normal living possible. In the ideal case, there could be an energy chart for each individual, listing basic energy-structure, energy-receipt and energy-expenditure, although much scientific work would need to be done to get a more accurate picture of energy-structure and energy-processes, on which some speculative remarks were made in this study.

Peace and a continued individual and social equilibrium seem to be within our grasp at the present time, but much hard work and good will is needed to make the possibility a reality. We live no longer in a world of vague illusions and a cruel and inhuman reality, but we still live in a world in which the possible and the real are far apart, and in this distance lies our greatest danger. The term "danger" is justified because the masses are growing increasingly aware of this reality, and what is needed most is that it is presented to them in sober and simple terms.

The masses neither want to be spoilt or coddled, nor treated more harshly than necessary, but what they want above all is to be treated honestly and to be told that the future does not consist of more pleasures for more people but that the laws of Nature create limits, within which human life must operate if it is to gain the permanence which we want for ourselves as well as for our children.

These limits are the same for all people, and within them there is enough room for growth, for change, for all possible ideologies, cultural patterns and individual idiosyncracies.

It is neither heaven nor hell which is within the reach of modern Man but a well-regulated livable world which offers fair rewards for fair efforts, and freedom for the price of moderate stoicism.

If the foundation of the future world is sought in the masses of the people, there is no special need for a world government, which is seen too much in the light of national governments but more for a renewal of a limited but valid legal system and a judicial body to which disputes are submitted because it is recognized that its findings are impartial and objective.

If the rights and duties of the individual under the dominant civilizational systems were defined, it might be found that the differences are less than if they are presented in the ideological terminology of these various civilizations. There are undoubtedly differences which would be consolidated in regional legal systems like Western law, Communist law, Mohammedan law, Chinese law and Indian law, and from these systems a common denominator could be culled in order to form the basis of a new type of international law, to be read from the cases of regional courts of which there are already some in existence.

Also in law, we find the same difference between individualistic-equalitarian and structural thinking, and it could be submitted that a reconsideration of the legal organization of global society in the light of structural factors is most urgently needed.

The legal system corresponds to the rate of social change, and if this rate is changing — as is being argued in this analysis — a new legal approach will needs emerge upon the basis of the rights and duties of the individual as interpreted in their structural function rather than by a positivistic law which is always a few steps behind reality.

Western law, especially in its continental form, is too much a product of a rationalism which is in contrast not only with modern science but also with the dictates of a society which seeks equilibrium.

Change is ignored by Western international law instead of being incorporated into it and of having its own specific legal expression. The power of the individual states is not a constant but a variable, and this fact is beginning to find a hesitant expression in some of the regional organizations but not in global society. Over a period of many years, very gradual changes are likely to occur which would stress functional interdependence rather than a fictitious equality which increases instead of diminishes social distance, as became evident within the Western nation states of the late nineteenth century.

The problem of "functional social distance" rather than of equality is the crucial one which the modern world has to solve and which can be reached only by a spreading of technological power. If nuclear power were no longer behind a veil of secrecy, each nation or group of nations would possess no more or less of it than corresponded to its actual power, and its use for the waging of war would almost automatically disappear, since wars arise from tensions caused by maladjustments for which there is no functional outlet. If the status in global society of the various nations were made to correspond to their functional power, the reason for friction would disappear.

We hesitate always between principles which express either a desire for dynamic or for static conditions but we overlook that a system — civilizational and legal — could be created which would allow for moderate change as a normal, legally regulated activity. At present, a premium is put on power possessed against power desired, and there is no international system which allows for normal change. It would be equally rational to regard the growing up of an individual as criminal as it is to assume that only a structure which aims at the perpetuation of the status quo is legal.

It would be too idealistic to expect these developments in regard to global society, but they are already taking place within regional groupings, and there seems to be the greatest, immediate possibility of functional integration. A basic common philosophy is needed for integration, and while we have regional philosophies, there is no global one as yet in sight, although it might emerge from a compromise between regional systems via an organization like the United Nations.

Perhaps it could be argued that the desire for *one* world-philosophy at the present time is still a form of a not overly subtle form of imperialism, and that the variety of philosophies or ideologies is a normal expression of cultural variety which does not preclude arrangements of a practical nature via a well-established legal system. Within mature societies, the individual can develop a philosophy of his own, but this fact does not prevent the regulation of the practical sides of his life by contracts which are adhered to from a normal feeling of give-and-take.

Within a social group, extreme behavior-forms are avoided because the group-structure creates habitual behavior-forms which make anti-social behavior in the long run almost impossible. Between the nations, a comparable development could occur if a general philosophy were developed which is based upon the right of self-determination of the dominant civilizations, with due respect for that same right in the case of others. Out of such a development, new social forms would arise by themselves while the theoretical blueprint used at present never translates itself into a tangible reality for the great masses of our world.

There is a need for a new international liberalism which wants to build freedom upon a solid economic foundation. It has been said that "Man must eat to live but not live to eat". In the same way, the economic basis of our life is essential but the economy is not the purpose of life. Its elevation to this status has created the dismal competition for power which is nothing but the extension of the competition of the so-called free individuals of the 19th century to highly organised super-states.

The fiction of freedom and equality rendered its service in the building of the modern economy at the cost of the suffering of many but it should be heard no more. The goal of a developed technology has been reached, and it could be made to render its service to all of mankind by making life livable but not by forcing the masses into a new slavery, defended by hysterical allusions to a fictitious prosperity or a meaningless equality.

Prosperity comes by itself if the idea of war is banned from the minds of people, as is proved quite convincingly by some countries. War is the eternal companion of the lust for power which cannot be controlled by laws or conventions, by treaties or assemblies, but only by creating an equilibrium in the individual as well as society which aims at a control of passions and desires.

What is really the meaning of power? We cannot rule over other people; we can only make them do certain things under a threat of death or under the promise of fictitious rewards which, in the long run, also lose their efficacy. This "power" might have been desirable or defendable when there were not enough goods for the survival of all men. If there are now — and we are assured by the economists of the truth of this assertion — power is no more than a nightmarish dream of the past, an obsession resulting from the slavery of bygone ages from which our habitual thought-patterns cannot yet free themselves.

Perhaps this is the deeper reason why Nature shows us now with frightening clarity that the desire for power and death go hand in hand. The death that modern technology has created does not doom some of us but all of us. Therefore it is also up to all of us to decide that we want to live in peace by respecting our fellow-creatures so much that we no longer want to deny them the same rights which we desire for ourselves.

The individual is at the root of all things, and it is the individual who can create a world in which we can all live with a reasonable amount of satisfaction if we expect no more than life has to offer: our daily bread, some dreams, some play, and some companionship.

# BIBLIOGRAPHICAL NOTES

CHAPTER I

1.  Cp. Lerner, Daniel, and Harold D. Lasswell (editors), *The policy sciences*. Stanford, Cal. 1951.
2.  This problem is investigated by sociology of knowledge and by the much older discipline of epistemology. The literature on the latter topic is too vast for any satisfactory mention in a footnote. On sociology of knowledge, we refer to Scheler, Max, *Die Wissensformen und die Gesellschaft. Probleme einer Sociologie des Wissens*. Leipzig (Der Neue Geist Verlag) 1926, and the chapter on Sociology of Knowledge in: Barnes, Harry Elmer, and Howard Becker, *Contemporary Social Theory*. New York 1940.
For more recent publications, bibliographical data can be found in *Current Sociology*, 1-4. Paris (UNESCO).
3.  Cp. Mannheim, Carl, *Ideology and Utopia*. 5th impression, London 1949; *Man and society in an age of reconstruction*. London 1951.
4.  The idea of structure prevailed strongly in Greek social thought as well as in the thinking of the Middle Ages. It then was expressed again in German Romanticism and in a great number of collectivistic theories. In an empirical version it seems to becoming to the fore in some branches of American sociology: cp. on this recent development: Merton, R. K., *Social theory and Social structure*. Glencoe, Ill. 1949; Murdock, G. P., *Social structure*. New York 1949; Parsons, Talcott, *Essays in sociological theory pure and applied*. Glencoe, Ill. 1949; The professions and social structure, in *Social Forces*, Vol. XVII, May 1939, p. 457-467; *The structure of Social Action*. Glencoe, III. 1949; Warner, W. Lloyd, *Structure of American Life*. Edinburgh 1952; Levy, I. Marion, *The structure of society*. Princeton 1952.
The concept of structure implies functional interrelatedness. Cp. p. 50-58 in Levy, I. Marion, *The structure of society*. Princeton 1952.
5.  The problem of "determinism" in relation to human action has emerged in innumerable forms. In early civilizational patterns the "idea" is frequently regarded as the determining factor in human life; in religious systems it is generally the deity although opposing forces occur in various forms. On the other side, we find numerous theories about economic, political, geographic, linguistic and social factors as being the decisive ones while modern social anthropology tends to find the explanation for human action in the human need-structure of the group, rather than of the individual.
Cp. on metaphysical theories: Freeman, Kathleen, *God, Men and State. Greek concepts*. London 1952; Hobhouse, L. T., *Social Evolution and Political theory*. New York 1918; McKeon, R. P., *The philosophy of Aristotle*. Chicago 1940; Ritter, C., *The essence of Plato's philosophy*. Translated by A. Allen. New York 1940; Stewart, I. A., *Plato's doctrine of ideas*. Oxford 1909. On the religious factor: Taylor, Henry Osborn, *The mediaeval mind. A history of the development of thought and emotion in the Middle Ages*. London 1911; Funck-Brentano, Frantz, *La société au Moyen-Age*. Paris 1937; Gilson, Etienne, *The spirit of mediaeval philosophy*. New York 1936; Hearnshaw, F. J. C., *The social and political ideas of some great mediaeval thinkers*. London [1928]; Power, Eileen, *Mediaeval people*. London 1946; Hobhouse, Walter, *The church and the world in idea and in history*. London 1916.
Economic, political, geographic, linguistic and social factors are dealt with in: Sorokin, Pitirim O., *Social and cultural dynamics*. New York 1937; Sumner, William Graham, and Albert Galloway Keller, *The science of society*. New Haven 1927. 4 vols; Barnes, Harry Elmer, *Introduction to the History of Sociology*. Chicago [1948]; Barth, Paul, *Die Philosophie der Geschichte als Soziologie*. I, 4. Auflage. Leipzig 1922; and numerous other general treatises on social thought.
In contemporary social anthropology great stress has been placed by Malinowski

on the need-structure as a determining factor. Cp. Malinowski, B., *The dynamics of culture change*. New Haven and London 1946; Chapple, E. D., and C. S. Coon, *Principles of anthropology*. New York 1942; Linton, R., *The study of Man*. New York 1936; F. Boas et al., *General anthropology*. Boston, etc. 1938; Goldenweiser, A. A., *History, Psychology and Culture*. New York 1933; Thurnwald, R. C., *Die menschliche Gesellschaft in ihren ethnosoziologischen Grundlagen*. Berlin 1932.

6. Cp. Toynbee, Arnold I, *A study of history*. Oxford 1934—39. 6 vols.

7. Cp. Thomas, W. I., *Primitive behavior*. New York 1937; Mauss, Marcel, *Manuel d'ethnographie*. Paris 1947; Murdock, G. P., *Our primitive contemporaries*. New York 1934; Lowie, R. H., *Primitive society*. New York 1920; Bernard, L. L., *Instinct*, New York 1924; and numerous anthropological case-studies.

8. Cp. Landheer, B., *Der Staats- und Gesellschaftsbegriff Platons*. Rotterdam 1926; Wild, John, *Plato's theory of Men. An introduction to the realistic philosophy of culture*. Cambridge, Mass. 1946; Taylor, A. E. *Plato and his work*. London 1948.
Plato gives a social typology, according to a certain basic differentiation but he explains this in *The Republic* in a mythological rather than in an exact science manner.

9. Apart from social anthropology, biology and social psychology have dealt with the organic bases of Man's behavior. Cp. Kluckhohn, Clyde, and Henry A. Murray, *Personality in nature, society and culture*. London 1953; Sapir, Edward, *Selected writings in language, culture and personality*. Berkeley 1948; Cooley, C. H., *Human nature and the social order*. 1902; Mead, George H., *Mind, Self and Society*. Chicago-Cambridge 1934; Young, Kimball, *A handbook of social psychology*. London 1946; Cannon, W. B., *Wisdom of the body*. New York 1939; Dorsey, J. M., *The foundations of human nature*. London 1935; Jennings, H. S., *The biological basis of human nature*. London 1930; Murphy, G., L. B. Murphy and T. Newcomb, *Experimental social psychology*. New York 1937.

10. This suggestion is offered as a speculative one, as there seems to be no evidence at present in its support in biology or related sciences. Cp. Carr-Saunders, A. M., *The biological basis of human nature*. L. T. Hobhouse Memorial Trust Lecture, London 1942; Hogben, L., *Nature and Nurture*. London 1939; Schwesinger, G. C., *Heredity and Environment*. New York 1933; Bauer, E., F. Fischer and F. Lenz, *Human heredity*. London 1931.

11. An attempt to relate social processes to neural ones was made by Alfred Korzybski in his *Science and Sanity. An introduction to Non-Aristotelian systems and general semantics*, second edition. New York 1941. Cp. also Lins, Mario, *Integration of theory and research in sociology*. Paper presented at the First Brazilian Congress of Sociology, Sâo Paulo, June 21-27, 1954. From the point of view of social psychiatry a number of contributions have been made. Cp., for instance, Bain, Read, Sociopathy and world organization, in *American Sociological Review*, Volume 9, April 1944, p. 127-138; Frank, Lawrence M., *Society as the Patient*. New Brunswick, N.J. 1948; Bricker, George, *Is Germany curable*. New York 1944; and numerous publications in the field of social pathology. In a way one could also refer to Malthus, T. S., *Essays on the principles of population as it affects the future improvement of society*. New York 1927. 2 vols.

12. Cp. Giddings, F. H., *The principles of sociology*. New York 1896; Abel, Theodore, The significance of the concept of consciousness of kind, in *Social Forces*, Vol. IX, 1930, p. 1-10.

13. The concept of the "most effective social group" was used by the author in: Sociology of War; p. 598-616 in Caldwell, Morris G., and Laurence Foster, *Analysis of Social Problems*. Harrisburg, Pa. 1954.

14. Reference is made to the sociological investigations which have concentrated on the relation between frustration and aggression. Cp. Murphy, G., L. B. Murphy and T. M. Newcomb, *Experimental social psychology*. New York 1937; Dollard, John, et al., *Frustration and Aggression*. London [1944]; Pavlov, I. P., *Lectures on conditioned reflexes*. Translated by W. H. Gantt. London 1929; Chapter V in Ogburn, William F.,

and Meyer F. Nimkoff, *A handbook of sociology,* 2nd edition. London 1950.

15. Cp. on sociological analysis of small groups: Bales, Robert F., *Interaction Process Analysis: a method for the study of small groups.* Cambridge, Mass.; Lewin, Kurt, *The conceptual representation and measurement of psychological forces.* Durham, N. C. 1938.

16. Cp. *Intern. Conciliation,* March 1955 (no. 521: Higgins, Benjamin, and Wilfred Molenbaum, *Financing economic development*).

17. An excellent analysis of these problems is given in: Lazarsfeld, Paul F. (editor), *Mathematical thinking in the social sciences.* Glencoe, Ill. 1954 Cp. particularly Chapter IV.: Marschak, Jakob, *Probability in the Social Sciences.* It stresses the utility function of decisions upon the basis of past experience. "Especially in social science there has been a temptation to use statistical tools for laborious rediscovery of the trivial, or the recording of the useless. One should not brush away as "utilitarian" or "pragmatic" the reminder that we ought to help in the making of socially important decisions." (p. 215, o.c.)

18. The old controversy between the exact and the social sciences seems to have lost some of its poignancy by the observation that the difference is a relative rather than an absolute one and that it can be regarded as a function of the rate of change of observer and observed phenomenon in a system of mutual dependency.

CHAPTER II

19. Cp. Scheler, Max, *Die Wissensformen und die Gesellschaft.* Leipzig 1926; *Versuche zu einer Sociologie des Wissens.* München 1924; *Die Stellung des Menschen im Kosmos.* Darmstadt 1928; *Zur Sociologie und Weltanschauungslehre.* Leipzig 1922, 4 vols. *Wesen und Formen der Sympathie.* 2. Auflage. Bonn 1923. Reference here is more specifically to *Die Stellung des Menschen im Kosmos* which contains his "philosophic anthropology" and relates to the problems dealt with in this chapter.

20. A philosophy of "social stages" was developed by Plato and Aristotle, in regard to history by Polybius and Ibn-Khaldun; more philosophically by Vico, Heger and Comte, to some extent also by the "theory of progress" of Turgot, Condorcet and other French rationalists.

21. Cp. p. 18-23 in Scheler, *Die Stellung des Menschen im Kosmos.*

22. Bauch, Bruno, *Das Substanzproblem in der griechischen Philosophie.* Heidelberg 1910; Hartmann, Nicolai, *Platos Logik des Seins.* Giessen 1909; Robin, L., *La théorie platonicienne des idées et des nombres d'après Aristote.* Paris 1908; Stenzel, J., *Zahl und Gestalt bei Platon und Aristoteles.* Leipzig und Berlin 1924; Susemihl, F., *Die genetische Entwicklung der platonischen Philosophie.* Leipzig 1855.

23. Cp. Schneider, Herbert, *Religion in various cultures.* New York 1932.

24. These observations are made purely as deductions from the field of social observation. Whether they have any value from the point of view of neurology could not be ascertained as this field is too complex for additional study.

25. In the period of Rationalism, this view was presented in terms of Deistic theories. Cp. Lecky, W. E. H., *History of rationalism in Europe.* London 1869, 2 vols; Leland, J.,*A view of the principal deistical writers.* London 1764, 2 vols; Fabre, J., *Les pères de la Révolution.* Paris 1910; M'Giffert, A. C., *Protestant thought before Kant.* New York 1911.

26. Cp. Beekmann, I., *A history of inventions.* London 1846; Hobhouse, L. T., G. C. Wheeler and M. Ginsberg, *Material culture and social institutions of the simpler peoples.* London 1930; Mumford, L., *Technics and civilisation.* London 1934; Walles, G., *Our social heritage.* London 1921; Wissler, C., *Man and culture.* New York 1928.

27. Cp. The section on Buddhism in Schneider, Herbert W., *Religion in various cultures.* New York 1932.

28. This point was brought out first in the writings of Benjamin Kidd and Hobhouse. Cp. Kidd, Benjamin, *Social evolution.* New York 1920, and *Principles of*

*Western civilization.* New York 1902; also Hobhouse, E. T., *Mind in evolution.* London 1913, 2 vols; *Morals in evolution,* London 1915, 2 vols; *The metaphysical theory of the state.* London 1918; Carter, Hugh, *The social theories of L. T. Hobhouse.* Chapel Hill, N.C. 1927.

29.  Cp. Weber, Max, *Gesammelte Aufsätze zur Religionssociologie.* Tübingen 1922-23 (3 vols), Vol. I, part I. transl. by T. Parsons as *The Protestant Ethic and the spirit of Capitalism.* London 1931; Abel, T. F., *Systematic Sociology in Germany.* New York 1929; Salomon, Albert, Max Weber's methodology, in: *Social Research,* Vol. I, 1934, p. 147-168.

30.  Cp. Scheler, Max, *Die Stellung des Menschen im Kosmos,* p. 46: "Das, was den Menschen zum Menschen macht, ist in allem Leben überhaupt entgegengesetztes Prinzip, das man als solches überhaupt nicht auf die "natürliche Lebensevolution" zurückführen kann, sondern das nur auf den obersten Grund der Dinge selbst zurückfällt — auf denselben Grund also, dessen Teil-Manifestation auch das "Leben" ist."

31.  Cp. Harrison, Jane, *Prolegomena to the study of Greek religion.* Cambridge 1908, and her work: *The religion of ancient Greece.* London 1915.

32.  Cp. Caird, Edward, *The evolution of theology in the Greek philosophers.* Glasgow 1904, 2 vols; Freeman, Kathleen, *God, Man and State. Greek Concepts.* London 1952; Stenzel, J., *Zahl und Gestalt bei Platon und Aristoteles.* Leipzig und Berlin 1924; Natorp, P., *Platons Ideeenlehre,* Leipzig 1921; Windelband, W., *Platon.* Stuttgart 1900. Fromanns Klassiker IX.

CHAPTER III

33.  Cp. Menzel, A., *Kallikles. Eine Studie zur Geschichte der Lehre vom Rechte des Stärkeren.* Wien 1922; Untersuchungen zum Sokrates-Prozesse, in: *Sitzungsberichte der Akademie der Wissenschaften in Wien,* Klasse Prt. CXVI, Wien 1902; Cornford, F. M., *Principium Sapientiae. The origins of Greek philosophical thought.* Cambridge 1952; Hardie, W. A., *Study of Plato.* Oxford 1936; Burnet, John, *Early Greek philosophy.* New York 1930; Santayana, George, *Platonism and the Spiritual Life.* New York 1927.

34.  For further reading on the subject of this chapter, the following works are suggested:

Alexander, Franz, *Our Age of Unreason. A study of the irrational forces in social life.* Philadelphia-New York (J. B. Lippincott Co.) 1942.

Barnes, Harry Elmer, *Historical Sociology. Its origins and development. Theories of social evolution from cave life to atom bombing.* New York (Philosophical Library) 1948.

Bernal, J. D., *The Social Function of Science.* New York (The Macmillan Co.) 1939.

Butler, N. M., *Development of the International Mind.* 1923.

Dawson, Christopher, *The Judgement of the Nations.* New York (Sheed and Ward) 1942.

Eliot, T. S., *The Idea of a Christian Society.* London (Faber and Faber, Ltd) 1939.

Flewelling, Ralph Tyler, *The Survival of Western culture.* New York (Harper and Brothers) 1943.

Gannon, Robert I., Ross J. S. Hoffman et al., *Men and modern secularism.* New York (Trinity Press, Inc.).

Hayes, Carlton J. H., *A Generation of Materialism, 1871-1900.* New York and London (Harper and Brothers) 1941. The Rise of Modern Europe Series.

Jung, Carl Gustav, *Modern Man in search of a soul.* London 1933.

Jung, Carl Gustav, *Psychological Types. Or the Psychology of Individuation.* New York 1923.

Jung, Carl G., *The Integration of the Personality.* Translated by Stanley Dell. London (Kegan Paul, Trench, Trubner and Co., Ltd.) 1940.

Kohn, Hans, *World order in Historical Perspective.* Cambridge (Harvard University Press) 1942.

Krutch, Joseph Wood, *The modern temper. A study and a confession*. New York 1929.
Krzesinski, Andrew J., *Is modern culture doomed?* New York (Devin Adair Co.) 1942.
Radhakdrishnan, S., *The Hindu View of Life*. New York 1927.
Scheler, Max, *Vom Umsturz der Werte*. Abhandlungen und Aufsätze. Zweite durch-
gesehene Auflage. Leipzig (Der Neue Geist) 1919.
Thorndike, E. L., *Human Nature and the Social Order*. New York (The Macmillan
Co.) 1942.
Weber, Max, *Essays in Sociology*. Translated, edited and with an introduction by
H. H. Gerth and C. Wright Mills. London (Kegan Paul, Trench, Trubner and Co.,
Ltd) 1948. International Library of Sociology and Social Reconstruction.
Wells, H. G., *The New World*. New York (Alfred A. Knopf) 1940.
Wells, H. G., *The Shape of things to come. The ultimate revolution*. London (Hut-
chinson and Co., Ltd.) 1935.
Wickes, Frances G., *The Inner World of Man*. New York (Harry Holt and Co.) 1948.

CHAPTER IV

35.  Cp. Natorp, P., *Platon's Ideenlehre*. Leipzig 1921; Hartmann, Nicolai, *Plato's
Logik des Seins*. Giessen 1909; Stenzel, J., *Platon, der Erzieher*. Leipzig 1928; Nietzsche,
Friedrich, *Der griechische Staat*. Leipzig; Wilamowitz, M. von, I. Kromager und A.
Heisenberg, *Staat und Gesellschaft der Griechen und Römer bis zum Ausgange des
Mittelalters*. Leipzig-Berlin 1925; Willmann, O., *Geschichte des Idealismus*. Braun-
schweig 1907.
36.  Cp. Cassirer, Ernst, *Language and myth*. Transl. by Suzanne K. Langer. New
York 1946; Jespersen, Otto, *Language. Its nature, development and origin*. New York
1921; Lee, Irving F., *Language habits in human affairs. An introduction to general
semantics*. New York [etc. 1941]; Morris, Charles, *Signs, language and behavior*. New
York 1946; Ogden, C. R., and I. A. Richards, *The meaning of meaning*. 8th ed.
London 1946.
37.  Cp. Alexander, Franz, (ed.), *Dynamic psychiatry*. Chicago 1952; Benedict, Ruth,
*Patterns of culture*. Boston 1934; Cooley, Charles Horton, *Social Organization: A
study of the larger mind*. New York 1924; Dollard, John, and Neal E. Miller, *Social
learning and society*. Ed. by Arthur Livingston. New York 1935, 4 vols.; Reichenbach,
Hans, *Experience and prediction: An analysis of the foundations and the structure
of knowledge*. Chicago 1938; Korzybski, Alfred, *Science and sanity. An introduction
to Non-Aristotelian systems and general semantics*. Lancaster, Penn. 1930, 2nd ed.
1941; Wiener, Norbert, *Cybernetics; or Control and Communication in the Animal
and the Machine*. New York 1948.
38.  Cp. Cantril, Handley, *The invasion from Mars*. Princeton 1940.
39.  This point has been stressed strongly by Benjamin Kidd and E. T. Hobhouse.
40.  Cp. the works on philosophy of history of Toynbee, Spengler, Turgot, Condorcet, Vico and Polybius.
41.  Cp. Herzler, *The social thought of early civilisation;* Breasted, James Henry, *A
history of Egypt from the earliest times to the Persian Conquest*. New York 1912.
42.  Cp. Wiener, Norbert, *Cybernetics or Control and Communication in the Animal
and the Machine*. New York 1948.
43.  See Whitney, G. T., and D. F. Bowers (editors), *The heritage of Kant*. Princeton
1939; Caird, E., *The critical philosophy of Immanuel Kant*. New York 1909. 2 vols.
Cp. Kant's essay *On the common saying*.
44.  Sorokin in his *Social and cultural dynamics*, New York [etc. 1937-1941], made a
comparable division into ideational, idealistic and sensate cultures while Spengler
distinguishes Apollonian, Magian and Faustian cultures.
45.  General bibliographical references for Chapter IV:
Arnold, E. Vernon, *Roman stoicism*. Cambridge 1911.
Aristotle, *The Basic Works of Aristotle*. Translated by R. P. McKeon. New York 1941.

Cary, M., and T. J. Haarhoff, *Life and thought in the Greek and Roman World.* New York (Thomas & Crowell Co.).

Clark, Gordon H., *Selections from Hellenistic Philosophy.* New York 1940.

Cornford, F. M., *Before and after Socrates.* Cambridge 1932.

Cornford, Francis Macdonald, *Plato's Cosmology.* The Timaeus of Plato translated with a running commentary. London (Routledge and Kegan Paul, Ltd.) 1937.

Freeman, Kathleen, *God, Man and State. Greek concepts.* London (Macdonald and Co., Ltd.) 1952.

Freeman, Kathleen, *The Pre-Socratic Philosophers.* Oxford (Basil Blackwell) 1946.

Gittler, Joseph B., *Social thought among the early Greeks.* Athens, Geo. (University of Georgia Press) 1941.

Hobhouse, L. T., *Morals in Evolution. A study in comparative ethics.* With a new introduction by Morris Ginsberg. London (Chapman and Hall) 1951.

Hobhouse, L. T., *Social Development. Its nature and conditions.* London (George Allen and Unwin, Ltd.) 1924.

Hobhouse, L. T., *Social Evolution and Political Theory.* New York (Columbia University Press) 1911.

Kidd, Benjamin, *Principles of Western Civilization.* London (Macmillan and Co., Ltd.) — New York (The Macmillan Co.) 1902.

Kidd, Benjamin, *Social Evolution.* New and revised edition. London (Macmillan and Co., Ltd.) — New York (The Macmillan Co.) 1898.

McKeon, R. P., *The Philosophy of Aristotle.* Chicago 1940.

Oakeley, Hilda D., *Greek ethical thought.* London 1925.

Ritter, C., *The Essence of Plato's Philosophy.* Translated by A. Allen. New York 1933.

Robin, Léon, *Aristote.* Paris (Presses Universitaires de France) 1944.

Robin, Léon, *La Pensée Hellénique des Origines à Epicure. Questions de méthode, de critique et d'histoire.* Paris (Presses Universitaires de France) 1942.

Rostovtzeff, M., *A History of the Ancient World.* Second edition. Oxford (Clarendon Press) 1930. 2 vols.

Sorokin, Pitirim A., *Social and cultural Dynamics.* New York [etc.] (American Book Co.) 1937. 4 vols.

Spengler, Oswald, *The Decline of the West.* New York 1926-1928. 2 vols.

Stewart, J. A., *Plato's Doctrine of Ideas.* Oxford 1909.

Taylor, A. E., *Plato. The Man and his work.* Fifth edition. London (Methuen and Co., Ltd.) 1948.

Werner, Jacob, *Paideia. The ideals of Greek culture.* New York 1939-1944. 3 vols.

Wild, John, *Plato's theory of Man. An introduction to the realistic philosophy of culture.* Cambridge, Mass. (Harvard Univ. Press) 1946.

Zimmern, Alfred, *The Greek Commonwealth. Politics and economics in Fifth Century Athens.* Fifth edition, revised. London (Oxford University Press - Geoffrey Cumberlege) 1931.

CHAPTER V

46. Selective reading-list:

Cassirer, Ernst, *Language and Myth.* Translated by Susanne K. Langer. New York and London (Harper and Brothers) 1946.

Davis, Kingsley, *Human Society.* New York (Macmillan Co.).

Durkheim, Emile, *De la Division du Travail Social.* 6me édition. Paris (Félix Alcan) 1932.

Hayakawa, S. I., *Language in Action. A guide to accurate thinking.* New York (Harcourt Brace and Company) 1939.

Jespersen, Otto, *Efficiency in Language Change.* Kopenhagen (Ejnar Munksgaard) 1941.

Jespersen, Otto, *Language. Its nature, development and origin.* New York 1921.

Jespersen, Otto, *Mankind, Nation and Individual. From a linguistic point of view.* London (George Allen and Unwin, Ltd.) 1946.

Korzybski, Alfred, *Science and Sanity. An introduction to Non-Aristotelian systems and general semantics.* Second edition. New York (The International Non-Aristotelian Library Publishing Co.) 1941.

Lee, Irving J., *Language habits in Human Affairs. An introduction to general semantics.* New York (Harper and Brothers) [1941].

Lewis, M. M., *Language in Society. The Linguistic Revolution and Social Change.* New York (Social Science Publishers) 1948.

Lippmann, Walter, *Essays in The Public Philosophy.* Boston and Toronto 1955.

Merton, R. K., *Social theory and social structure.* Glencoe, Ill. (The Free Press) 1949.

Morris, Charles, *Signs, Language and Behavior.* New York (Prentice Hall, Inc.) 1946.

Murdock, G. P., *Social structure.* New York (Macmillan) 1949.

Ogden, C. K., and I. A. Richards, *The meaning of meaning. A study of the influence of language upon thought and of the science of symbolism.* Eight edition. London (Kegan Paul, Trench, Trubner and Co., Ltd.) 1946.

Parsons, Talcott, *Essays in Sociological Theory pure and applied.* Glencoe, Ill. (The Free Press) 1949.

Parsons, Talcott, The professions and Social Structure, in: *Social Forces,* Volume XVII, May 1939.

Parsons, Talcott, *The Structure of Social Action.* (Reprint) Glencoe, Ill. The Free Press) 1949.

Piaget, Jean, Bärbel Inhelder and Alina Szeminska, *La géométrie spontanée de l'enfant.* Paris 1948.

Sumner, William Graham, and Albert Keller, *The Science of Society.* New Haven (Yale University Press) 1927. 4 vols.

Toynbee, Arnold J., *A Study of History.* Oxford (Oxford University Press) 1934-1939. 6 vols.

Warner, W. Lloyd, *Structure of American Life.* Edinburgh (At the University Press) 1952.

Whitehead, Alfred North, *Symbolism. Its meaning and effect.* Cambridge (The University Press) 1928.

**CHAPTER VII**

47. General selective reading-list:

Boissonnade, P., *Life and work in mediæval Europe.* Translated by E. Power. London 1927.

Case, S. J., *Makers of Early Christianity.* New York 1934.

Cave, R. C., and H. H. Coolson, *A source book for mediæval economic history.* 1936.

Chapman, Dom John, *Saint Benedict and the sixth century.* London (Steed and Ward) 1929.

Chesterton, C. K., *St. Francis of Assisi.* London 1923.

Chesterton, C. K., *St. Thomas Aquinas.* London 1933.

Coker, F. W., *Organismic Theories of the State.* New York 1910.

Dawson, C., *Mediæval religion.* New York 1934.

DeWolf, M., *History of mediæval philosophy.* Translated by E. Messenger. New York 1935.

Duchesne, Louis, *Early History of the Christian Church.* New York 1923. 3 vols.

Dunning, W. A., *A history of political theories.* New York 1902-20. 3 vols.

Emerton, Ephraim, *The "Defensor Pacis" of Marsiglio of Padua. A critical study.* Cambridge, Mass. (Harvard University Press) 1920.

Funck-Brentano, Frantz, *La Société au Moyen-Age.* Paris (Flammarion) 1937.

Gilson, Etienne, *La philosophie au moyen-âge. Des origines patristiques à la fin du XIVe siècle.* 3me édition. Paris (Payot) 1947.

Gierke, O. von, *Political theories of the Middle Age.* New York 1936.

Green, J. R., *Town Life in the XVth Century.* London 1894.

Guardini, Romano, *Unterscheidung des Christlichen.* Mainz 1935.

Hearnshaw, F. J. C. (ed.), *The social and political ideas of some great mediaeval thinkers.* London [etc.] (George C. Harrap and Co., Ltd.) 1949.

Homans, George Caspar, *English villagers of the Thirteenth Century.* Cambridge, Mass. (Harvard University Press) 1942.

Huizinga, J., *Herfsttij der Middeleeuwen.* Haarlem 1928.

Latourette, Kenneth Scott, *A history of the expansion of Christianity.* New York 1943. 4 vols.

Mckeon, Richard (ed.), *Selections from mediæval philosophers.* New York 1930. 2 vols.

Pegis, Anton C., *Saint Thomas and the Greeks.* Milwaukee (Marquette University Press) 1939.

Pirenne, Henri, *A history of Europe from the invasions to the 16th century.* London 1939.

Pirenne, Henri, *Histoire économique de l'occident médiéval.* [Brugge] (Desclée de Brouwer) 1951.

Pirenne, Henri, *Les Villes du Moyen Age. Essai d'histoire économique et sociale.* Bruxelles (Maurice Lamerton) 1927.

Power, Eileen, *Mediæval people.* Eighth edition. London. (Methuen and Co. Ltd.) 1946.

Renan, Ernest, *Histoire des origines du Christianisme.* Paris (Calmann Lévy. Ancienne Maison Michel Lévy Frères) 1883. 8 vols.

Rodgers, Edith Copperrider, *Discussion of Holidays in the Middle Ages.* New York (Columbia University Press) 1940.

Sertillanges, A. D., *The foundations of Thomistic philosophy.* Translated by G. Anstruther. Saint Louis 1931.

Schilling, V., *Die christlichen Sociallehren.* Köln-München-Wien 1926.

Schwer, Wilhelm, *Catholic social theory.* Translated by Bartholomew Landheer. St. Louis-London 1940.

Sombart, Werner, *Der moderne Kapitalismus. Historisch-systematische Darstellung des gesamteuropäischen Wirtschaftslebens von seinen Anfängen bis zur Gegenwart.* München-Leipzig (Dunker und Humblot).

Taylor, Henry Osborn, *The mediaeval mind. A history of the development of thought and emotion in the Middle Ages.* London 1911, 2 vols.

Tornay, Stephen, *Ockham. Studies and selections.* La Salle. Illinois 1938.

Thompson, J. W., *Economic and social history of Europe in the later Middle Ages.* 1931.

Thompson, J. W., *Economic and social history of the Middle Ages, 300-1300.* 1928.

48. For the material of this and the following sections reference is made to the above mentioned works of H. O. Taylor, J. W. Thompson and W. Schwer.


CHAPTER VIII

49. Carr, H. W., *Leibniz.* Boston 1929.

*Cartwrightiana.* Edited by Albert Peel and Leland H. Carlson. London (George Allen and Unwin, Ltd.) 1951.

Daire, M. Eugène, *Physiocrates. Quesnay, Dupont de Nemours, Mercier de la Rivière, L'Abbé Baudeau, le Trosne. Avec une introduction sur la doctrine des physiocrates, des commentaires et des notices historiques.* Paris (Librairie Guillaumin) 1846. 2 vols.

Davis, Jerome, *Capitalism and its culture.* New York (Farrar and Rinehart) 1935.

Descartes. *The Philosophical Works of Descartes.* Translated by E.S. Haldane and G. R. T. Ross. Cambridge 1911.

Faltz, Werner, Democracy and Capitalism in Max Weber's Theory, in: *Sociological Review,* Volume XXVII, October 1935.

Gibson, A. B., *The Philosophy of Descartes*. London 1932.

Gras, N. S. B., *Business and Capitalism*. New York (F. S. Crofts and Co.) 1939.

Leibniz, *The philosophical writings of Leibniz*. Translated by Mary Morris. New York 1934.

Luther, Martin. *Conversations with Luther; selections from recently published sources of the Table Talk*. New York 1915.

Martin, Alfred von, *Sociology of the Renaissance*. New York (Oxford University Press) 1944.

Quesnay, François, *Physiocratie ou Constitution naturelle du Gouvernement le plus advantageux au genre humain*. Yverdon 1768. 4 vols.

Tawney, R. H., *Religion and the rise of capitalism*. Pelican American edition. 1947.

Taylor, Henry Osborn, *Thought and Expression in the Sixteenth Century*. New York 1920. 2 vols.

Weber, Max, *The Protestant Ethic and the Spirit of Capitalism*. London 1930.

Wolf, A., *A History of Science, Technology and Philosophy in the 16th, 17th and 18th centuries*. New York 1935-1938. 2 vols.

50. Cp. p. 257. Hobhouse, Walter, *The church and the world*. London 1910.

CHAPTER X

51. *Cambridge economic history of Europe*. 1941.

Daire, M. Eugène, *Physiocrates. Quesnay, Dupont de Nemours, Mercier de la Rivière, L'Abbé Baudeau, Le Trosne, Avec une introduction sur la doctrine des physiocrates, des commentaires et des notices historiques*. Paris (Librairie de Guillaumin) 1846. 2 vols.

Davis, Jerome, *Capitalism and its culture*. New York (Farrar and Rinehart) 1935.

Fichte, J. G., *The popular works of J. G. Fichte*. London 1889.

Gonnard, René, *Histoire des doctrines économiques*. 4me édition. Paris (Librairie générale de droit et de jurisprudence) 1943.

Gras, N. S. B., *Business and capitalism*. New York (F. S. Crofts and Co.) 1939. 408 pp.

Gray, Alexander, *The Socialist tradition; Moses to Lenin*. New York. (Longmans, Green and Co.) 1946.

Heaton, Herbert, *Economic history of Europe*. Revised edition. New York (Harper and Brothers) 1948.

Malthus, T. R., *Principles of political economy considered with a view to their practical application*. Second edition. Oxford (Basil Blackwell) — New York (Augustus M. Relly, Inc.) 1951.

*(A handbook of) Marxism being a collection of extracts from the writings of Karl Marx, Friedrich Engels and the greatest of their followers, V. I. Lenin and J. Stalin*. Emile Burns, editor. London (Gollancz) 1935.

Nussbaum, F. L., *A history of the economic institutions of modern Europe*. New York 1933.

Polanyi, Karl, *Origins of our time. The great transformation*. London (Gollancz) 1944.

Quesnay, François, *Physiocratie ou Constitution naturelle du Gouvernement le plus advantageux au genre humain*. Yverdon 1768. 4 vols.

Ricardo, David, *The works and correspondence of David Ricardo*. Edited by Piero Sraffa with the collaboration of M. H. Dobb. Cambridge (The University Press) 1951. 9 vols.

Schenk, H. G., *Progress and disenchantment. A comparative study of European romanticism*. London (Kegan Paul, Trench and Trubner and Co., Ltd.) International Library of Sociology and Social Reconstruction.

Schleiermacher, Friedrich, *Sämmtliche Werke*. Berlin (G. Reimer) 1846. 9 vols.

Schmidt-Warneck, F., *Die Sociologie Fichte's*. Berlin (Puttkammer und Mühlbrecht) 1884.

Smith, Adam, *The Wealth of Nations*. Numerous editions.

Spann, O., *Haupttheorien der Volkswirtschaftlehre auf lehrgeschichtlicher Grundlage*. Leipzig 1911.

Stark, W., *The History of Economics in its relation to social development*. London (Kegan Paul, Trench and Trubner and Co., Ltd.) [1945]. International Library of Sociology and Social Reconstruction.

Tawney, R. H., *Religion and the rise of capitalism*. Pelican American edition. 1947.

Turgot, A., *On the progress of the human mind*. Hanover, Vermont 1929.


CHAPTER XI


52. Berkeley, George. *The works of George Berkeley D.D., Formerly Bishop of Cloyne. Including his posthumous works*. Edited by Alexander Campbell Fraser. Oxford (Clarendon Press) 1901. 4 volumes.

Caird, E., *The critical philosophy of Immanuel Kant*. New York 1909. 2 vols.

Cassirer, Ernst, *Das Erkenntnisproblem in der Philosophie und Wissenschaft der neueren Zeit*. Berlin 1906-1920. 3 vols.

Cassirer, Ernst, *Die Philosophie der Aufklärung*. Tübingen 1932.

Descartes, *The Philosophical works of Descartes*. Translated by E. S. Haldane and G. R. T. Ross. Cambridge 1911.

Dilthey, Wilhelm, *Weltanschauung und Analyse des Menschen seit Renaissance und Reformation*. Leipzig 1921.

Ficino, Marsilio, *Marsilio Ficino's commentary on Plato's Symposium*. The text and a translation, with an introduction by Sears Reynolds Jayne. Columbia (University of Missouri) 1944. *The University of Missouri Studies,* Vol. XIX, No. 1.

Gibson, A. B., *The Philosophy of Descartes*. London 1932.

Gierke, O. F. von, *Johannes Althusius und die Entwicklung der naturrechtlichen Staatstheorien*. Breslau 1913.

Hearnshaw, F. J. C. (ed.), *The social and political ideas of some great French thinkers of the age of reason*. London 1930.

Joël, Karl, *Wandlungen der Weltanschauung*. Tübingen 1928-29. 2 vols.

Kant, Immanuel, *Critique of practical reason and other writings in moral philosophy*. Translated by Beck. Chicago 1949.

Lecky, W. E. H., *History of the Rise and Influence of the Spirit of Rationalism in Europe*. London 1890. 2 vols.

Meinecke, Friedrich, *Die Idee der Staatsräson in der neueren Geschichte*. München 1924.

Stephen, Leslie, *History of English thought in the eighteenth century*. London 1902. 2 vols.

Whitney, G. T., and D. F. Bowers (editors), *The Heritage of Kant*. Princeton, N.J. (Princeton Univ. Press) 1939.

53. Cp. Cassirer, Ernst, *Das Erkenntnisproblem in der Philosophie und Wissenschaft der neueren Zeit*. Berlin, 1906-1920 (3 vols.) for these and subsequent passages of this chapter.


CHAPTER XII


54. Amiel, Henri-Frédéric, *Jean-Jacques Rousseau*. New York 1922.

Bogardus, Emory S., *The development of social thought*. Second edition. New York [etc.] (Longmans, Green and Co.) 1947.

Carr, H. W., *Leibniz*. Boston 1929.

Chandler, Albert R., *The clash of political ideals. A source book on democracy, communism and the totalitarian state*. New York (D. Appleton-Century Co.) 1940.

Hearnshaw, F. J. C. (ed.), *The social and political ideas of some great thinkers of the Renaissance and Reformation.* London [etc.] (George C. Harrap and Co. Ltd.).

Hearnshaw, F. J. C. (ed.). *The social and political ideas of some great thinkers of the sixteenth and seventeenth centuries.* London [etc.] (George C. Harrap and Co., Ltd.).

Hegel, *The philosophy of history.* Translated by J. Sibrec. New York (The Colonial Press) 1899.

Hegel, G. W. F., *The Philosophy of Right.* Translated by T. M. Knox. Oxford 1942.

Hobbes, Thomas. *Hobbes' tripos in three discourses:* the First, Humane Nature; the Second, De corpore Politico; the Third, of Liberty and Necessity. 3rd edition. London (Matt. Gilliflower, Henry Rogers and Theo. Fox) 1684.

Mckeon, Richard, *The philosophy of Spinoza. The unity of his thought.* New York [etc.] (Longmans, Green and Co.) 1928.

Marcuse, Herbert, *Reason and Revolution. Hegel and the rise of social theory.* London [etc.] (Oxford University Press) 1941.

Marx, Karl, *Selected Works.* Prepared by the Marx-Engels-Lenin Institute, Moscow [1933] Under the editorship of V. Adoratsky. Editor english edition C. P. Dutt. London (Lawrence and Wishart) [1943]. 2 vols.

Merton, R. K., *Social theory and social structure.* Glencoe, Ill. (The Free Press) 1949.

Murdock, G. P., *Social structure.* New York (Macmillan) 1949.

Parsons, Talcott, An analytical approach to the theory of social stratification, in *The American Journal of Sociology,* Volume XLV, May 1940, p. 841-862.

Parsons, Talcott, *Essays in Sociological Theory Pure and Applied.* Glencoe, Ill. (The Free Press) 1949.

Robbins, Lionel, *The economic basis of class conflict and other essays in political economy.* New York (Macmillan Co.) 1939.

Schaub, Edward L. (ed.), *Spinoza, the Man and his Thought.* Addresses delivered at the Spinoza tercentenary sponsored by the philosophy club of Chicago. Chicago (The Open Court Publishing Co.) 1933.

Spinoza. *Selections.* John Wild, editor. New York 1930.

Spinoza. *The philosophy of Spinoza.* Selections from his chief works. With a life of Spinoza and an introduction by Joseph Ratner of Columbia University. New York (The Modern Library) 1927.

Wolfson, H. A., *The philosophy of Spinoza. Unfolding the latent processes of his reasoning.* Cambridge, Mass. (Harvard Univ. Press) 1934. 2 vols.

55. This is strongly stressed by Walter Lippmann in his *The public philosophy. On the decline and revival of the Western society.* Boston and Toronto 1955.

## CHAPTER XIII

56. Condorcet, *De la République ou un Roi est-il nécessaire à la conservation de la Liberté?* [Paris 1791].

Condorcet, *Esquisse d'un tableau historique des progrès de l'esprit humain. Suivi de réflexions sur l'esclavage des nègres.* Paris (Masson et fils) 1822.

Condorcet, *Vie de Monsieur Turgot.* London [n.p.] 1786.

Gannon, Robert I, Ross J. S. Hoffman et al., *Man and modern secularism.* New York (Trinity Press, Inc.).

Henry, Charles (ed.), *Correspondance Inédite de Condorcet et de Turgot, 1770-1779.* Publié avec des notes et une introduction. Paris (Perinet Cie) [n.d.].

Mumford, Lewis, *Techniques and civilization.* London (George Routledge and Sons, Ltd.) 1946.

Murray, Rosalind, *The Forsaken Fountain.* London (Hollis and Cartes) 1948.

Schapiro, J. Solwyn, *Condorcet and the Rise of Liberalism.* New York 1934.

Turgot, A., *On the progress of the human mind.* Hanover, Vermont 1929.

CHAPTER XIV

57. Ashton, E. B., *The Fascist, his State and his Mind*. New York (Putnam) 1937.
Bain, Read, Sociopathy and world organization in: *American sociological review*, Volume 9, April 1944, p. 127-138.
Barnes, Harry Elmer, *The Genesis of the world war. An introduction to the problem of war guilt*. New York (Alfred A. Knopf) 1926.
Barnes, Harry Elmer, *World politics in modern civilization. The contributions of nationalism, capitalism, imperialism and militarism to human culture and international anarchy*. New York (A. A. Knopf) 1930.
Carr, Edward Hallett, *The bolshevik revolution, 1917-1923*. London (Macmillan and Co.) 1950-1952. 2 vols.
Chandler, Albert R., *The clash of political ideals. A source book on democracy, communism and the totalitarian state*. New York (D. Appleton-Century Co.) 1940.
Davis, Kingsley, *Human society*. New York (Macmillan Co.).
Ebenstein, William, *The Nazi State*. New York (Farrar and Rinehart) 1943.
Ford, Guy Stanton (ed.), *Dictatorships in the modern world*. Revised and enlarged. Minneapolis. (University of Minnesota Press) 1939.
Freytag-Loringhoven, Hugo von, *Deductions from the world war*. London (Constable and Co., Ltd.) 1918.
Gini, Corrado, *Problemi Sociologici della Guerra*. Bologna (Zanichelli) [n.d.].
Hart, Liddel, *A history of the world war, 1914-1918*. 2nd enlarged edition. London (Faber and Faber) 1934.
Hobbs, William Herbert, *The world war and its consequences*. Being lectures in the course on patriotism delivered at the University of Pittsburg during the summer session of 1918. With an introduction by Theodore Roosevelt. New York-London (G. P. Putnam's Sons) 1919.
Kohn, Hans, *The Idea of Nationalism. A study in its origins and background*. New York (The Macmillan Co.) 1945.
Kohn, Hans, *Revolutions and Dictatorship. Essays in contemporary history*. Cambridge (Harvard Univ. Press) 1939.
MacIver, R. M., *Leviathan and the people*. Baton Rouge, La. (Louisiana State University Press) 1939.
Murdock, G. P., *Social Structure*. New York (Macmillan) 1949.
Parsons, Talcott, *The Structure of Social Action* (Reprint). Glencoe, Ill. (The Free Press) 1949.
Sombart, Werner, *The quintessence of capitalism. A study of the history and psychology of the modern business man*. (Translation of Der Bourgeois) New York 1915.
Trotsky, Leon, *The history of the Russian revolution*. Translated by Max Eastman. New York 1932.


CHAPTER XVI

58. Barnes, Harry Elmer (ed.), *An Introduction to the History of Sociology*. Chicago (The University of Chicago Press) 1948.
Barnes, Harry Elmer, *Society in transition*. New York (Prentice Hall, Inc.) 1946.
Barnes, Harry Elmer, and Howard Becker, *Social Thought from Lore to Science*. Boston (D. C. Heath and Co.) 1938. 2 vols. •
Bernard, L. L., and Jesse Bernard, *Origins of American sociology. The social science movement in the United States*. New York (Thomas Y. Crowell Co.) 1943.
Carr, Edward Hallett, *The new society*. London (Macmillan and Co.) 1951.
*Chemins du Monde. Le destin de l'Individu*. Paris (Editions de Clermont) 1948.
Ghurye, G. S., *Culture and society*. New York (Oxford University Press) 1948.
Giedion, S., *Mechanization takes command*. New York (Oxford Univ. Press) 1948.
Hacker, L. M., *A short History of the New Deal*. New York (Crofts) 1939.

House, Floyd Nelson, *The Development of Sociology.* New York and London (Mc-Graw-Hill Book Co., Inc.) 1936.

Huxley, Aldous, *Science, Liberty and Peace.* New York and London (Harper and Brothers) 1946.

Kisker, George W. (ed.), *World tension. The Psychopathology of International Relations.* New York (Prentice Hall, Inc.) 1951.

Klineberg, Otto, *Tensions affecting International Understanding. A survey of research.* New York 1950. Social science research council bulletin, 62.

Laski, Harold J., *Liberty in the modern state.* New edition. London (George Allen and Unwin, Ltd.) 1948.

Linton, Ralph, *The study of Man.* New York-London (D. Appleton-Century Co., Inc.) 1937.

Lundberg, George A., Read Bain and Nels Anderson (eds.), *Trends in American sociology.* New York and London (Harper and Brothers) 1929.

Mackenzie, Findlay (ed.), *Planned society, Yesterday, today and tomorrow.* New York (Prentice Hall, Inc.) 1937.

Mckeon, Richard, *Freedom and History. The semantics of philosophical controversies and ideological conflicts.* New York (The Noonday Press, Inc.) 1952.

Mckeon, Richard, with the assistance of Stein Rokkan (eds.), *Democracy in a world of Tensions.* A symposium prepared by UNESCO. Chicago (The University of Chicago Press).

Mannheim, Karl, *Man and Society in an age of reconstruction. Studies in modern social structure.* London (Kegan Paul, Trench, Trubner and Co., Ltd.) 1940.

Mannheim, Karl, The Crisis of Culture in the Era of mass Democracies and Autarchies, in: *Sociological review* (British), Volume XXVI, April 1934, p. 105-129.

Maritain, Jacques, *The Twilight of Civilization.* New York (Sheed and Ward) 1943.

Mayo, Elton, *The social Problems of an Industrial Civilization.* London (Routledge and Kegan Paul, Ltd.) 1949. International Library of Sociology and Social Reconstruction.

Posnack, Emanuel R., *The 21st century looks back.* New York (William-Frederick Press) 1946.

Randall, John Herman, *Our changing Civilization. How science and the machine age are reconstructing modern life.* New York (Frederick A. Stokes Co.) 1929.

Rauschning, Hermann, *Time of Delirium.* Translated from the German by Richard and Clara Winston. New York-London (D. Appleton Century Co., Inc.) [1946].

Read, Herbert, *Art and Industry. The principles of industrial design.* 2nd edition. London (Faber and Faber) 1945.

Sorokin, Pitirim A., *Contemporary Sociological Theories.* New York-London (Harper and Brothers) 1928.

Sorokin, Pitirim A., *The Crisis of our Age. The social and cultural outlook.* New York (E. P. Dutton and Co., Inc.) 1945.

Toynbee, Arnold J., *A study of History.* Oxford (Oxford University Press) 1934.

Toynbee, Arnold J., *Civilization on trial.* New York (Oxford Univ. Press, Inc.) 1948.

CHAPTER XVII

59. Bryson, Lyman, Louis Finkelstein and R. M. Mac Iver, *Conflicts of Power in modern culture.* Seventh symposium. New York (Harper and Brothers) 1947.

Callis, Helmut G., The sociology of International Relations, in: *American sociological review,* Volume 12, June 1948, p. 323-334.

Carr, Edward Hallett, *Nationalism and after.* London (Macmillan and Co., Ltd.) 1945.

Chadwick, H. Munro, *The Nationalities of Europe and the growth of National Ideologies.* London (Cambridge University Press) — New York (Macmillan Co.) 1945.

Earle, Edward Mead (ed.), *Nationalism and Internationalism.* New York (Columbia University Press) 1950.

Hayes, C. J. H., *Essays on Nationalism*. New York (Macmillan) 1926.
Hayes, Carlton J., *The historical Evolution of modern Nationalism*. New York (The Macmillan Co.) 1948.
Hertz, Frederick, *Nationality in History and Politics. A study of psychology and character*. New York (Oxford Univ. Press) [1945].
Jordan, Virgil, *Manifesto for the Atomic Age*. (Rutgers University Press) 1946.
Kohn, Hans, *The Idea of Nationalism. A study in its origins and background*. New York (The Macmillan Co.) 1945.
Mander, Linden A., *Foundations of modern world society*. Stanford University, Calif. (Stanford Univ. Press) London (Cumberlege).
Nantet, Jacques, *Bataille pour la Faiblesse*. Paris (Librairie Gallimard) 1948.
Pillsbury, W. B., *The Psychology of Nationalism and Internationalism*. New York-London (D. Appleton and Co.) 1919.
Ralston, Jackson A., *A quest for International Order*. Washington D.C. (John Bryne and Co.) 1941.
Rocker, Rudolf, *Nationalism and Culture*. Translated by Ray E. Chase. New York (Covici-Friede Publishers) 1937.
Roucek, Joseph S. (ed.), *Twentieth century Political Thought*. New York (Philosophical Library) 1946.
*Tensions that cause wars*. Common statement and individual papers by a group of social scientists: Gordon W. Allport, George S. Gurvitch, etc. brought together by UNESCO. Edited by Hadley Cantril Urbana. (University of Illinois Press) 1950.
Ward, Barbara, *The West at Bay*. New York (W. W. Norton and Co., Inc.) 1948.
White, Lyman Cromwell, assisted by Maria Ragonett Zocca, *International Non-Governmental Organizations. Their purposes, methods and accomplishments*. New Brunswick, New Jersey (Rutgers University Press) 1951.

CHAPTER XVIII

60. Bentwich, Norman, and Andrew Martin, *A Commentary on the Charter of the United Nations*. New York 1951.
Besterman, Theodore, *UNESCO. Peace in the minds of Men*. London (Methuen and Co., Ltd) 1951.
Boasson, Ch., *Sociological aspects of Law and International Adjustment*. Amsterdam (North Holland Publishing Company) 1950.
Cecil, Lord Robert, *The moral Basis of the League of Nations*. London (Lindsey Press) 1923.
Davis, Kingsley, *Human society*. New York (Macmillan Co.) 1949.
Eagleton, Clyde, *International Government*. Revised edition. New York (Ronald Press) 1948.
Enock, C. R., *Can we set the world in order? The need for a constructive world culture. An appeal for the development and practice of a science of corporate life, as contrasted with perennial economic strife, waste and warfare: a new science of human geography and industry planning, or constructive economic biology*. London (Grant Richards Ltd.) 1916.
Fischer, Eric, *The Passing of the European Age. A study of the transfer of western civilization and its renewal in other continents*. Revised edition. Cambridge, Mass. (Harvard University Press) 1948.
Holborn, Hajo, *The Political Collapse of Europe*. New York (Alfred A. Knopf) 1951.
Leonard, L. Larry, *International organization*. New York [etc.] (McGraw-Hill) 1951.
Levi, Werner, *Fundamental world organization*. Minneapolis, Minn. (University of Minnesota Press) 1950.
Lippmann, Walter, *The Cold War*. New York (Harper) 1947.
McMullen, Laura Waples (ed.), *Building the World society. A handbook of international relations*. New York (McGraw-Hill) 1931.

Mander, Linden A., *Foundations of modern World society*. Revised edition. Stanford University, California (Stanford Univ. Press) 1947.

Muzumdar, Haridas T., *The United Nations of the world*. Second edition. New York (Universal Publishing Co.) 1944.

Ray, Jean, La Communauté Internationale d'après les traités du XVIe siècle à nos jours, in: *Annales sociologiques (Collection de l'année sociologique)*, Part III, Sér. C, 1938.

Ruyssen, Théod., Les caractères sociologiques de la Communauté humaine. Paris (Recueil Sirey) 1939. *(Recueil des Cours de l'Académie de droit international*, 67, p. 121-232.)

Schevill, Ferdinand, Jacob Viner, Charles C. Colby, Quincy Wright, J. Fred Rippy and Walter H. C. Loves, *The Foundations of a more stable world order*. Chicago (University of Chicago Press) 1941.

Schuman, Frederick L., *The Commonwealth of Man. An inquiry into power politics and world government*. New York (Alfred A. Knopf) 1952.

Toynbee, Arnold J., *A study of History*. Oxford (Oxford University Press) 1934-1939. 6 vols.

West, Ranyard, *Conscience and Society. A study of the psychological prerequisites of law and order*. London (Methuen and Co., Ltd.).

Wilkie Wendell, *One World*. New York 1943.

Woodward, Ernest Llewellyn, J. Robert Oppenheimer, Edward Hallet Carr, et al., *Foundations for world order*. Denver (University of Denver Press) 1949.

Wright, Quincy (ed.), *The World Community*. Chicago (University of Chicago Press) 1948.

York, Elizabeth, *Leagues of Nations — Ancient, mediæval, modern*. London (The Swarthmore Press, Ltd.) 1919.

Ziff, William B., *Two worlds. A realistic approach to the problem of keeping the peace*. New York (Harper and Brothers) 1946.

# GENERAL INDEX

Idea, 3, 17, 18, 22, 24, 25, 27, 30, 31, 32, 38, 39, 40, 48, 52, 88, 93, 96, 107, 119, 122, 123, 129, 130, 131, 132, 134, 145, 148, 149, 150, 153, 159, 160, 161, 163, 167, 183, 224, 230, 233, 236, 237, 238, 239, 246, 249.
Idealism, 86, 96, 98, 100, 129, 131.
Ideals, Christian-, 84, 85, 87, 89, 90.
Ideological thinking, see: Thinking.
Ideology, 60, 94, 135, 136, 177, 179, 191, 194, 215, 223, 236, 238, 253, 254.
Ideology, of the U.S.S.R., 166.
Ideology, American-, 166.
Ideology, Class-, 187, 188, 195.
Ideology, National-, 35, 60, 223.
Imagination, 6, 22, 24, 25, 39, 43, 49, 56, 84, 140, 141, 143, 146, 150, 170.
Imaginative reaction, see: Reaction.
thinking, see: Thinking.
Increase in population, see: Population.
India, 24, 50, 211, 223, 231, 239, 240, 241, 243, 244, 251, 253.
Indians, Plains-, 50.
Individual, 3, 4, 5, 8, 9, 10, 11, 12, 14, 16, 19, 21, 22, 25, 27, 31, 35, 37, 40, 44, 47, 52, 55, 56, 57, 63, 65, 82, 91, 95, 97, 99, 101, 105, 107, 108, 122, 123, 124, 125, 130, 134, 137, 138, 147, 155, 156, 158, 159, 163, 164, 165, 169, 173, 175, 180, 183, 210, 211, 212, 214, 218, 220, 223, 232, 233, 250, 252, 253, 254, 255, 256.
Individual equilibrium, see: Equilibrium.
freedom, see: Freedom.
rights, see: Rights.
symbolism, see: Symbolism.
Individualism, 24, 85, 89, 95, 96, 98, 100, 101, 103, 124, 126, 128, 129, 130, 131, 133, 134, 135, 162, 211, 213, 214, 229, 245, 252.
Individualistic attitude, see: Attitude.
economy, see: Economy.
period, see: Period.
thinking, see: Thinking.
Industrial economy, see: Economy.
Industry, 99, 100, 105, 122, 123, 124, 157, 166, 239.
Innocentius III (Pope), 88.
Inquisition, 90, 91.
Integration, 133, 154, 188, 189, 191, 193, 194, 195, 213, 215, 216, 217, 218, 220, 225, 227, 229, 230, 231, 234, 235, 236, 238, 240, 243, 250, 254.
Integration in intern. society, 215, 216.
Integration in national society, 215.
Integration, Cultural-, 238.

Integration, Economic-, 225, 252.
Integration, Global-, 188, 193, 227, 243.
Integration, International-, 194, 215.
Integration, Regional-, 189, 214, 215, 219, 225, 231, 233, 245.
Integration, World-, see: Integration, Global-.
Intellect, 7, 16, 25, 37, 42, 46, 140, 142, 144, 149, 161, 170, 171, 172, 179, 190, 193, 209, 210.
Intellectual function, see: Function.
leaders, see: Leaders.
reaction, see: Reaction.
International integration, see: Integration.
law, see: Law.
organization, see: Organization.
society, see: Society.
Integration in-, see: Integration.
symbols, see: Symbols.
Internationalism, 166.
Inventions, 25, 64, 97, 124, 144, 157, 168, 171, 176, 220, 249.
Investiture, 88.
Ireland, 88.
Italy, 92, 156, 194, 228.

Japan, 238, 240.
Jews, 84, 223.
John of Jandun, 92.
Justice, 107, 108, 109, 110, 111, 112, 113, 114, 115, 116, 117, 118.

Kant, 37, 47, 96, 130, 148, 149, 150, 216.
Kant's philosophy, see: Philosophy.
Keppler, 145.
Kleist, H. von: 107.
Knowledge, 6, 7, 13, 17, 21, 22, 23, 26, 27, 29, 30, 31, 32, 37, 38, 40, 41, 51, 56, 61, 85, 104, 108, 118, 120, 133, 138, 139, 143, 144, 146, 147, 148, 149, 150, 151, 152, 168, 169, 170, 171, 181, 188, 190, 230.
Knowledge, Control-, 17, 21, 50, 51, 56, 57, 64, 171, 180, 189.
Kohlhaas, Michael, 107-119.
Korea, 224.

Labor, 96, 97, 125, 127, 128, 131, 132, 134, 135, 153, 162, 163, 164, 175, 228, 244.

6158

# Date Due

|  |  |  |  |
|---|---|---|---|
|  |  |  |  |
|  |  |  |  |
|  |  |  |  |
|  |  |  |  |
|  |  |  |  |
|  |  |  |  |
|  |  |  |  |
|  |  |  |  |
|  |  |  |  |
|  |  |  |  |
|  |  |  |  |
|  |  |  |  |
|  |  |  |  |
|  |  |  |  |
|  |  |  |  |
|  |  |  |  |
|  |  |  |  |